The Seven Weld Brothers

The Seven Weld Brothers

Six Generations of Descendants
of
William Fletcher Weld
George Richards Minot Weld
Stephen Minot Weld
Thomas Swan Weld
Christopher Minot Weld
Francis Minot Weld
John Gardner Weld

ⓛⓛⓛ
1800 to 2000
ⓛⓛⓛ

A Contemporary Genealogy
compiled by
Nicholas Benton

THE WELDS OF HARVARD YARD
by Craig Lambert

iUniverse, Inc.
New York   Lincoln   Shanghai

The Seven Weld Brothers
1800 TO 2000

iUniverse, Inc.

For information address:
iUniverse, Inc.
2021 Pine Lake Road, Suite 100
Lincoln, NE 68512
www.iuniverse.com

Cover: Two Weld landmarks at Harvard:
The Weld Boathouse (see page 1)
Larz Anderson Bridge accross the Charles. (See page 3)
Photo taken by the author at his 50th Harvard reunion,
6 June 2001.

ISBN: 0-595-31390-6 (Pbk)
ISBN: 0-595-66306-0 (Cloth)

For Rose Weld Baldwin,
the family enthusiast.
They don't come any better.

CONTENTS

INTRODUCTION

HOW IT BEGAN. This genealogy is the result of a modest but challenging request by my wife's aunt, Eloise Weld Choate: "Can you give me a list of living Weld relatives <u>outside</u> the Stephen Minot Weld, Jr. family?" In short Stephen's aunts, uncles, cousins and their descendants.

SELECTING PARAMETERS. Seeking some parameters to the request, I stepped back one generation to the Seven Weld Brothers of Roxbury, MA, one of whom was Stephen's father (Stephen, Sr.) After three years (1987-90) I was able to complete the project to the best of my ability. The first of the seven brothers, William, was born in 1800. Since that date there have been six generations of descendants for each of the brothers down to 1990. Importantly there are two exceptions to this group, specifically Stephen Minot Weld, Sr. and Thomas Swan Weld. The descendants of these two have been extended an additional decade—up to 2002. Reason: I had completed and previously published another Weld genealogy, *The Call of the Weld*, which took the Stephen Minot Weld, Jr. family line up to the year 2000. In the case of Thomas Swan Weld, I am most grateful to James Warren Gould, a fine family historian, and the spouse of a descendant (see page 105) who was able to extend that branch into the 21st century as a result of his meticulous proofreading of the entire genealogy.

SIBLINGS…There was an eighth Weld brother, Clark Minot Weld, who died age 20 in Vera Cruz, Mexico as a midshipman in the Mexican Navy. The brothers also had three sisters: two were both named Margaret; one died young and the other did not marry. The third sister, Anna Minot, married in 1845 the Rev. Joseph H. Allen. They had six children all with the surname of Allen. None of these siblings are in this book.

…AND ANCESTORS. The seven Weld brothers are the eighth generation of Edmund Weld of Sudbury, Suffolk, England. His son, Joseph, was the first

Weld to emigrate from England to the New World and settle down in Roxbury, outside of Boston in 1635. He brought his wife, Elizabeth Wyse, and five members of his young family with him. Herewith the line that goes directly back to Edmund: William Gordon[7], Eleazer[6], Joseph[5], Joseph[4], John[3], Capt. Joseph[2], Edmund[1]. All of these men were prominent citizens, owning and farming vast tracks of land in the town of Roxbury, MA.

CONTEMPORARY GENEALOGY. How reliable is it? After all, we are dealing here mostly with the living whose public records and vital statistics are fairly hard to come by. Many states for obvious reasons will not give out such records to strangers. In addition another important barrier is the formidable mountain of fees required to obtain birth, marriage and death certificates. There are only two modes of transportation for contemporary information: mail and phone. Mail can prove to be frustrating. Recipients tend to put questionnaires aside to fill out and send another day. They rarely come back. The phone, on the other hand, is a godsend. I must have talked to some 300 people (read strangers) and was turned down by only two (curiously both in the Philadelphia area) who felt my call was an invasion of privacy. The tactful course is to agree with them. Try to assure them that your inquiry for genealogy purposes is honorable. There are other sources you can count on to get the information you seek.

CAVEAT LECTOR. For serious genealogists these are two words to keep permanently in mind regarding contemporary research. Of all the people I spoke to, I would venture that less than five percent were shaky in their facts and family history; they were, however, probably, in the ballpark. Fortunately many of the facts about all the descendants of the Seven Weld Brothers could be confirmed through such public sources as newspapers (particularly good for marriages) Who's Who, Social Registers, college class reports (when easily available), alumni offices, the Social Security Death Index and occasionally a vital record if the particular state was willing to part with it. (See Sources.)

HARVARD INFLUENCE. There is a remarkable feature within this genealogy, namely the number of men and women—both Weld family members and their spouses—who graduated from Harvard over this 200 year period. Readers can sense this by the Harvard Class dates which appear in brackets after each name. My research was brought to the attention of Editor Craig Lambert of *Harvard Magazine* who was planning an article for that publication about one prominent Harvard family to coincide with the 100th anniversary of the magazine. A delightful article entitled *The Welds of Harvard Yard* appeared in the November 1998 issue and is reprinted here with Lambert's and the Harvard Magazine's express permission. I am most grateful for their spirited send-off.

ACKNOWLEDGMENTS. Almost every page includes a name that extended important information to me. I thank them all. Most helpful to me in my research were the Peck family of Cincinnati, and Wyoming, OH, Mrs. Ruth MacDowell of Pauling, NY and her daughter, Anne MacDowell Jaster of Schenectady, NY, Mrs. Emily Strawbridge Clothier of Philadelphia, Charles Dawes Dunlap of New Orleans, LA and especially William Richard Eyre of London, England who gave me virtually all the missing descendants of Arthur Cyril Gordon Weld whose first wife divorced him and took their two daughters off to Rome (resulting in many interesting lines in Italy, Germany and England.) It is people like these who make contemporary genealogy so fascinating.

TWO IMPORTANT ASSISTANTS. When I had completed the manuscript—when the last Weld was in position—I looked at the manuscript and said "This is hopeless." It was incomprehensible, virtually impossible to follow my numbering. What I needed was a fresh pair of eyes who could translate my data into the standard format used by the New England Historic Genealogical Register. I found just such a clear-headed person, Maciej Simm, a student at SUNY Buffalo who, as an undergraduate, was preparing to enter medical school. How he took my rough manuscript and literally "crow-barred" it into the Register format through his computer, I'll never quite understand. But I am most appreciative. If there are errors (and there are, sadly, bound to be) they are mine alone, not Simm's.

Every genealogist knows there are never enough eyes when it comes to the final product. And I got the best pair of eyes of all—namely those of James Warren Gould of Cotuit, MA (mentioned above). I am especially grateful to Jim who found at least three factual or typographical errors on every page. He would question style inconsistencies which had to be resolved; he was able to fill-in so many of my blank spaces. I quake to think that I might have gone to press without him.

Nicholas Benton
New York, NY

January 2004

THE WELDS OF HARVARD YARD

History through a family lens
by
Craig Lambert

There have been some rogues: on the eve of the unveiling of John Harvard's statue in 1884, a young fellow named Weld allegedly sneaked under the drapery and placed a chamber pot beneath the namesake's chair. But the large, sprawling Weld family has also spawned more than its share of distinguished members of the Harvard family. Two Harvard buildings and two professorships bear the surname. The clan's history is closely linked to the history of Harvard itself.

Welds have been at Harvard almost since the first classroom opened its door—and the family's genealogy goes back even further than that: one William Weld was sheriff of London in 1352. Three centuries later, the first of the family to attend Harvard, John Weld (born in 1625), found himself on the other end of the constable's stick. In 1644, he and a classmate robbed two houses of 11 pounds in money and 30 shillings' worth of gunpowder. When found out, they were expelled from the College after having been whipped by President Henry Dunster himself. John Weld returned to England, where he became a minister in the bishopric of Durham.

The first Weld to graduate was Edmund Weld (1631-1668), A.B. 1650, who became a minister in Ireland. During the seventeenth and eighteenth centuries, 18 more Welds and three Weld spouses followed Edmund through the Yard, but we can conveniently begin the saga of the modern day dynasty with William Gordon Weld (1775-1825) and Hannah (Minot) Weld (1780-1860). This pivotal couple produced one daughter and eight sons; one boy was killed in Mexico, but the remaining seminal septet sired 813 descendants.

A handful of these descendants are profiled here. Source material varies: the portraits of earlier Welds depend on documents; those covering more recent offshoots benefitted from interviews. The privately printed 1938 book *Weld Collections*, by a Weld spouse, Charles Francis Robinson, is an invaluable source of genealogical and biographical data. We owe an even greater debt of gratitude to a singular genealogist and historian Nicholas Benton '51, another Weld spouse. He is the husband of Kitty (Bigelow) Benton (granddaughter of Rudolph Weld '05) and the father of Emily Weld Benton '84 and Louisa Barclay Benton '86.

This summer (1998), Emily Weld Benton married John Morgan at the Bentons' summer home in Wareham, Massachusetts, near Cape Cod. The cottage, known as *West House*, is one of six separate houses at Indian Neck in Wareham; the group of homes amount to a family compound of sorts, and if the Weld clan has a family seat, this is it. Indian Neck commands a majestic view of Bourne Cove and the Atlantic Ocean. In 1881 "the General"—Stephen Minot Weld Jr. (see below)—and his cousin William Minot bought the property. Generations of Welds have lived here, although in recent decades a preponderance of female off-spring in the New England branches of the family has made the Weld surname rare at Indian Neck; the graceful cottages now house Bigelows, Bentons, and Baldwins, by coincidence, all Harvard spouses.

One former denizen of Indian Neck, Anna (Reed) Parsons (1858-1958), shows how the events of a single lifetime can telescope history. As a young girl, she witnessed Abraham Lincoln's funeral cortege. In time she married William Barclay Parsons Jr., chief engineer of both the New York City subway system and the Cape Cod Canal. Their daughter, Sylvia, married Rudolph Weld '05, son of "the General," and their daughter Sylvia-who is now 89-may be the oldest living member of the Weld family. During the 1930's the younger Sylvia recalls, she once visited her grandmother Anna in New York City and happened to mention that she planned to vote for Franklin Delano Roosevelt, earning herself a scathing rebuke. Sylvia then suggested that her grandmother's political guidance was predictable, because she had always supported the Republican Party. "No, I haven't!" the older woman burst out. "Only since McKinley!"

WILLIAM FLETCHER WELD (1800-1881)

Ironically, William Fletcher Weld, who built the first great Weld fortune and Weld Hall in Harvard Yard, never attended college. He had prepared for Harvard, as one of the sons of dynasty-founders Hannah (Minot) and William Gordon Weld, a prosperous ship master and ship owner. During the War of 1812, however, a British frigate cruising off Boston harbor captured one of the family's ships-with the patriarch himself in command-carrying a valuable cargo of wine and Spanish silver dollars. This financial disaster canceled young William's college plans.

At 15 he became a clerk for an importer in Boston; by 22, he had set himself up in the dry-goods trade. But a partner's badly managed ventures mired the young company in debt, and Weld did not find his way to affluence until he entered the shipping trade that had once enriched his father. By 1833, he had made enough money to build the *Senator,* the largest ship of its time.

Weld eventually became one of the most successful merchant-ship owners in the country, with 51 sailing vessels and 10 steamers. Yet in time he foresaw the decline of American shipping and sold off his fleet to focus on urban real estate and railroads, in particular the Boston and Albany and Boston and Maine lines.

At his death, he left an estate estimated at $20 million. He had married twice, fathering six children by his first wife, Mary (Perez Bryant), and one son by his second wife, Isabella (Walker). That son-George Walker Weld (see below)-donated the Weld Boathouse. Thus, although legions of Welds have attended the University over the centuries, this father-son pair are responsible for the two Harvard buildings that bear the family name.

STEPHEN MINOT WELD A.B. 1826; A.M. 1829 (1806-1867)

Tours of the Old Yard often pause near Weld Hall while the guides note that John F Kennedy '40 lived there during his freshman year. The building's namesake, Stephen Minot Weld, was another of the sons of William Gordon and Hannah Weld. In 1870, Stephen's eldest brother, William, donated the funds to erect Weld Hall in his memory. Constructed between 1871 and 1872, it carries this inscription:

STEPHANO MINOT WELD
VIRO DE VNIVERSITAT OPTIME MERITO
FRATRI FRATER

(To Stephen Minot Weld, a man deserving well of the University, his brother [dedicates this] to his brother.)

As an undergraduate, Stephen was, according to a classmate, "the most popular member of his class, and this without seeking it, without any concession of principle, by virtue of his sterling worth, his elastic spirits, and his strong social sympathies." These qualities must have served him well as master of the private school in Roxbury that he founded in 1827 and taught at for the ensuing three decades. More than a thousand boys from all parts of the country, and even Cuba and Mexico, attended the school, many in preparation for Harvard.

Weld also had a keen business sense and accumulated a sizable estate through shrewd investments in Jamaica Plain real estate. The Massachusetts legislature twice elected him to the Governor's Council. He was a presidential elector on the Lincoln ticket in 1864, and helped raise recruits for the Union cause in which his eldest son, Stephen Jr., distinguished himself. After Appomattox, Weld belonged to the committee that raised a quarter-million dollars to fund the construction of Memorial Hall in honor of Harvard's

Union war dead; many believed the money could not have been raised without his enthusiasm and energy.

William Weld honored his brother's memory with a building for the College in part because of Stephen's great reputation among Harvard men. An Overseer from 1855 until his death, Stephen was the prime mover in a 14-year effort that secured passage of the 1865 law authorizing Harvard alumni to elect the members of the Board of Overseers-a reform that wrested control away from the Commonwealth and thus in an important way established Harvard as a private college.

On December 5, 1867, while attending a reading in Boston by Charles Dickens, Weld caught a cold that turned into pneumonia, causing his death a week later. At his funeral and memorial service on December 17, there was a great public gathering in Jamaica Plain; his obituary in the *Boston Evening Transcript* described a "bright, cheerful, warm-hearted man who preserved, as a winning grace, his childlike simplicity to the last," recalling that he had "in every way a genial nature" and noting "the beaming pleasantness of his companionship."

GEORGE WALKER WELD, A.B. 1860
(1840-1905)

At his death at age 64, an obituary noted that George Walker Weld—as founder of the Weld Boat Club in 1889—was "the greatest benefactor Harvard ever had in rowing." In 1889 he also funded the construction of a boathouse, later moved upstream to make way for the current Weld Boathouse, opened in 1906. The same obituary called him "an advocate of healthy, clean sport of a kind that would attract a large number of students." Weld Boathouse has, indeed, been a key venue for the democratization of rowing at Harvard. Today it houses the Radcliffe and intramural crews and is the center for instruction in recreational and competitive sculling, open to all members of the University. Young George matriculated in 1856, only four years after the first intercollegiate athletic contest in the United States: the 1852

Harvard-Yale boat race at Lake Winnipesaukee, New Hampshire. By 1889 that regatta had become a popular annual event, yet there were few opportunities for undergraduates eager to row. When Weld's boathouse opened its doors, with 21 new shells, young athletes who had been cut from the varsity and class crews could continue to train in eights, fours, pairs, and singles.

Weld himself had been athletic at Harvard and for some years afterward. But around age 40 "a grave malady" afflicted him. Records do not clarify the nature of his illness, which required a long hospital stay and left him a paralytic. (Although an undated Boston newspaper item notes that "The illness of George Walker Weld has assumed a sad form and he has been carried to the Somerville insane asylum," psychiatric diagnosis was then an even less exact science than it is today, and no other evidence suggests that Weld suffered from mental illness.) He bore his infirmity with cheerfulness, and throughout his life continued to attend Harvard athletic events in a wheelchair or carriage.

As a wealthy Boston bachelor, Weld seems to have greatly enjoyed life. He belonged to several downtown clubs and was a founding member of the Boston Athletic Association, organizers of today's Boston Marathon. He often invited friends to cruise on his 80-foot steel schooner, *Chanticleer*, considered one of the finest steam yachts in the United States. He belonged to the New York Yacht Club and was part of the syndicate that built the America's Cup defender *Puritan*.

In 1903 Weld fractured his thigh and his health deteriorated; his obituary attributed death "to a general breaking down." Although he left no direct descendants, he had a family connection to another enduring Harvard (and Charles River) legacy. His niece, Isabel Weld Perkins, was the wife of Larz Anderson, A.B. 1888, LL.B. 1891, donor of the Anderson Memorial Bridge, which has brought Boston traffic directly into Harvard Square since 1913. The carved stone bridge crosses the Charles next to the Weld Boathouse, and was purposely designed with "a high enough arch to admit the passage of all sorts of pleasure craft."

STEPHEN MINOT WELD, JR., A.B. 1860
(1842-1920)

On the honeymoon following his second marriage, in 1904, Stephen Minot Weld Jr. and his new bride, Susan Edith Waterbury, toured Civil War battlefields where 40 years earlier the 62-year-old groom had made war, not love. Weld was a first-year student at Harvard Law School when the conflict broke out. He was eager to join the action, and as a member of the Army of the Potomac from 1861 to 1865, he participated in many major conflicts, including the Second Battle of Bull Run, Antietam, and Gettysburg. Twice he was captured by Confederate troops, and twice exchanged; a bullet once pierced his boot and he had his horse shot from under him.

Weld rose rapidly from second lieutenant to lieutenant colonel to colonel, and at his discharge in 1865 he was breveted a brigadier general-at age 23. Even today, members of the Weld clan refer to him simply as "the General."

"The General," however, was no abolitionist, and had "little liking for those he considered antislavery zealots," writes David Herbert Donald. In his foreword to Weld's Civil War diary and letters, republished by the Massachusetts Historical Society in 1979, the Warren professor of American history emeritus observes, "When abolitionist Senator Charles Sumner made an appearance at the Harvard class day exercises in 1860, Weld was a member of the graduating class that booed and hissed him. Like most conservative upper-class New Englanders, Weld disliked slavery, but he had no special sympathy for the sufferings of blacks; he felt that, if left alone, the South's 'peculiar institution' would die out of its own accord." Throughout his war diary which the General first published himself in 1912 in an edition of 50 copies for relatives-it is clear that he viewed the Union cause as essentially one of putting down a rebellion, not freeing slaves.

Weld prepared for Harvard at his father's boarding school, and entered the College at 14 years of age. He was an abstemious young man: "I did not touch a drop of wine or liquor all through my college career until about a month before I graduated, nor did I smoke until then," he wrote. "I was up to a great deal of mischief, but got though all right...graduating, I believe, number 28 in a class of 108."

"The whole spirit between the Faculty and the students was one of war," Weld recalled in his reminiscences. "We looked on the Faculty as our oppressors, and we were-a great many of us-up to every devilment that we could think of, to trouble and bother them....The College then was more in the nature of a boarding school. There were about four hundred undergraduates, where now [1912] there are some four or five thousand."

His older cousin George Walker Weld was a classmate, and one night came to Stephen's room with a plan to "screw in one of the tutors, named Pearce. The plan was to take a hinge and screw one part to the bottom and the other to the sill of the door, so that in the morning...[Pearce] would find himself locked in and unable to attend prayers, and so could not mark us for our absence." But tutor Pearce was on the lookout, heard George and his friend Osborne at their work, and chased them down the stairs. At the bottom of the flight, George grabbed a banister and swung under the stairs, while Pearce pursued Osborne out into a heavy snowfall. "Osborne plunged into a snow-drift and stuck there, and Pearce jumped on him. They had a row and a good deal of scuffling, and in it Pearce, who wore a red wig, lost it. It got lost in the snow and was never found until the next spring." Osborne was expelled and got his degree many years later, but George Weld's quick wit in swinging beneath the stairs saved him from discipline.

In Stephen Weld's senior year, Cornelius Felton, professor of Greek, was appointed president of Harvard. "We felt very much aggrieved," Weld wrote, "because, at the inauguration ceremonies, which were to take place the day before our graduation, the Latin oration, which had always by universal custom been given to the graduating class, was given to the class below us because our first scholar had not taken Latin as an elective. It caused a great deal of feeling. The members of our choir refused to sing and our class would not take part in the inauguration ceremonies, so they were postponed until the day after our graduation. At a meeting of the Alumni held in University Hall on that day, we proposed a vote of censure on the Faculty for their treatment of us as a class, which was exceedingly ill-advised."

After the Civil War, Weld returned home to misfortune. His beloved father died in 1867; soon thereafter, a felting mill in which he had inherited about $14,000 worth of the stock failed. "[T}he mortification was almost more than I could bear," he recalled. He made a new start by borrowing $25,000 from friends to buy a cotton mill that was connected with the felting mill. "I literally had not a cent left in the world," he wrote. But bad luck dogged him again; a pond two miles upstream broke its dam and the ensuing flood swept the cotton mill away.

Yet this turned out to be a blessing in disguise. To pay his debts, Weld began working as a cotton salesman. Eventually he built a fortune as a successful cotton and woolen broker, opening branches even in Bombay and Japan. There were some huge setbacks, including the embezzlement of $326,000 by an old friend who had become a business partner. But overall, the downtown Boston firm of S. M. Weld and Company prospered and made the General a wealthy man.

In 1869 Weld married Eloise Rodman. The couple lived on a 52-acre estate in Dedham, most of which was surrounded by a high stone wall. Here, Weld indulged his passion for horticulture, creating one of the finest rock gardens in the country. The estate employed eight gardeners year-round, and had a water tower and a dozen greenhouses, one of which was dedicated to growing table grapes all year long. (MIT now owns and operates the property as a conference center known as Endicott House.) Weld became president of the Massachusetts Horticultural Society' in 1906, and worked closely with Harvard professor Charles Sargent, founder of the Arnold Arboretum, in building the arboretum's collection.

Eloise Weld died in 1898, having borne six boys and one girl. The General sustained other personal losses. Twins Stephen and Alfred succumbed to rheumatic fever at 17 and tuberculosis at 32, respectively. Eight-year-old Lothrop Motley Weld drowned in the channel at Bourne Cove in Wareham in 1882, just one year after the family had purchased property there for a summer residence. Daughter Eloise died in England at the age of 28, in 1907.

In 1904 the General married Susan Edith Waterbury, who was 24 years his junior and had been governess to his younger sons. In his later years, he spent much of his time at the family compound he had established at Indian Neck. There he created another spectacular garden and built a private 18-hole golf course as well as several comfortable houses. In addition to fishing, golf, and shooting, another hobby was buying beautiful land and then selling it at cost to friends who would take care of it; in this way he acquired and transferred hundreds of acres along the shores of Buzzards Bay.

The General preserved not only land but many of the older values; he was a transitional figure between the nineteenth century and the modern era. He died in the winter of 1920 in Boca Grande, Florida. Fittingly, at his funeral, as his body was carried from the church, a lone bugler sounded *Taps*. Shortly thereafter, five of his grandchildren, the offspring of his youngest child, Philip Balch Weld '08, came to live at the Dedham estate. "[T]he coachman met us at Back Bay station with the eight-seater depot omnibus drawn by a pair of chestnuts," recalled Philip Saltonstall Weld '36, one of those children. "The auto was still suspect in Boston and environs."

LOTHROP MOTLEY WELD 1920-(1898-1947)

HOLLYWELD:
Few people realize that a Hollywood star—Tuesday Weld—was actually a member of the Harvard Weld family. Her father, Lothrop Motley Weld 1920, was one of General Stephen Minot Weld's grandsons— the namesake of the little boy who drowned in Bourne Cove at the age of eight.

Lothrop Weld prepared for Harvard at St. Mark's and served in World War I. After completing college he married and fathered yet another Lothrop Motley Weld, Jr. Harvard 1950, while working as a salesman for S.M. Weld and Company (cotton brokers) in Boston. After a few years he moved to the oil business and to the upper East Side of Manhattan. He had taken a second wife in 1929 and a third, an 18-year old bride in Arkansas in 1932. (Weld omitted mention of this short-lived marriage in his class reports.) In 1934 he married for the fourth time (Yosene Balfour Ker) and made another career transition— to gentleman farmer in Wellfleet, MA. By 1945 he had retired and returned to Manhattan. He was the father of five children by his four marriages, the youngest of whom was two-year old Susan Ker Weld, the future actress.

TUESDAY WELD (b.1943) began her show business career as a fashion and catalog model at age 3. Many know Weld's motion picture roles and her famous 1950s teenage blonde-goddess incarnation as Thalia Menninger on *The Many Loves of Dobie Gillis*. Although her movie credits include featherweight fare like *Sex Kittens Go To College* (1960), they also embrace more serious work such as *Play It As It Lays* (1972) based on Joan Didion's novel, and *Who'll Stop the Rain* (1978), the screen version of Robert Stone's *Dog Soldiers*.

"There is nothing remotely spiritual about the beauty of Tuesday Weld" *The New Yorker* cooed in 1989, adding that "in the late 1960s the star's teasing all-American unwholesomeness was at its peak." Her three husbands include film actor and pianist Dudley Moore and concert violinist Pinchas Zuckerman.

PHILLIP SALTONSTALL WELD A.B. 1936 (1914-1984)

On winter Sunday afternoons in Marblehead, Massachusetts, the frost-bite dinghy regattas were not a terribly popular form of sailboat racing. "You'd go zinging around the harbor-four races, back to back-in the freezing cold," recalls Annie (Weld) Bell, who some-times crewed for her father, Philip Weld. He wanted to hone his racing skills and, as the daughter laughingly recalls, "He had to look hard to find a crew."

Yet the bone-chilling preparation paid off in 1980 when Weld won a 3,000-mile race with no crew at all. At age 65, he beat 89 younger competitors in the *London Observer*-sponsored OSTAR (Observer Singlehanded TransAtlantic Race) on his 50-foot trimaran, *Moxie*. By crossing the Atlantic in a record time of 17 days, 23 hours, he became "the fastest sailor in the history of the world."

Weld, who described this race in his memoir, *Moxie*, had a singular talent for taking on chaotic forces and finding a way through the most daunting troubles. Single-handed sailing was exhilarating; he was not attracted to America's Cup racing, with its big organizations and crews. "He was so good in high stress situations: keeping a level head, sorting out what needed to be done. He did not lose his cool," says Bell. In long-distance sailing he was against the elements, and something in him loved that kind of challenge, being out in that wild territory.

At times the elements nearly won. In 1976, en route to an earlier OSTAR, a huge rogue wave north of Bermuda capsized Weld's trimaran *Gulf Streamer* stranding him and a crewman for five days before a British container ship rescued them. Weld was unflappable. He had spoken with many sailors who had been in distress and, as he relates in the documentary film *American Challenge*,

"You've got to see at least nine ships before you're rescued." At the suggestion of his wife, Anne (Warren), he christened his next trimaran *Rogue Wave*.

Phil Weld came from doubly old New England stock: his mother's family were Saltonstalls. (Massachusetts governor, and later U.S. Senator, Leverett Saltonstall '14, LL.B. '17, LL.D. 42, was his mother's cousin.) Yet he was "not the normal, quiet, self-effacing Yankee," says his daughter Eloise (Weld) Hodges '62 ('82). "He was a volcanic presence. He had very strong opinions and was impatient with those who couldn't keep up with him, or with complacent people who didn't have the vision to see what was coming down the pike. My father was always 10 to 15 years ahead of the moment. When he blew up about something, he didn't burn bridges-he bombed them."

At Harvard, Weld was president of the Porcellian Club and a reasonably diligent scholar-a consequence of landing on permanent probation after some drink-inspired hijinks on the first weekend of his freshman year. "I knew if I missed one class I was out," he later admitted. He never finished his senior thesis on Lord Byron, but essayed a romantic adventure of his own: one summer, accompanied by a friend from Harvard and Milton Academy, he ascended the Amazon to Ecuador and set out for the untamed haunts of the Jivaro Indians.

In World War II, impatient with the numbing routine of a training camp in Oregon, Weld volunteered as a commando, and parachuted behind Japanese lines in Burma. He enlisted as a private and was discharged as a second lieutenant, thrice decorated for valor as part of the celebrated Merrill's Marauders.

After the war, Weld resumed the newspaper career he had begun in Chicago in the late 1930s. Eventually he owned several town papers on Boston's North Shore and in New Hampshire. He and Anne moved to Dolliver's Neck in Gloucester in 1954, where, by the ocean, they raised a son and four daughters. After the *Gulf Streamer* calamity in 1976, Weld decided to simplify his estate in the event of another, more final, accident, and sold his publishing interests for $10 million in 1978.

His publishing savvy benefitted this magazine, which he served as volunteer president and publisher between 1967 and 1972, and as a member of its governing boards until his death. He was instrumental in hiring John T. Bethell '54, the magazine's editor from 1966 to 1994; as a teenager in the late 1940s, Bethell had a job bundling and distributing copies of the *Cape Ann Summer Sun*, one of Weld's papers, and had later been an editor at another, the *Beverly Times*.

"He never wanted *Harvard Magazine* to become the mouthpiece of a monolithic Harvard and not have the guts to print anything critical of what Harvard was doing," Hodges recalls. "He didn't want Harvard to ever get self-complacent and feel it could get away without criticism. In 1969 when the police bust and student strike roiled the Yard, *Harvard Magazine* covered the story vividly in photographs and an eyewitness account by Bethell, and despite protests from officials and alumni who would have preferred the magazine to look the other way, Weld stood squarely behind the coverage, noting bluntly that "the motto of this institution is *Veritas*."

During the 1970s, which Weld described as "the happiest decade of my happy life," he nonetheless had to face some troubling truths of his own. In 1971, his firstborn, Philip Jr. '60, slipped into chronic manic depression. Weld pere had regarded his son as the heir apparent ("It never occurred to him to have a daughter as heir apparent," Hodges wryly observes), and it was for many reasons deeply anguishing to see the young man disabled by illness and incapable of taking over the reins.

This may have been another reason for Weld's sale of his publishing interests and his increasing involvement with sailboat racing during the 1970s; on the ocean, one was completely absorbed by the conundrums of wind and water. And even there, Weld was a maverick. As an early convert to multihull boats, he relished not only the vastly greater speeds but the "outsider" status of the innovative catamaran and trimaran designs; he gleefully mocked traditional monohull boats as "heeler-keelers" as he whizzed past them in races.

In later years Weld became active in the nuclear disarmament movement. He also backed James Anderson, Philip S. Weld professor of atmospheric chemistry, in his pioneering work on ozone holes in the upper atmosphere (see "Reeling through the Stratosphere," January-February 1983). Weld endowed the chair Anderson now holds and, wanting to learn the relevant chemistry, hired an undergraduate to come to Gloucester and tutor him. He also underwrote the construction of an unmanned aircraft that could fly to high altitudes to document ozone depletion. Concerned about the nation's dependence on petroleum, he drew upon his sailing experience and plunged into the study of solar and wind energy-building a windmill, installing solar panels at home, and investing in U.S. Windpower, a utility that operated a string of windmills along the Southern California coast. "He felt wind had power," says Hodges. "He would read the *Odyssey* and quote the wind god Aeolus."

In a "retirement" that was actually a broadening out into several new careers, Weld had an array of exciting projects before him, making his sudden death at 69 especially unfortunate. On his last afternoon he attended a luncheon meeting of Harvard Magazine's board of incorporators, and again exhorted the editors to cover controversial issues; he even offered a cash prize for the best example of investigative reporting. Then, on his way through the Square to attend another meeting, he suffered a fatal heart attack. "We've always wondered whether he'd voted," says Hodges; her father died on Election Day 1984 and, typically, had been eager to vote for the underdog.

Susan Roosevelt Weld 1970; J.D. '74; PhD. '90

Another branch of the Weld family has its roots in New York. Susan Roosevelt Weld, herself a member of a distinguished Harvard family joined the New York Welds when she married William Floyd Weld 1966; J.D. '70

In 1948, as Mao's revolution roiled China, an airplane of the China National Aviation Corporation crashed in Hong Kong harbor. Quentin Roosevelt, grandson of Theodore Roosevelt and vice president of that airline, which served Chiang Kai-shek's government, perished in the crash. Sabotage was suspected; the planes had been airlifting rice to some of the last cities held by the Nationalists. "Everything was so confusing in Hong Kong then," says Roosevelt's youngest daughter, Susan (Roosevelt) Weld '70, J.D. '74, Ph.D. '90, who is now a research fellow in East Asian legal studies. When her father died she was only eight months old; although born in Oyster Bay, Long Island, she had been christened in Shanghai.

After Roosevelt's death, his widow returned to Oyster Bay, where the little girl and her three sisters grew up in a house with their grandmother, mother, and three aunts. At that time and place, and in that social set, widows were often the objects of social neglect: "My mother was not invited to dinner parties," Weld recalls. In contrast, her parents' Chinese friends in New York were very loyal, and Weld became good friends with their children. The experience helped guide her toward her later career: in addition to her Harvard appointment, Weld teaches Chinese and Japanese law at Boston College Law School. She specializes in China's early "warring states" period; in the last decade she has visited the country two or three times a year to examine ancient tablets, view archaeological sites, or attend conferences.

Her childhood surroundings were comfortable. After grade school she attended Concord Academy and applied to two colleges: Stanford and Radcliffe. "I decided to go to the most distant one," she says. But after two years in Palo Alto she felt that "Stanford wasn't dark enough, not shady and shadowy enough. I loved those Cambridge alleys that you could sneak down and no one would see you."

Hence she transferred to Radcliffe, moved from science into East Asian studies, and took a year in Taiwan. "In those days that's what you did, since we couldn't go to mainland China," Weld recalls. At Radcliffe she played a little squash and a lot of Pine Orchard Poison, a complicated two-pack game of solitaire. She remembers sitting on her bed listening to the demonstrations by Students for a Democratic Society (SDS) taking place outside. Weld opposed the Vietnam War and had picketed the Selective Service office in Oakland,

California, but, she says, "I remember the vulnerability and youth of the state police who were used to control the demonstrators. These 18-year-old recruits were shaking with fear, literally trembling. The idea that 'These are pigs and you have to be against them' was ridiculous. I think the cause is important all on its own, and doesn't have to involve demonizing ordinary people who are caught up in it one way or the other."

After college, government funding for graduate studies seemed to be drying up, so Weld took a law degree and practiced for five years. "I did everything under the sun," she says. "Pensions, tax, small corporations, litigation." After her 1975 marriage to William Weld '66, J.D. '70, the couple moved from New York City to Cambridge, where they bought a large old house "that was going cheap because of oil-crisis prices-it's still impossible to heat."

Her husband began his career as a lawyer and now practices in New York and Boston with McDermott, Will, & Emery. William Weld took time out to serve as a federal prosecutor and later as governor of Massachusetts (from 1990 to 1997), a job he resigned to pursue a quixotic, doomed bid to become U.S. ambassador to Mexico over the wishes of a fellow Republican, Senator Jesse Helms. Bill Weld comes by wealth and power congenitally: his middle name, Floyd, is the surname of a signer of the Declaration of Independence, and his paternal forebears founded the Wall Street investment house White, Weld & Company. He grew up on Long Island in a house whose driveway was a mile and a half long. Yet he has always had the common touch. Once, when Massachusetts Senate president William Bulger kidded Governor Weld publicly about his ancestors having come over on the *Mayflower*, Weld rose on the dais with a correction: "Actually they weren't on the *Mayflower*. They sent the servants over first to get the cottage ready." (He had honed his public persona at Harvard, where he earned a summa in classics and donned drag for Hasty Pudding shows-an experience that may have inspired his exhortation to seniors at 1998 Class Day exercises: "*Carpe diem*…do some high stepping, kick up your heels. Show a little leg.")

In Cambridge, the Welds have raised their children David '98 (see below), Ethel, Mary, Quentin, and Francis. The two youngest are at Milton Academy, Mary attends Yale, and Ethel, a graduate of Cambridge Rindge and Latin, the local public high school, is enrolled at New York University. "Ethel is very opposed to Ivy League schools," her mother notes. "She considers them elitist bastions."

David & Governor Weld

DAVID WELD 1998

"Our father used to tell us that all our ancestors were opium smugglers-it's pretty much the family business," says David Weld '98. "I've even had a hand in it myself." This example of drollery is only one of the ways that Weld pere et fils resemble each other: in both, the dead-pan humor comes packaged with high intellect. David Weld concentrated in physics, earned a magna, and may begin a Ph.D. program at Stanford after taking off to work for a computer company. "Physics is really cool," he says. "It's the most fundamental of the sciences, and it seem to use part of one's brain that other fields don't use. It's a strange trick to get equations to relate to the real world.

"There are so many different things in physics: you can do computer programming, build cool stuff, use machines. And people give you unbelievable quantities of money to do it! Physics graduate school is pretty much free for everybody, while medical school is unbelievably expensive."

At Harvard, Weld lived in Eliot House and joined the board of the *Advocate*, the College's oldest literary magazine. "I've written things myself, but have never submitted any for publication," he says. "I like to read literature." But he figured, "If I'm an English major, I'm never going to do anything with physics because you can't do that stuff on your own. As a physics major, I can always read." He also took two years of Chinese. "I was drawn to Chinese because it's so different from English," he explains. "In restaurants, my mother used to teach us how to draw ideograms on napkins." Weld began taking squash seriously in his sophomore year; as a junior and senior he played for Harvard's junior varsity team. He sometimes gets onto the court with his father. "Squash was really fun," he says. "In our branch of the Weld family, everybody is extremely bad at sports."

He displays a filial irreverence toward his dad's political career. "In 1979 my father ran for attorney general, and it was not a very successful outing," he says, grinning. "He lost by the largest margin of any statewide race in history, I think. Then (Democratic gubernatorial nominee) John Silber made some injudicious comments and Dad was suddenly governor." More soberly, Weld remembers standing on stage at the 1990 Massachusetts Republican Convention when "one guy was holding up a baby to my father, yelling, 'Hey, Bill, do you want to kill this baby?'" David Weld says the film *Wag the Dog*, in which a U.S. president starts a war to divert attention from domestic problems, is "not even a parody-it doesn't go far enough. I've heard some far more cynical things."

ROSE SALTONSTALL WELD 1990

This is loyalty to one's roots: born in Beverly Hospital in Beverly, Massachusetts, Rose Saltonstall Weld '90, M.D., now works there as a resident in family practice. In her branch of the family, Dr. Weld is a bit of a black sheep: grandfather Philip Saltonstall Weld, father Philip S. Weld Jr. '60, mother Elizabeth (New) Weld Nolan, sister Sarah Weld '87, even her stepfather-*Boston Globe* columnist Martin F. Nolan, IOP '78-are "all writers or newspaper types," she points out. "But I always had a lot of trouble with writing. Being at the bottom of the heap in this group was intimidating. So I went in my own direction."

At Harvard she concentrated in biological anthropology and played field hockey and lacrosse, briefly. Her college athletic career reached its pinnacle when, in her senior year, she coordinated the Mather House intramural sports program that captured the Straus Cup. Interest in a medical career did not germinate until the summer after her junior year, when she worked for a young neurobiologist in a laboratory at Tufts. After graduation, Weld took premedical courses at night at Harvard Extension School and Northeastern University while working days in a lab at Harvard Medical School. She eventually earned her M.D. from the University of Pittsburgh- "Harvard would not grant me an interview," she notes, without rancor. In fact, she found the change of venue "a good thing-I hadn't lived outside the Northeast."

The home turf had already offered vicissitudes aplenty. Her father's manic depression manifested itself when she was only 3 years old, and his condition, she says, "was not adequately diagnosed or aggressively treated." The paternal mood swings caused frightening experiences in her childhood. "My Dad was hospitalized many times when I was young," she recalls. "Lots of times I didn't know what the adults were talking about; they would say things like, 'Is he on his way up?'" After 17 years of marriage, Weld's parents divorced in 1980. Her mother remarried and her father moved to California, remarried, divorced again, and died in 1987 of a preleukemic blood disorder.

Rose Weld's own marital life has only just begun. In September she married classmate Michael Dorrington, whom she met when they were sophomores; he is now with the Boston law firm of Sullivan & Worcester. Their wedding ceremony took place in Boston, at King's Chapel on Tremont Street, the same church in which Anne Warren married Rose Weld's grandfather, Philip Saltonstall Weld, in 1937.

"I don't talk about the Welds that much because we're a big, prominent family, and most people my age aren't from big, prominent families," she says. "You go to school with people who may be the first in their family to attend— and you've got 10 generations of ancestors who went to Harvard."

The First Weld Brother
WILLIAM FLETCHER WELD
and his descendants

FIRST GENERATION

1. WILLIAM FLETCHER WELD was born in Roxbury, MA, 15 April 1800 and died in Philadelphia, PA on 12 December 1881, the son of William Gordon Weld and Hannah Minot. (He gave Weld Hall to Harvard in 1872 in memory of his brother, Stephen Minot Weld.) Married (1) in Boston, MA 5 December 1825 MARY PEREZ BRYANT who was born in Boston, MA in 1804 and died in Boston, MA circa 7 December 1836, daughter of Perez Bryant and Frances Goodwin Clark. Married (2) in Leominster, MA 9 September 1839 ISABELLA MELISSA WALKER who was baptized in Templeton, MA 9 May 1813 and died in Boston, MA on 13 October 1908, daughter of Lovell Walker and Elizabeth Russell of Rutland, MA.

Six children by Mary Perez Bryant:

2.   i.   WILLIAM GORDON born in Boston, MA 10 November 1827. Married CAROLINE LANGDON GODDARD.

    ii.   MARY MINOT was born in Boston, MA 11 September 1829 and died in Boston, MA 29 September 1853. (Unmarried).

    iii.   SARAH was born in Boston, MA 19 April 1831 and died 1831 in Boston, MA.

3.   iv.   SARAH MINOT born in Boston, MA 30 April 1832. Married GEORGE LANGDON PRATT.

    v.   FRANCES BRYANT was born in Boston, MA 10 August 1834 and died in Boston, MA 25 April 1857. (Unmarried).

4.   vi.   ANNA MINOT born in Boston, MA 8 November 1835. Married GEORGE HAMILTON PERKINS.

One child by Isabella Melissa Walker:

    vii.   GEORGE WALKER (H'60) was born in Boston, MA 3 September 1840 and died in Boston, MA 15 February 1905. A member of the Class of 1860 at Harvard, he gave the Weld Boat House to the college. (Unmarried).

SECOND GENERATION

2. WILLIAM GORDON WELD was born in Boston, MA 10 November 1827 and died in Boston, MA 16 April 1896. Married in Winchester, MA on 4 January 1854 CAROLINE LANGDON GODDARD who was born in Brookline, MA on 30 May 1831 and died in Boston, MA 14 April 1918, daughter of Charles Goddard of Portsmouth, NH and Caroline Ann LeRow of Boston, MA.

Two children:

    i.   WILLIAM FLETCHER (H'76) was born in Boston, MA 26 February 1855 and died in Brookline, MA 8 January 1893. (He established a Weld Professorship at Harvard Law School in 1882.) Married in Boston, MA 23 June 1886 ELLEN HOMER WINCHESTER who was born in Boston, MA 15 August 1861 and died in Bern, Switzerland 23 December 1927, daughter of Thomas Bradlee Winchester and Ellen D. Manson of Taunton, MA. No children. (She married the noted horseman, Herman B. Duryea (1856-1916) in London, England 30 April 1895.)

5.   ii.   CHARLES GODDARD (H'79) born in Boston, MA 20 August 1857. Married HANNAH PUTNAM TRAIN.

3. SARAH MINOT WELD was born in Boston, MA, 30 April 1832 and died probably in Boston, MA after 1895. Married in Brookline, MA, 8 November 1869 GEORGE LANGDON PRATT, who was born in Boston, MA, 1826 and died in Boston, MA, 4 November 1872, son of George Pratt and Abigail H. Lodge (who was a daughter of Giles Lodge of England).

One child:

6.   i.   MARY BRYANT born in Boston, MA 20 June 1871. Married (1) CHARLES FRANKLIN SPRAGUE. Married (2) EDWARD DESHON BRANDEGEE.

4. ANNA MINOT WELD was born in Boston, MA on 8 November 1835 and died in Brookline, MA on 20 October 1924. Married in Boston, MA on 25 July 1870 GEORGE HAMILTON PERKINS, who was born in Contoocock, NH on 20 October 1835 and died in Boston, MA on 28 October 1899, son of Judge Hamilton Eliot Perkins and Clara Bartlett George.

One child:

    i.   ISABEL WELD was born in Brookline, MA on 29 March 1876 and died in Boston, MA on 3 November 1948. Married in Boston, MA on 10 June 1897

LARZ ANDERSON (H'88) who was born in Paris, France on 15 August 1861 and died in White Sulphur Springs, WV on 13 April 1937, son of Gen. Nicholas Longworth Anderson and Elizabeth Coles (Kilgour) of Cincinnati, OH. Larz Anderson was the donor of the bridge (beside the Weld Boat House) which bears his name in Cambridge, MA. The bridge enabled Harvard students to get to the playing fields on the other side of the Charles River. Today it's a major thoroughfare for cars and commercial traffic. (No children.)

THIRD GENERATION

5. CHARLES GODDARD WELD (H'79) was born in Boston, MA 20 August 1857 and died in Brookline, MA on 18 June 1911. Married in Duxbury, MA on 11 April 1881 HANNAH PUTNAM TRAIN, who was born in Roxbury, MA on 31 January 1858 and died in Brookline, MA on 8 February 1943, daughter of William Graham Train and Mary Elizabeth Phipps.

One child:

7. i. MARY born in Brookline, MA on 5 April 1901. Married SUMNER ARTHUR PINGREE.

6. MARY BRYANT PRATT was born in Boston, MA on 20 June 1871 and died in Brookline, MA on 28 August 1956. Married (1) in Boston, MA on 25 November 1891 CHARLES FRANKLIN SPRAGUE (H'79) who was born in Boston, MA on 10 June 1857 and died in Providence, RI on 31 January 1902, the son of Seth Edward Sprague and Harriet Boardman (Lawrence). Married (2) in Boston, MA on 17 November 1904 EDWARD DESHON BRANDEGEE (H'81) who was born in Utica, NY 10 October 1857 and died in Brookline, MA on 10 September 1933 son of John Jacob Brandegee and Martina Louisa Condict of Utica, NY.

Two children by Charles Franklin Sprague:

8. i. MARION, born in Beverly, MA on 20 June 1893. Married JOHN EDWARD BOIT.

9. ii. ELEANOR, born in Washington, DC on 27 March 1898. Married (1) Dr. WILFRED SEFTON. Married (2) JOHN HENDERSON STEWART. Married (3) EDWARD TAYLOR HUNT TALMADGE, Jr.

Two children by Edward Deshon Brandegee:

10. i. MARTINA LOUISE, born in Brookline, MA 9 October 1906. Married JAMES LAWRENCE, JR.

ii.   JOHN LANGDON was born in Brookline, MA 15 June 1908 and died in Jamaica Plain, MA on 4 December 1964. Married (1) in 1933/34 (divorced 1946) EDITH S. BROOKE who was born in London, England, 1911, daughter of Stopford Brooke and Helen Ellis. (She then married Roy. W. Baker of Falmouth, MA 10/23/46. They lived in Antrim, NH until 1961.) Married (2) in Reno, NV circa 1946 (divorced 1962) MARGARET DOBBINS WHITTEMORE who was born in Boston, MA on 12 September 1921 and died in Waquoit, Falmouth, MA on 17 July 1976, daughter of David L. Whittemore and M. Dolores Dobbins of Newton, MA. (No children).

FOURTH GENERATION

7. MARY WELD was born in Brookline, MA on 5 April 1901 and died in So. Hamilton, MA on 6 April 1978. Married in Boston, MA on 26 March 1927 SUMNER ARTHUR PINGREE who was born in Ermita, Cuba on 4 January 1894 and died in Beverly, MA on 18 February 1965, son of Ernest H.A. Pingree and Addie B. Siders.

Three children:

11.   i.   SUMNER ARTHUR, JR. born in Boston, MA on 11 September 1928. Married (1) JANET FORD. Married (2) VIRGINIA LEE CASWELL (BRUSH).

12.   ii.   CHARLES WELD born in Boston, MA on 1930. Married ANN COVELL COPELAND.

13.   iii.   JOHN RANDOLPH born in Boston, MA on 25 May 1933. Married (1) MARGARET CARTER JONES. Married (2) DIANE DELLE TUZIK (OBER).

8. MARION SPRAGUE was born in Beverly, MA on 20 June 1893 and died in Boston, MA on 30 April 1968, Married in Chestnut Hill, MA on 5 June 1920 JOHN EDWARD BOIT (H'12) who was born Brookline, MA 20 November 1889 and died in Boston, MA 25 June 1978, the son of Robert Apthrop Boit and Lillian Willis of Brookline, MA.

Five children:

i.   LILLIAN WILLIS was born in Beverly, MA on 19 March 1921 and died in Albuquerque, NM circa 1984. Not married.

14.   ii.   MARY born in Boston, MA on 7 September 1922. Married (1) WILLIAM JOHN BINGHAM (H'44). Married (2) WILLIAM VINCENT

McDermott, Jr. ('38).

iii.   Eleanor was born Boston, MA on 15 August 1924. Married in Brookline, MA on 24 June 1956 (divorced 1963) to Thomas Francis Lane, Jr. who was born in Boston, MA on 11 August 1925, son of Thomas Francis Lane and Margaret M. Hannaford. (No children).

15.   iv.   Robert Sprague (twin)(H'53), born Boston, MA on 4 April 1931. Married (1) Drucilla Moore Buffington. Married (2) Agnes Bundy Harding.

16.   v.   Charles Sprague (twin)(H'53) born in Boston, MA on 4 April 1931. Married (1) Marka Spalding. Married (2) Christina Grote (Lombard). Married (3) Nancy Kunkle (Stout).

9. Eleanor Sprague was born in Washington, D.C. on 27 March 1898 and died in Hampton, NJ on 28 April 1959. Married (1) in Chestnut Hill, MA on 31 May 1919 (divorced) Dr. Wilfred Sefton who was born in Auburn, NY on 14 July 1892 and died in Auburn, NY on 4 November 1942, son of Frederick Sefton and Maude Fitch. Married (2) in Cambridge, MA on 20 November 1936 to John Henderson Stewart who was born in Pittsburgh, PA on 4 June 1891 and died in New York, NY on 1 November 1939, son of John Henderson Stewart and Virginia Hay. Married (3) in Mendham, NJ on 2 April 1942 Edward Taylor Hunt Talmage, Jr.(P'17) who was born in Brooklyn, NY on 4 January 1895 and died in Princeton, NJ on 27 June 1964, son of Edward T.H. Talmadge and Mary Bliss Prentice.

Two children by Dr. Wilfred Sefton:

17.   i.   Katharine, born in South Auburn, NY on 26 February 1920. Married (1) Richard Jackson Theobald (H Law'33). Married (2) William Francis Payson.

ii.   Charles Sprague was born in South Auburn, NY on 27 February 1922 and died near Hutchinson, Kansas on 24 May 1945 (plane crash). St. Paul's School '40; Ensign in USNR 1945.

10.Martina Louise Brandegee was born in Brookline, MA on 9 October 1906 and died in Brookline, MA on 5 March 1959. Married in Brookline, MA on 9 September 1933 to James Lawrence, Jr.(H'29) who was born Hyde Park, MA on 30 May 1907 and died in Brookline, MA on 29 January 1995, son of James Lawrence (H'01) and Marion L.Peabody.

Four children:

18. i. JAMES, III (H'58) born in Boston, MA on 9 August 1936. Married JANE SCUDDER BURGIN (H'62).

19. ii. MARTINA LEE (H'61), born in Boston, MA on 16 April 1939. Married NILE LUDLOW ALBRIGHT (H'61).

20. iii. EDWARD PEABODY (H'63), born in Boston, MA on 15 December 1941. Married VIRGINIA MIDDLETON MALONEY.

     iv. ROBERT PRESCOTT was born in Boston, MA on 14 February 1950.

FIFTH GENERATION

11. SUMNER ARTHUR PINGREE, JR. was born in Boston, MA on 11 September 1928. Married (1) in Dedham, MA on 6 June 1950 (divorced 1960) JANET FORD who was born in Newton, MA on 22 March 1928, daughter of Rev. Fred B. Ford and Mary O. Lynch. Married (2) in Estill, SC on 27 April 1961 VIRGINIA LEE CASWELL (BRUSH) who was born in Havana, Cuba on 30 May 1930, daughter of William Watson Caswell and Elizabeth Norfleet.

Two children by Janet Ford:

21. i. CHARLES FORD, born in Boston, MA on 10 January 1952. Married ROCHELLE MARIE JOHNSON.

22. ii. SUMNER ARTHUR, III born in Boston, MA on 26 June 1953. Married SALLY JOAN EMELIA ALEXANDRA ENGELHARD.

One child by Virginia Lee Caswell:

     i. RICHARD CASWELL was born in Savannah, GA on 27 December 1968.

12. CHARLES WELD PINGREE was born in Boston, MA on 19 August 1930. Married in Palmerton, PA on 15 June 1957 ANN COVELL COPELAND who was born in Palmerton, PA on 22 May 1931, daughter of Lewis Covell Copeland and Katherine Frances Pitcher.

Three children:

23. i. WILLIAM LEWIS, born in Salem, MA on 29 May 1958. Married LUCY GURNEY CUMMINGS.

ii.   CHRISTOPHER WELD was born in Salem, MA on 26 July 1959.

24.   iii.   JAY COPELAND, born in Salem, MA on 13 September 1961. Married SHARON FARRAR.

13. JOHN RANDOLPH PINGREE was born in Boston, MA on 25 May 1933. Married (1) in Orleans, France on 7 July 1956 (divorced) MARGARET CARTER JONES who was born in Fayetteville, TN on 20 November 1933, dau. of James Charles Jones and Nellie May Orr. Married (2) in Hamburg, NJ on 10 October 1969 DIANE DELLE TUZIK who was born in Perth Amboy, NJ on 2 May 1934 daughter of Dr. Theodore Hugo Tuzik and Marjorie Elizabeth Delle (Whaley).

Three children by Margaret Carter Jones:

25.   i.   JOHN RANDOLPH JR. born in Miami, FL on 17 January 1957. Married DEBRA LYNN DETTNER.

26.   ii.   ALEXANDER WELD born in Salem, MA on 13 February 1958. Married CINDY LYNN BIETZ.

27.   iii.   MARY ORR born in Salem, MA on 26 April 1960. Married EDWARD WINSOR FISHER.

14. MARY BOIT was born in Boston, MA on 7 September 1922 and died in Boston, MA on 1 September 1984. Married (1) in Brookline, MA on 26 December 1944 (divorced) WILLIAM JOHN BINGHAM, JR.(H'44) who was born in Belmont, MA on 16 April 1921, son of William John Bingham and Florence Patee. Married (2) in Dedham, MA on 1 June 1976 to WILLIAM VINCENT MCDERMOTT, JR.(H'38) who was born in Salem, MA on 7 March 1917, son of William Vincent McDermott and Mary A. Feenan. (He marries Frances Weld Gardner in Dedham, MA on 16 January 1989. See page 61.)

Three children by William John Bingham, Jr.:

28.   i.   WILLIAM JOHN, III, born Boston, MA on 14 April 1946. Married MARY ADA JILES.

29.   ii.   ROBERT BOIT, born in Boston, MA on 16 July 1948. Married JULIE ANN CHAPMAN.

iii.   CHARLES SPRAGUE was born in Boston, MA on 16 April 1954.

15. ROBERT SPRAGUE BOIT (twin) (H'53) was born in Boston, MA on 4 April 1931. Married (1) in Boston, MA on 1 January 1955 (divorced 1967) DRUCILLA MOORE BUFFINGTON who was born in Evanston, IL on 21 June 1934, daughter of George Nicholas Buffington and Sarah Louise Buffington (cousins). Married (2) in Brookline, MA on 6 April 1968 AGNES BUNDY HARDING who was born in Summit, NJ on 28 September 1941, daughter of Henry W. Harding and Agnes Burke.

Two children by Drucilla Moore Buffington:

i.   NICHOLAS BUFFINGTON was born in Boston, MA on 28 July 1958.

ii.   PEGGY was born in Boston, MA on 6 October 1960.

Two children by Agnes Bundy Harding:

i.   SAMUEL HARDING (H'91), was born in Boston, MA on 22 May 1969.

ii.   JOHN HARDING was born in Boston, MA on 6 August 1970.

16. CHARLES SPRAGUE BOIT (twin) (H'53) was born in Boston, MA on 4 April 1931. Married (1) in Falmouth, MA on 25 August 1955 (divorced) MARKA SPALDING who was born in Hartford, CT on 8 March 1935, daughter of Oakes Ames Spalding (H'27) and Dorothy Goodrich. Married (2) in White Post, VA on 6 May 1966 (divorced) CHRISTINA GROTE (LOMBARD) who was born in Berlin, Germany in 1937, daughter of Count Friedrich F. Grote and Rachel Derby Smith. Married (3) in Dedham, MA on 1 January 1980 NANCY KUNKLE (STOUT) who was born in Waterbury, CT in 1936, daughter of Lawrence G. Kunkle and Marion Arber.

Two children by Marka Spalding:

30. i.   CHRISTOPHER SPRAGUE (H'78), born in Boston, MA on 26 July 1956. Married AMY GRACE BROWN.

31. ii.   PETER GOODRICH, born in Boston, MA on 20 January 1960. Married JENNIFER L. SCHNEIDERS.

One child by Christina Grote (Lombard):

i.   CHARLES-FREDERICK DAVID (H'90) was born in Boston, MA on 3 April 1967.

17. KATHARINE SEFTON was born in South Auburn, NY on 26 February 1920 and died

in Boston, MA on 24 April 1981. Married in Mendham, NJ on 4 April 1945 (divorced) (1) RICHARD JACKSON THEOBALD (H.Law'33) who was born In Columbus, OH on 31 October 1912, son of Adolph Theobald and Mrs. Harvey Cashatt. Married (2) in Washington, D.C. on 27 January 1966 WILLIAM FRANCIS PAYSON who was born in Short Hills, NJ on 22 January 1912, son of Harold Payson and Lavina Hodgkinson. (Payson now lives in Jaffrey, NH.)

Three children by Richard Jackson Theobald:

32.   I.   GRETCHEN, born in Morristown, NJ on 16 January 1946. Married (1) JIMMIE LEE HOAGLAND. Married (2) PETER FRANK RIENT (H'60).

   ii.   PENELOPE was born in Morristown, NJ on 19 October 1947 and died in Peterborough, NH on 27 July 1974. Married in Peterborough, NH on 16 December 1971 THOMAS ALLEN MAY who was born in New York, NY on 8 May 1944, son of Thomas S. May and Mary B. Barden. (No children).

33.   iii   SPRAGUE JACKSON, born in Boston, MA on 6 June 1951. Married THAYER McDOUGAL (TANTON).

18. JAMES LAWRENCE, III (H'58) was born in Boston, MA on 9 August 1936. Married in Milton, MA on 20 April 1963 JANE SCUDDER BURGIN (H'62) who was born in Boston, MA on 14 April 1940, daughter of Clarence Rodgers Burgin (H'21) and Helen Swain of Milton, MA.

Two children:

   i.   LANGDON SWAIN, born in Evreux, France on 29 June 1966.

   ii.   JAMES, IV (H'92), born in Baltimore, MD in 1970.

19. MARTINA LEE LAWRENCE (H'61) was born in Boston, MA on 16 April 1939. Married in Brookline, MA on 15 June 1963 NILE LUDLOW ALBRIGHT (H'61) who was born in Boston, MA on 5 August 1939, son of Hollis Ludlow Albright and Elin M. Petersen.

Three children:

   i.   MARTINA BRANDEGEE (H'90) was born in Boston, MA on 18 July 1968.

   ii.   TARA LAWRENCE was born in Boston, MA on 28 August 1969.

iii.   LARS LAWRENCE was born in Boston, MA on 3 October 1974.

20. EDWARD PEABODY LAWRENCE (H'63) was born in Boston, MA on 15 December 1941. Married in Gladwyne, PA on 1 April 1967 (divorced) VIRGINIA MIDDLETON MALONEY who was was born in Philadelphia, PA in 1942, daughter of Paul Maloney and Virginia Wells.

Two children:

i.   ABBOTT WELLS (H'93) was born in Boston, MA on 22 August 1970.

ii.   ELOISE PAUL was born in Boston, MA on 2 June 1973.

SIXTH GENERATION

21. CHARLES FORD PINGREE was born in Boston, MA on 10 January 1952. Married in North Haven, ME on 28 June 1975 ROCHELLE MARIE JOHNSON who was born in Minneapolis, MN on 2 April 1955, daughter of Harry Marvin Johnson and Dorothy Marie Henderson.

Three children:

i.   HANNAH MARIE was born in Belfast, ME on 18 October 1976.

ii.   CECILY was born in Camden, ME on 30 August 1979.

iii.   ASA ROBERT was born in Camden, ME on 14 June 1981.

22. SUMNER PINGREE, III was born in Boston, MA on 26 June 1953. Married in Bernardsville, NJ on 4 February 1978 SALLY JOAN EMELIA ALEXANDRA ENGELHARD who was born in New York, NY on 8 December 1953, daughter of Charles William Engelhard and Jane Reis Brian.

Two children:

i.   ALBERT HUGO was born in New York, NY on 4 July 1981.

ii.   KATHERINE ENGELHARD was born in Washington, D.C. on 9 February 1983.

23. WILLIAM LEWIS PINGREE was born in Salem, MA on 29 May 1958. Married in Cold Spring Harbor, NY on 20 August 1983 LUCY GURNEY CUMMINGS who was born in Glen Cove, NY on 1 October 1957, daughter of Edward Gurney Cummings and Karen Gjeillerup.

Two children:

i.   CAROLINE WELD WAS born in Salem, MA on 24 October 1985.

ii.   Child expected in Salem, MA in April 1990.

24. JAY COPELAND PINGREE was born in Salem, MA on 13 September 1961. Married in Marblehead, MA on 3 June 1984 SHARON FARRAR who was born in Marblehead, MA on 16 November 1958, daughter of Richard Farrar and Mary Ellen Peach.

One Child:

i.   CAITLIN MARGARET was born in Salem, MA on 25 June 1985.

25. JOHN RANDOLPH PINGREE, JR. was born in Miami, FL on 17 January 1957. Married in Granite City, IL on 25 April 1981 DEBRA LYNN DETTNER who was born in East St. Louis. MO on 20 April 1959, daughter of Frederick George Dettner and Marjorie Edna Pick.

One child:

i.   JOHN RANDOLPH, III was born in Marietta, GA on 21 November 1988.

26. ALEXANDER WELD PINGREE was born in Salem, MA on 13 February 1958. Married in Tuscumbia, AL on 3 March 1979 CINDY LYNN BIETZ who was born in Ft. Lauderdale, FL on 22 August 1958 daughter of Frederick M. Bietz and Dorothy Virginia Chaisson.

Three children:

i.   AMANDA JOY was born in Sheffield, AL on 12 February 1981.

ii.   TIFFANY WELD was born in Sheffield, AL on 15 December 1983.

iii.   AUBREY LYNN was born in Sheffield, AL on 4 September 1987.

27. MARY ORR PINGREE was born in Salem, MA on 26 April 1960. Married in Hamilton, MA on 15 October 1987 EDWARD WINSOR FISHER who was born in Boston, MA on 27 July 1959, son of John Noble Fisher and Cynthia Groener.

One child:

i.   EDWARD WINSOR, JR. was born in Hanover, NH on 30 October 1988.

28. WILLIAM JOHN BINGHAM, III was born in Boston, MA on 14 April 1946. Married in Grantsburg, WI on 31 July 1976 (divorced 1983) MARY ADA JILES who was born in Jefferson, Iowa on 15 December 1948, daughter of William Michael Jiles and Ida Lorraine Johnson.

One child:

i.   SKYE BOIT was born in Frederick, WI on 9 June 1979.

29. ROBERT BOIT BINGHAM was born in Boston, MA on 16 July 1948. Married in Wayzata, MN on 24 December 1980 JULIE ANN CHAPMAN who was born in Minneapolis, MN on 20 November 1953, daughter of Loyall Chapman and Mitzi Hanson.

Two children:

i.   JESSICA BOIT was born in Minneapolis, MN on 23 July 1984.

ii.   MAX WYATT was born in Minneapolis, MN on 14 July 1986

30. CHRISTOPHER SPRAGUE BOIT (H'78) was born in Boston, MA on 26 July 1956. Married in Wellesley, MA on 12 September 1987 AMY GRACE BROWN who was born in Boston, MA on 29 October 1959, daughter of Jacob B. Brown and Dianne A. McCraken.

One child:

i.   ANDREW was born in Boston, MA on 5 October 1989.

31. PETER GOODRICH BOIT was born in Boston, MA on 20 January 1960 Married in Kennilworth, IL on 25 June 1988 JENNIFER L. SCHNEIDERS who was born on 23 June _____, daughter of _____.

Child expected in Darien, CT in 1989.

32. GRETCHEN THEOBALD was born in Morristown, NJ on 16 Jaunary 1946. Married (1) in McLean, VA on 10 October 1970 (divorced 1979) JIMMIE LEE HOAGLAND (1970 Pulitzer Prize winner) who was born in Rock Hill, SC on 22 January 1940, son of Lee Roy Hoagland and Edith Irene Sullivan (now Estes). Married (2) in Washington, D.C. on 27 September 1980 PETER FRANK RIENT (H'60) who was born in Moscow, Russia on 12 March 1938, son of Mandakulatur Vishvanata Gangadharan (born in Madras, India on 6 September 1906) and Gertrude Rient (Mansfield) (born in Brno, Czechoslavakia on 2 February 1912.)

Two children by Peter Frank Rient:

i.   SPRAGUE MANSFIELD was born in Washington D.C. on 6 December 1981.

ii.   NELL INDIA was born in Washington, D.C. on 4 March 1984.

33. SPRAGUE JACKSON THEOBALD was born in Boston, MA on 6 June 1951. Married in Newport, RI on 6 December 1986 THAYER MCDOUGAL (TANTON) who was born in Detroit, MI on 21 October 1946, daughter of Leslie Paxton McDougal and Nancy Randell.

One child:

i.   SEFTON BUCKLAND was born in Newport, RI on 19 October 1988.

Two stepchildren:

i.   CHAUNCEY TANTON was born in Newport, RI on 29 September 1977.

ii.   DOMINIQUE TANTON was born in Newport, RI on 2 October 1980.

The Second Weld Brother
GEORGE RICHARDS MINOT WELD
and his descendants

FIRST GENERATION

1. GEORGE RICHARDS MINOT WELD was born in Boston, MA on 18 April 1803 and died in West Roxbury, MA on 16 December 1853, son of William Gordon Weld and Hannah Minot. Married in Roxbury, MA on 2 June 1833 HARRIET LOWDER who was born in Roxbury, MA on 21 January 1816 and died in Boston, MA after 1870, daughter of John Lowder and Charlotte Johnson. (Harriet Lowder Weld married 14 September 1870 Anni Willard of Woodstock, VT.)

Eight children:

2.   i.   ELLEN MINOT, born in West Roxbury, MA on 1 June 1834. Married BENJAMIN EDDY.

       ii.   A child was born in Jamaica Plain, MA in March 1836 and died in Jamaica Plain, MA on 13 April 1836.

       iii.   HARRIET JULIA was baptized in Jamaica Plain, MA on 28 May 1837 and died young, in Jamaica Plain, MA.

3.   iv.   SUSAN MINOT, born in Boston, MA on 15 June 1839. Married FRANKLIN WALTER.

4.   v.   ISABELLA MINOT, born in Boston, MA circa 1841. Married GEORGE HERBERT STEARNS.

5.   vi.   HARRIET EMILY, born in Boston, MA in 1845. Married HIRAM DAVID PECK.

       vii.   GEORGE RICHARDS MINOT, JR. was born in Boston, MA circa 1847 and died in New York, NY on 13 March 1922. (Unmarried).

       viii.   GORDON ELLIOT was born in Jamaica Plain, MA in 1852 and died in Boston, MA on 25 January 1899. (Unmarried).

SECOND GENERATION

2. ELLEN MINOT WELD was baptized in West Roxbury, MA on 1 June 1834 and died poss. in Groton, MA between 1880-1900. Married in Boston, Ma on 11 February 1854 BENJAMIN EDDY, who was born in Boston, MA on 26 January 1829 and died poss. Groton, MA after 1900, son of Caleb Eddy (1784-1859) and Caroline Gay (1792-1862).

Three children:

6   i.   CHARLES BENJAMIN, born in Medford, MA on 13 October 1854. Married LUCY ANN COREY.

     ii.   MARY CAROLINE was born in Roxbury, MA on 4 December 1855 and died after 1860. Place unknown, poss. Groton, MA.

     iii. NELLIE was born in Chelsea, MA on 28 February 1860 and died. (Place and date unknown, poss. Groton, MA.)

3. SUSAN MINOT WELD was born in Boston, MA on 15 June 1839 and died poss. Brookline, MA before 1903. Married in Boston, MA on 29 October 1863 to FRANKLIN WALTER who was born in Philadelphia, PA on 19 January 1839 and died in Brookline, MA on 4 March 1903, son of Edwin Walter and Hannah Ann Newlin.

Eight children:

     i.   FRANKLIN, JR. was born in Philadelphia, PA on 16 October 1864 and died in Brookline, MA on 31 May 1932. Married in Brookline, MA on 3 September 1902 ANNE VICTORIA FROUDE who was born in Clifford, Ontario on 19 April 1873 and died in Brookline, MA on 27 June 1958, daughter of Thomas Froude and Mary Matilda Biggar. No children.

     ii.   MINOT WELD was born in Philadelphia, PA on 3 January 1866 and died in Boston, MA on 26 December 1905. Married in Brookline, MA on 4 June 1890 ALICE WINCHESTER RICHARDS who was born in Saugus, MA on 3 May 1867 and died in Scituate, MA on 6 July 1894, daughter of J. Dudley Richards and Julia Born Saunders. No children.

7.   iii. ISABEL WELD, born in Philadelphia, PA on 4 February 1867. Married EDWARD LYMAN BROWN.

8.   iv.   BERTHA GORDON, born in New York, NY on 5 June 1869. Married FREDERIC

HEAP STRAWBRIDGE.

9. v. ANNA WHARTON, born in Philadelphia, PA on 31 December 1872. Married ALEXANDER FOSTER CROSMAN JR.

    vi. GEORGE WELD (H'00) was born in Philadelphia, PA on 21 November 1877 and died in Brattleboro, VT on 1 January 1926. (Not married).

10. vii. CORNELIA FRANKLIN, born in Germantown, PA on 13 June 1879. Married EDWIN PRESCOTT TRIPP.

11. viii. HARRY, born in Brookline, MA on 11 July 1880. Married (1) HENRIETTA MALLISON. Married (2) GRACE HOVEY ROGERS.

4. ISABELLA MINOT WELD was born in Boston, MA circa 1841 and died poss. in Wyoming, OH after 1880. Married (prob. MA or OH) on 15 April 1874 GEORGE HERBERT STEARNS, who was born in Cincinnati, OH on 14 March 1845 and died poss. Wyoming, OH after 1901, son of George Sullivan Stearns and Amelia Stevenson.

Three children:

    i. GEORGE MINOT WELD was born in Cincinnati, OH 20 August 1876 and died in Cincinnati, OH circa 1928. Married in Hamilton, OH circa 1920 EDNA WATERS (Gimble) who was born in Kentucky on 7 April 1898 and died in Cincinnati, OH on 7 August 1974, daughter of Silas B. Waters and Laura Bruner. No children.

    ii. MABEL was born in Cincinnati, OH on 18 October 1877 and died in San Jose, CA on 5 September 1970. Married in Boston, MA on 16 October 1918 WINALOE ULYSSES STONEHILL who was born in Washington, D.C. in 1883 and died probably in Los Angeles, CA between June-December 1939, son of Henry Stonehill and Emma D. Held. No children.

12. iii. GORDON WELD born in Wyoming, OH on 20 November 1880. Married MIRIAM CLARA Hobart.

5. HARRIET EMILY WELD was born in Boston, MA in 1845 and died in Cincinnati, OH on 12 January 1914. Married in Boston, MA on 19 November 1868 to HIRAM DAVID PECK, (H.Law'65) who was born in Cynthiana, KY on 23 March 1844 and died in Cincinnati, OH on 11 October 1914, son of John Wellington Peck and Nancy Jane Veach.

Three children:

i.   EDITH WELD was born in Cincinnati, OH in 1871 and died in Murray, KY on 23 October 1962. (Unmarried).

13.   ii.   JOHN WELD (H'96) born in Wyoming, OH on 5 February 1875. Married (1) NELLE WRIGHT. Married (2) ALMA HELM.

14.   iii.   ARTHUR MINOT born in Cincinnati, OH on 5 April 1877. Married MARGUERITE COMSTOCK.

THIRD GENERATION

6. CHARLES BENJAMIN EDDY was born in Medford, MA on 13 October 1854 and died in Groton, MA on 16 May 1936. Married in Groton, MA on 26 August 1877 LUCY ANN COREY who was born in Groton, MA on 30 August 1856, died in Groton, MA on 10 August 1923, daughter of Andrew C. Corey (a farmer) and Sarah C_____(Nashua, NH).

One child:

15.   i.   HELEN MINOT, born in Groton, MA on 7 July 1890. Married to ARTHUR OLAF CHRISTENSEN.

7. ISABEL WELD WALTER was born in Philadelphia, PA on 4 February 1867 and died in Brookline, MA on 20 February 1923. Married in Brookline, MA on 22 November 1893 EDWARD LYMAN BROWN who was born in Boston, MA on 25 March 1867 and died in Boston, MA on 13 March 1942, son of Edward Jackson Brown (son of Benjamin) and Mary E. Brown (daughter of Charles).

Three children:

16.   i.   CHARLES FARWELL, born in West Medford, MA on 23 July 1895. Married SARAH SOUTHWICK RODMAN.

17.   ii.   ELLIOT WELD, born in Weston, MA on 16 November 1897. Married (1) ELIZABETH DEGROAT. Married (2) CHRISTINE MARTIN QUIRK.

18.   iii.   EDWARD LYMAN, JR. born in Waltham, MA on 11 April 1899. Married ELIZABETH MAY JACK.

8. BERTHA GORDON WALTER was born in New York, NY on 5 June 1869 and died in Chestnut Hill, PA on 12 November 1946. Married in Brookline, MA on 5 June 1894 FREDERIC HEAP STRAWBRIDGE who was born in Chestnut Hill, PA on 24 October 1866 and died in Chestnut Hill, PA on 21 December 1958, son of Justus Clayton Strawbridge and Mary S. Lukens.

Five children:

19.   i.   JUSTUS CLAYTON, born in Chestnut Hill, PA on 17 April 1895. Married MARGARET LARUE.

20.   ii.   FREDERIC HEAP, Jr. born in Chestnut Hill, PA on 18 November 1897. Married EMILY EARNSHAW CLOTHIER.

21.   iii.   ANNA WELD, born in Philadelphia, PA on 3 October 1900. Married JOHN WINTHROP CLAGHORN.

22.   iv.   GORDON WELD, born in Philadelphia, PA on 4 Novmeber 1901. Married (1) ELIZABETH MOSCHEL ECHTERNACH. Married (2) NANCY STUDEVANT MEYER. Married (3) ELIZABETH ALMA FISHER.

23.   v.   EDWARD RICHIE born in Philadelphia, PA on 22 November 1903. Married (1) BARBARA WARD PERRY. Married (2) JOYCE HELEN TRAUGER.

9. ANNA WHARTON WALTER was born in Philadelphia, PA on 31 December 1872 and died circa 1954 in Mt. Airy, PA. Married in Philadelphia, PA on 10 June 1896 (divorced) to ALEXANDER FOSTER CROSMAN, JR. who was born in Portsmouth, NH on 1 August 1871 and died in Oswego, IL on 2 August 1980, son of Alexander Foster Crosman and Frances Strader Foster (daughter of composer, Stephen Foster).

One child:

24.   i.   DOROTHY WELD, born in Montreal, Quebec, Canada on 12 April 1908. Married HERBERT ARTHUR WOODBURY, JR.

10. CORNELIA FRANKLIN WALTER was born in Germantown, PA in 13 June 1879 and died in North Falmouth, MA on 11 January 1966. Married in Philadelphia, PA on 31 January 1902 EDWIN PRESCOTT TRIPP who was born in New Bedford, MA on 5 December 1879 and died in Falmouth, MA on 11 December 1953, son of Eliphlet A. Tripp and Henrietta M. Vincent.

Two children:

25.   i.   EDWIN PRESCOTT, Jr. born in Boston, MA on 27 December 1912. Married (1) THERESA MOCHAK. Married (2) EDITH POWELL.

26.   ii.   MINOT WELD, born in Boston, MA on 9 March 1915. Married MARTHA JANE SWANSON.

11. HARRY WALTER was born in Brookline, MA on 11 July 1880 and died in Brookline, MA on 28 February 1941. Married (1) in Newton, MA on 12 October 1910 HENRIETTA MALLISON who was born in England on 26 March 1882 and died in Boston, MA on 25 June 1914, daughter of Frank Mallison and Annie Ashworth; married (2) in Brookline, MA on 16 January 1918 GRACE HOVEY ROGERS who was born in Brookline, MA on 31 January 1881 and died in North Falmouth, MA on 20 March 1981, daughter of George Rogers and Sarah Foster Guild.

One child:

        i.   BERTHA GORDON was born in Boston, MA on 5 October 1912. Married in Newton, MA on 15 June 1957 HOWARD ERNEST ETTER who was born in Everett, MA on 8 May 1913, son of John Conrad Etter and Ray Marshall. (No children).

12. GORDON WELD STEARNS was born in Wyoming, OH on 20 November 1880 and died poss. Wyoming, OH after 1907. Married in Newton, MA on 14 June 1905 MIRIAM CLARA HOBART who was born in Newton MA on 3 May 1885 and died in Newton, MA on 9 January 1973, daughter of Kirk Wood Hobart and Henrietta Hamilton.

One child:

27.   i.   MIRIAM VERE, born in Newton, MA on 2 April 1907. Married WALTER JACK HETHERINGTON TURNBULL.

13. JOHN WELD PECK was born in Wyoming, OH on 5 February 1875 and died in Cincinnati, OH on 10 August 1937. Married (1) in Cincinnati, OH on 7 January 1899 NELLE WRIGHT who was born Cincinnati, in 1871 and died in Cincinnati, OH on 26 October 1931, daughter of Cyrus Mansfield Wright and Mary Julia Tanner. Married (2) in Cincinnati, OH on 5 August 1933 ALMA HELM who was born in Indiana on 17 April 1885 and died in Cincinnati, OH on 29 August 1979, daughter of Andrew Helm and Anna Ilzhoeffer.

Two children:

28.   i.   JANE WRIGHT, born in Cincinnati, OH on 29 March 1902. Married HERBERT SMEAD ALCORN.

29.   ii.   EMILY NELLE, born in Cincinnati, OH on 21 February 1905. Married LUCIEN HOLIDAY MINOR.

14. ARTHUR MINOT PECK was born in Cincinnati, OH on 5 April 1877 and died in Wyoming OH on 28 October 1962. Married (poss. in Cleveland, OH) in 1902 MARGUERITE COMSTOCK who was born in Cleveland, OH on 30 October 1879 and died in Cincinnati, OH on 13 April 1939, daughter of Frank Dunham Comstock and Marguerite G. Congley (of New Orleans, LA).

Three children:

30.   i   HAROLD DAVID, born in Cincinnati, OH on 16 February 1908. Married ELLEN POAGE.

31.   ii.   JOHN WELD, II born in Cincinnati OH on 23 June 1913. Married (1) BARBARA ANN MOESER. Married (2) JANET ALCORN.

32.   iii.   ARTHUR MINOT, JR. born in Wyoming, OH on 19 December 1918. Married (1) ELIZABETH BULLOCK. Married (2) JANET ANN SCHOENBERG.

FOURTH GENERATION

15. HELEN MINOT EDDY was born in Groton, MA on 7 July 1890 and died in September 1973 in Groton, MA. Married in Groton, MA on 25 January 1911 ARTHUR OLAF CHRISTENSEN (H'06) who was born in Beaufort, SC on 12 December 1882 and died in Beaufort, SC on 26 April 1971, son of Niels Christensen and Abby Mandana Holmes.

One child:

i.   MINOT HOLMES was born in Groton, MA on 1 June 1912 and died in Groton, MA on 5 November 1933.

16. CHARLES FARWELL BROWN was born in W. Medford, MA on 23 July 1895 and died in Newton, MA on 24 October 1962. Married in Brookline, MA on 14 May 1921 SARAH SOUTHWICK RODMAN who was born in Wellesley Hills, MA on 1 August 1894 and died in Norwalk, CT on June 1976, daughter of Dr. Warren A. Rodman and

Caroline Southwick.

Two children:

33.   i.   CHARLES FARWELL, JR. born in Boston, MA on 17 March 1922. Married JANICE GLENN ST. CLAIR.

      ii. RODMAN WELD (H'45) was born in Jamaica Plain, MA on 10 May 1924 and died in Glendale, CA in June/July 1988. (Unmarried).

17. ELLIOT WELD BROWN was born in Weston, MA on 16 November 1897 and died in Plymouth, MA on 19 January 1987. Married (1) in Boston, MA on 7 January 1933 ELIZABETH DEGROAT who was born in Passaic, NJ in 1901 and died in Boston, MA on 3 February 1938, daughter of Floyd Elmer DeGroat and Minnie Phelps Swan. Married (2) in Wellesley, MA on 27 February 1946 CHRISTINE MARTIN QUIRK who was born in Oswego, NY on 17 June 1904 and died in Massachusetts in March 1987, daughter of John Henry Quirk and Nelle Goble.

One child by Elizabeth DeGroat Brown:

      i.   DIANA DEGROAT was born in Boston, MA on 23 January 1938.

18. EDWARD LYMAN BROWN, JR. was born in Waltham, MA on 11 April 1899. Married in Beverly, MA on 8 May 1937 ELIZABETH MAY JACK who was born in Manchester, MA on 2 March 1907, daughter of Thomas Reid Jack (of Scotland) and Elizabeth Wood Stenhouse.

One child:

      i.   EDWARD REID was born in Beverly, MA on 20 March 1939.

19. JUSTUS CLAYTON STRAWBRIDGE was born in Chestnut Hill, PA on 17 April 1895 and died in Newport, RI on 22 July 1981. Married in Germantown, PA on 16 April 1918 MARGARET LARUE who was born in Germantown, PA on 2 April 1895 and died in Newport, RI on 1 May 1974, daughter of Walter LaRue and Helen Fruit.

One child:

34.   i.   MARGARET, born in Merion, PA on 3 February 1919. Married MANCHA MADISON CLEWS.

20. FREDERIC HEAP STRAWBRIDGE, JR. was born in Chestnut Hill, PA on 18 November 1897 and died in Wynnewood, PA on 11 August 1980. Married in Randor, PA on 5 October 1920 EMILY EARNSHAW CLOTHIER who was born in Villa Nova, PA on 1 June 1901, daughter of Morris Lewis Clothier and Lydia May Earnshaw.

Six children:

35.   i.   EMILY CLOTHIER, born in Philadelphia, PA on 18 February 1922. Married THOMAS JOSEPH WRIGHT.

      ii. LYDIA LAWRENCE was born in Philadelphia, PA on 2 June 1924.

36.   iii. MARY, born in Philadelphia, PA on 30 August 1925. Married PETER PAGE SCHAUFFLER.

37.   iv. ALEXANDRA CUMMINS, born in Philadelphia, PA on 16 January 1937. Married THOMAS JOSEPH WRIGHT.

      v.   ELIZABETH WALTER was born in Philadelphia, PA on 29 January 1939 and died in Bryn Mawr, PA on 5 August 1974. Married in Wynnewood, PA on 5 September 1970 CHARLES WILLIAMS FRANK who was born in Jacksonville, IL on 12 February 1943, son of Charles Edward Frank and Dorothy Berry.(No children).

      vi. FREDERICA WAS born in Philadelphia, PA on 4 July 1941 and died in Philadelphia, PA on 23 May 1984. (Not married).

21. ANNA WELD STRAWBRIDGE was born in Philadelphia, PA on 3 October 1900 and died in Philadelphia, PA in March 1989. Married in Philadelphia, PA on 8 October 1919 to JOHN WINTHROP CLAGHORN who was born in Philadelphia, PA on 6 September 1898 and died in Philadelphia, PA on 2 September 1986, son of John William Claghorn and Agnes Ellis Boyd.

Five children:

38.   i.   ANNE STRAWBRIDGE, born in Philadephia, PA on 19 July 1920. Married WILLIAM THACHER LONGSTRETH.

39.   ii.   ELIZABETH LIVINGSTON, born in Philadelphia, PA on 24 October 1922. Married ALAN MCILVAIN.

40.   iii.   JOHN WINTHROP JR., born in Philadephia, PA on 28 December 1923. Married MARGERY ELIZABETH RICHARDSON.

41.   iv.   SUSAN MINOT WELD, born in Philadelphia, PA on 7 December 1925. Married (1) RICHARD E. PILLING. Married (2) THEODORE BIRD AITKEN.

42.   v.   FREDERICK STRAWBRIDGE, born in Philadelphia, PA on 9 November 1926. Married KATHARINE TAWS.

22. GORDON WELD STRAWBRIDGE (HBS'24) was born in Philadelphia, PA on 4 November 1900. Married (1) in Elkton, MD on 3 February 1926 ELIZABETH MOSCHEL ECHTERNACH who was born in Germantown, PA on 19 March 1906 and died in Palo Alto, CA on 3 March 1943, daughter of William Echternach and Caroline Hartenstein. Married (2) in 1943, (divorced 1960) NANCY STURDEVANT MEYER, who was born in New Haven, CT in 1923, daughter of John Meyer and Florine Greer. (She subsequently married Howard Haven Jewell in 1965.) Married (3) in Mill Valley, CA on 22 June 1963 (divorced 1980) ELIZABETH ALMA FISHER, who was born in Maine on 4 April 1918, daughter of Daniel W. Fisher and Lottie Blanchard.

One child by Elizabeth Moschel Echternach:

43.   i.   SALLY WELD, born in Germantown, PA on 10 November 1926. Married CHARLES WALTER MAGNESON.

Two children by Nancy Sturdevant Meyer:

44.   ii.   DAPHNE GREER, born in Eureka, CA on 13 January 1945. Married ROGER MALCOLM STEWART.

45.   iii.   ROGER CLAYTON, born in San Francisco, CA on 3 April 1947. Married WENDY LOVE.

Stepchild (daughter of Elizabeth Alma Fisher):

    i.   NANCY ELLEN MADDOCK was born in New Jersey on 18 January 1948, daughter of Charles Maddock and Elizabeth Alma Fisher. Married in San Rafael, CA on 18 January 1969 MICHAEL THOMAS CALDWELL who was born in

California on 6 August 1946, son of Charles Caldwell and Bertha Shanks.

23. EDWARD RICHIE STRAWBRIDGE was born in Philadelphia, PA on 22 November 1903. Married (1) in Whitemarch, PA on 16 April 1941 BARBARA WARD PERRY who was born in Germantown, PA on 13 July 1917 and died in Germantown, PA on 28 November 1949, daughter of Ward Tyson Perry and Laura Thomas; Married (2) in Mill Valley, CA on 5 April 1956 to JOYCE HELEN TRAUGER who was born in Ambler, PA on 14 January 1929, daughter of George Halverson Trauger and Antoinette Klinger.

Two children by Barbara Ward Perry:

    i.   SANDRA was born in Chestnut Hill, PA on 17 February 1945. Married in Chestnut Hill, PA in 1968 (divorced 1974) PETER YOVU who was born in New York, NY on 14 February 1949, son of George Yovu and Mary Breare.

46.   ii.   FREDERIC JUSTUS, born in Chestnut Hill, PA on 13 November 1946. Married PATRICIA SHANNON.

24. DOROTHY WELD CROSSMAN was born in Montreal, Canada on 12 April 1908. Married in Paris, France on 28 July 1928 HERBERT ARTHUR WOODBURY, JR. who was born in Council Bluffs, IA on 19 March 1901 and died in Alton, IL on 2 August 1980, son of Herbert Arthur Woodbury and Bessie Conklin.

Three children:

47.   i.   PATRICIA MINOT, born in Philadelphia, PA on 15 June 1929. Married WILLIAM DAVID BIRD.

    ii.   ALEXANDER CROSMAN was born in Philadelphia, PA on 8 September 1932.

    iii.   EDMUND WHITNEY was born in Philadelphia, PA on 14 August 1936.

25. EDWIN PRESCOTT TRIPP, JR. was born in Boston, MA on 27 December 1912. Married (1) in Hartford, CT circa 1935-40 (divorced) THERESA MARIE MOCHAK who was born in Westfield, MA on 24 September 1914 died in Falmouth, MA on 28 July 1978, daughter of Stanislav Mochak and Gabriella Thriesak. Married (2) in Plymouth, MA on 28 October 1965 EDITH POWELL (HAMPTON) who was born in Everett, MA on 30 December 1924, daughter of Henry M. Powell and Roseley M. Taylor.

Two children by Theresa Marie Mochak:

48.   i.   ELIZABETH ANN, born in Wareham, MA on 9 August 1943. Married WALTER COACHMAN PRICE, Jr.

        ii.   EDWIN PRESCOTT, III WAS born in Wareham, MA on 3 May 1945. Married in Melrose, MA on 23 October 1976 DARRYL DONNELLY who was born in Lynn, MA on 2 October 1946, daughter of Leonard T. Donnelly and Evelyn Marie Daggatt. No children.

26. MINOT WELD TRIPP was born in Boston, MA on 9 March 1915. Married in Falmouth, MA on 2 September 1938 MARTHA JANE SWANSON who was born in Youngsville, PA on 9 October 1916, daughter of Frederick E. Swanson and Hazel Sweet.

Two children:

49.   i.   MINOT WELD, Jr born in Cambridge, MA on 18 June 1939. Married MALLORY ANN PENFIELD.

50.   ii.   SUSAN VINCENT, born in Newton, MA on 4 August 1947 married LYLE BYRON SNIDER.

27. MIRIAM VERE STEARNS was born in Newton, MA on 2 April 1907 and died in Boston, MA on 24 July 1973. Married in Boston, MA on 31 August 1935 WALTER JACK HETHERINGTON TURNBULL who was born in Boston, MA on 18 February 1907 and died in Brookline, MA on 25 January 1980, son of Walter Hetherington Turnbull and Kathleen Elizabeth Keats.

Two children:

        i.   GUY HOBART HETHERINGTON was born in Boston, MA on 16 January 1938. Married in Brookline, MA on 10 November 1974 CONSTANCE ELEANOR DZIOK who was born in Woonsocket, RI on 19 December 1946, daughter of Theodore J Dziok and Elizabeth Szpakowski. (No children.)

51.   ii.   GWENDOLYN STEARNS, born in Boston, MA on 2 December 1940. Married PETER LAURENCE FENNINGER.

28. JANE WRIGHT PECK was born in Cincinnati, OH on 29 March 1902. Married in Wyoming, OH on 27 October 1928 HERBERT SMEAD ALCORN who was born in

Wyoming OH on 25 May 1900 and died in Naples, FL on 31 December 1982, son of Herbert Alcorn and Grace Smead.

Two children:

52. i. HERBERT RICHARD, born in St. Louis, MO on 24 October 1933. Married (1) JOANNE KELLER. Married (2) ROSETTA ELIZABETH FALKENRATH (KREISEL). Married (3) PATRICIA GEDOS (BERLY).

53. ii. WILLIAM WRIGHT, born in St. Louis, MO on 2 February 1936. Married (1) MARY ELIZABETH JONES. Married (2) SUSAN WHITE.

29. EMILY NELLE PECK was born in Cincinnati, OH on 21 February 1905. Married in Wyoming, OH in 1925 (divorced 1936) LUCIEN HOLIDAY MINOR, who was born in Charlottesville, VA in 1900 and died circa 1975-78.

Three children:

54. i. LUCIEN WELD, born in Charlottesville, VA on 6 November 1926. Married BARBARA MASON BRENT.

55. ii. PATRICIA JEANNE, born in Covington, KY on 21 November 1928. Married WALTER JACKSON TAYLOR, JR.

56. iii. JOHN WELD PECK, born in Cincinnati, OH on 29 June 1935. Married (1) VIRGINIA GREENE. Married (2) SUSAN LYNN KUEHL.

30. HAROLD DAVID PECK was born in Cincinnati, OH on 16 February 1908 and died in Wyoming, OH on 29 December 1988. Married in Wyoming, OH on 9 December 1938 ELLEN POAGE who was born in Cincinnati, OH on 9 March 1917, daughter of C. Dean Poage and Marion Mitchell.

Four children:

57. i. DAVID WINCHESTER, born in Wyoming, OH on 1 June 1936 Married BEVERLY JEAN AYERS.

58. ii. MARY ELLEN, born in Wyoming, OH circa 1940. Married JOHN THOMAS STONE.

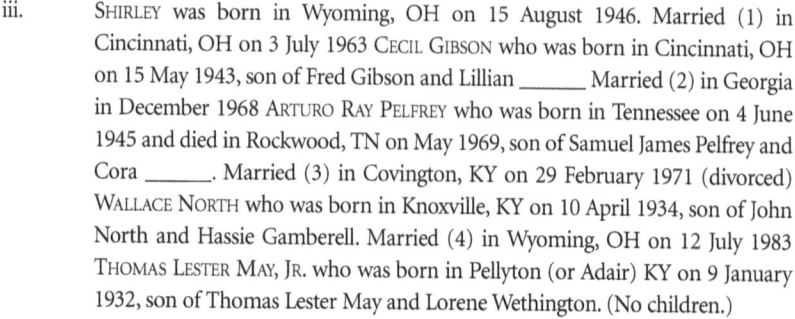

iii.   SHIRLEY was born in Wyoming, OH on 15 August 1946. Married (1) in Cincinnati, OH on 3 July 1963 CECIL GIBSON who was born in Cincinnati, OH on 15 May 1943, son of Fred Gibson and Lillian _____ Married (2) in Georgia in December 1968 ARTURO RAY PELFREY who was born in Tennessee on 4 June 1945 and died in Rockwood, TN on May 1969, son of Samuel James Pelfrey and Cora _____. Married (3) in Covington, KY on 29 February 1971 (divorced) WALLACE NORTH who was born in Knoxville, KY on 10 April 1934, son of John North and Hassie Gamberell. Married (4) in Wyoming, OH on 12 July 1983 THOMAS LESTER MAY, JR. who was born in Pellyton (or Adair) KY on 9 January 1932, son of Thomas Lester May and Lorene Wethington. (No children.)

iv.   WILLIAM GLEN was born in Wyoming, OH on 15 May 1948.

31. JOHN WELD PECK II was born in Cincinnati, OH on 23 June 1913. Married (1) in Cincinnati, OH on 25 March 1941 to BARBARA ANN MOESER who was born in Cincinnati, OH on 15 August 1915 and died in Cincinnati, OH on18 April 1981, daughter of Edgar R. Moeser and Edna Kearns. Married (2) in Cincinnati, OH on 29 January 1982 JANET ALCORN who was born in Cincinnati, OH on 23 April 1913, daughter of Robert S. Alcorn and Edith Maish.

Three children by Barbara Ann Moeser:

59.   i.   JOHN WELD III, born in Cincinnati, OH on 29 January 1944. Married (1) SUSAN BELT. Married (2) SUE ANN BLOCKER.

60.   ii.   JAMES HIRAM, born in Cincinnati, OH in 1945. Married BARBARA TROMBLY.

61.   iii.   CHARLES EDWIN, born in Cincinnati, OH in 1948 Married MARY ELLEN HAGEN.

32. ARTHUR MINOT PECK, JR. was born in Wyoming, OH on 19 December 1918. Married (1) in Ft. Worth, TX on 16 August 1941 (divorced 1962) to ELIZABETH BULLOCK who was born in Toledo, OH on 5 April 1917, daughter of Holt Bullock and Gladys Graves. Married (2) in Cincinnati, OH on 20 August 1965 JANET ANN SCHOENBERG (ROBINSON) who was born in Harrison, OH on 24 November 1926, daughter of George Walter Schoenberg and Cordinda Lee; Married (3) in Cincinnati, OH on 4 September 1970 ROSEMARY TATE STEFENS (COSTETTER) who was born in Cicero, IN on 1 February 1917, daughter of Roy Carlton Stefens and Margaret Tate.

Three children of Elizabeth Bullock:

62.   i.   NANCY MINOT, born in Cincinnati, OH on 1 March 1948. Married JOHN AMOS LONG, JR.

63.   ii.   ELIZABETH GRAVES, born in Cincinnati, OH on 27 August 1949. Married TERRY ALAN DUNLAP.

64.   iii.   CHRISTINE WELD, born in Cincinnati, OH on 9 November 1951. Married CARL HINZ MARGRAF, JR.

FIFTH GENERATION

33. CHARLES FARWELL BROWN, JR. (H'45) was born in Boston, MA on 17 March 1922. Married in Newton, MA on 26 February 1944 JANICE GLENN ST. CLAIR who was born in Coshocton, OH on 17 July 1922, daughter of Clinton Draper St. Clair and Margaret J. Glenn.

Two children:

65.   i.   CHARLES ST. CLAIR, born in Boston, MA on 10 December 1944. Married JACQUELINE ANN STONE.

66.   ii.   JAMES SOUTHWICK, born in Boston, MA on 24 April 1948. Married CYNTHIA CONWAY GROSS.

34. MARGARET STRAWBRIDGE was born in Merion, PA on 3 February 1919. Married in Woods Hole, MA on 5 September 1940 MANCHA MADISON CLEWS who was born in Paris, France on 27 October 1915, son of Henry Clews Jr. and Marie Elsie Whelen (Goelet).

Three children:

67.   i.   CHRISTOPHER STRAWBRIDGE, born in Bryn Mawr, PA on 16 November 1944. Married NOELE DOYLE.

68.   ii.   HENRY MADISON, born in Bryn Mawr, PA on 19 November 1944. Married HENRIETTA BOOTH THOMPSON.

       iii.   SYLVIA was born in Bryn Mawr, PA on 30 April 1953.

35. EMILY CLOTHIER STRAWBRIDGE was born in Philadelphia, PA on 18 February 1922 and died in Philadelphia, PA in May 1951. Married in Narberth, PA in April 1948 THOMAS JOSEPH WRIGHT who born in Narberth, PA on 10 April 1923, son of Edward V. Wright.

One child:

69.   i.   FREDERIC STRAWBRIDGE WRIGHT, born in Philadelphia, PA on 25 November 1949. Married DIANE MARIE DIMASCIO.

36. MARY STRAWBRIDGE was born in Philadelphia, PA on 30 August 1925. Married in Philadelphia, PA on 2 July 1958 PETER PAGE SCHAUFFLER who was born in New York, NY on 13 October 1922, son of Bennet Fellows Schauffler and Marjorie Page.

Three children:

i.   RICHARD PAGE, born in Philadelphia, PA on 1 May 1959.

ii.   DAVID ESTES, born in Philadelphia, PA on 29 June 1961.

iii.   FLORENCE, born in Philadelphia, PA on 1 November 1963.

37. ALEXANDRA CUMMINS STRAWBRIDGE was born in Philadelphia, PA on 16 January 1937. Married (1) in Narberth, PA on 19 September 1953 (divorced) THOMAS JOSEPH WRIGHT who was born in Narberth, PA on 10 April 1923, son of Edward V. Wright (Previously married to Alexandra's sister, Emily C. Strawbridge). Married (2) in Wynnewood, PA on 1 January 1968 (divorced) DAVID STEWART SMITH, who was born 24 February 1939.

Six children by Thomas Joseph Wright; all subsequently adopted by David Stewart Smith:

70.   i.   ALEXANDRA MARIE (WRIGHT) SMITH, born in Philadelphia, Pa on 17 August 1954. Married KURT WENZEL.

71.   ii.   TIMOTHY JAMES (WRIGHT) SMITH, born in Philadelphia, PA in September 1955. Married CATHERINE MCFALL.

72.   iii.   GREGORY GIRARD (WRIGHT) SMITH, born in Philadelphia, PA on 12 March 1957. Married PAMELA RAE SNYDER.

iv.   JOHN ANTHONY (WRIGHT) SMITH was born in Philadelphia, PA on 20 March 1958. Married in Coudersport, PA in June 1980 SONJA ROHRER who was born in

Lancaster, PA on 16 March 1961, daughter of Clyde Rohrer and Eleanor_____.

v.   PAUL BENEDICT (WRIGHT) SMITH was born in Philadelphia, PA on 13 August 1959.

73.   vi.   ELIZABETH ANN (WRIGHT) SMITH, born in Philadelphia, PA on 26 February 1964. Married KENNETH RUTER.

Child by David Stewart Smith:

i.   DAVID LEWIS SMITH was born in Bryn Mawr, PA on 25 September 1970.

38. ANNE STRAWBRIDGE CLAGHORN was born in Philadelphia, PA on 19 July 1920. Married in Chestnut Hill, PA on 21 June 1941 WILLIAM THACHER LONGSTRETH who was born in Haverford, PA on 4 November 1919 and died in Florida 11 April 2003, son of William Church Longstreth and Nelle Thacher Cameron.

Four children:

74.   i.   ANNE CLAGHORN, born in Philadelphia, PA on 13 May 1942. Married (1) JAY ALLEN ANDERSON. Married (2) ROBERT PAUL DeLAY.

75.   ii.   PETER STRAWBRIDGE, born in Philadelphia, PA on 15 October 1944. Married ELIZABETH ERICKSON STEEL.

76.   iii.   ELLEN KINCAID, born in Philadelphia, PA on 28 November 1945. Married EDWARD HOWARD GOODWIN, JR.

77.   iv.   WILLIAM THACHER, JR. born in Detroit, MI on 13 April 1949. Married ALICE BRECKINRIDGE GOODWIN.

39. ELIZABETH LIVINGSTON CLAGHORN was born in Philadelphia, PA on 24 October 1922. Married in Philadelphia, PA on 4 October 1947 ALAN McILVAIN, who was born in Downingtown, PA on 17 February 1922, son of Walter Biddle McIlvain and Alida Brown Baird.

Three children:

78.   i.   ALAN, JR. born in Philadelphia, PA on 28 June 1948. Married ANN HAVENS.

79. ii.   GORDON WELD, born in Philadelphia, PA on 4 February 1951. Married MARCIA H JORDAN.

80. iii.   JANET LIVINGSTON, born in Philadelphia, PA on 21 April 1954. Married DAVID OAKES O'HARA.

40. JOHN WINTHROP CLAGHORN, JR. was born in Philadelphia, PA on 28 December 1923. Married in Pocono Manor, PA on 22 June 1946 MARGERY ELIZABETH RICHARDSON who was born in Passaic, NJ on 13 December 1924, daughter of Hubert Townsend Richardson and Lydia Cheyney.

Four children:

81. i.   MARGERY RICHARDSON born in Philadelphia, PA on 4 May 1947. Married RANDALL WARREN ROBERTSON.

82. ii.   JOHN WINTHROP III born in Philadelphia, PA on 24 August 1950. Married MARGARET ELLEN JUMP.

83. iii.   DAVID TOWNSEND born in Boston, MA on 15 May 1953. Married ELIZABETH VANTASSEL WEISBECKER.

84. iv.   SUSAN STRAWBRIDGE born in Princeton, NJ on 2 July 1957. Married SUART WILLIAM FERGUSON.

41. SUSAN MINOT WELD CLAGHORN was born in Philadelphia, PA on 7 December 1925. Married (1) in Chestnut Hill, PA on 15 June 1946 RICHARD E. PILLING, who was born in Chestnut Hill, PA circa 1924 and died Somerville, NJ on 5 November 1951, son of George Platt Pilling, III and Lucille Bachman. Married (2) in Chestnut Hill, PA on 29 November 1952 THEODORE BIRD AITKEN who was born on 28 April 1923, son of John Aitken.

Three children by Richard E. Pilling (subsequently adopted by Theodore Bird Aitken):

i.   RICHARD was born in Philadelphia, PA on 8 May 1947.

ii.   STEPHEN STOCKTON was born in Philadelphia, PA.

iii.   JAMES LAWRENCE was born in Philadelphia, PA.

Two children by Theodore Bird Aitken:

i.   SUZANNE NIVEN was born in Philadelphia, PA on 29 September 1953.

ii.   THEODORE BIRD, JR. was born in Philadelphia, PA on 20 July 1956.

42. FREDERICK STRAWBRIDGE CLAGHORN was born in Philadelphia, PA on 9 November 1926. Married in *Andalusia,* Torresdale, PA on 25 June 1949 KATHARINE TAWS who was born in Philadelphia, PA on 9 June 1932, daughter of Edward Town Taws and Helen May Holmes.

Three children:

85.   i.   FREDERICK STRAWBRIDGE, JR. born in Philadelphia, PA on 8 March 1950. Married MARY HOLT SCOTT.

86.   ii.   EDWARD TAWS born in Philadelphia, PA on 29 May 1952. Married KATRINA ELIZABETH VAN BUREN.

      iii   JAMES LAWRENCE was born in Philadelphia, PA on 4 November 1953. Married in Carmel, CA on 7 April 1990 ANITA RACHEL ZICHICHI who was born in West Covina, CA on 13 April 1958, daughter of Lindy Zichichi and Mary Rita Giacalone.

43. SALLY WELD STRAWBRIDGE was born in Germantown, PA on 10 November 1926. Married in San Francisco, CA on 30 August 1947 CHARLES WALTER MAGNESON, who was born in Los Gatos, CA on 17 March 1923, son of Walter Charles Magneson and Hazel Downing.

Seven children:

87.   i.   LESLIE ELIZABETH born in Sacramento, CA on 6 June 1948. Married RONALD PETER CHILDS.

88.   ii.   NANCY LYNN born in Turlock, CA on 7 May 1950, Married JOHN BRADLEY CASSIDY.

89.   iii. ROBIN MOSCHEL born in Turlock, CA on 23 December 1951. Married WILLIAM NORMAN CENTER.

90.   iv.   SCOTT STRAWBRIDGE born in Turlock, CA on 1 May 1953. Married PAMELA

Ann Greenstreet.

91.   v.   John Forrest born in Ceres, CA on 18 March 1955. Married Patricia Lynn Gooch.

92.   vi.   Mark Downing born in Modesto, CA on 25 August 1956. Married Jan McKelvey.

      vii.   Eric Weld born in Modesto, CA on 20 August 1959.

44. Daphne Greer Strawbridge was born in Eureka, CA on 13 January 1945. Married in Mill Valley, CA on 24 November 1967 Roger Malcolm Stewart who was born in Oklahoma City, OK 9 April 1941, son of Roy Stewart and June Mayberry.

Three children:

i.   Jesse Gordon was born in Berkeley, CA on 2 April 1972.

ii.   Justin Nickolas was born in Menlo Park, CA on 30 May 1979.

iii.   Patrick Haven was born in Rolling Bay, WA on 30 December 1986.

45. Roger Clayton Strawbridge was born in San Francisco, CA on 3 April 1947. Married in Sausalito, CA on 10 May 1970 Wendy Love, who was born in Palo Alto, CA on 12 October 1940, daughter of David Love and Arah Manning.

One child:

i.   Arah Kate was born in Denver, CO on 1 June 1975.

46. Frederic Justus Strawbridge was born in Chestnut Hill, PA on 13 November 1946. Married in Maryland, on 14 February 1969 Patricia Shannon, who was born in Philadelphia, PA on 31 January 1947, daughter of Thomas Shannon and Laura Purves.

Two children:

i.   Jennifer Shannon was born in Overbrook, PA on 3 November 1969.

ii.   REBECCA PERRY was born in Overbrook, PA on 7 August 1973.

47. PATRICIA MINOT WOODBURY was born in Philadelphia, PA on 15 June 1929. Married in Alton, IL on 23 August 1952 (divorced) WILLIAM DAVID BIRD, who was born in Savannah, GA in 1925, son of Edmund Bird and Idel Miller.

One child:

93.   i.   LAURA WOODBURY, born in Chicago, IL on 6 June 1957. Married TERRY WAYNE BERNAIX.

48. ELIZABETH ANN TRIPP was born in Wareham, MA on 9 August 1943. Married in Falmouth, MA on 16 January 1968 (divorced 1990) WALTER COACHMAN PRICE, JR. who was born in Pittsburgh, PA on 18 May 1948, son of Walter Coachman Price and Janet Armstrong.

Four children:

i.   AMY ELIZABETH was born in Boston, MA on 28 March 1970.

ii.   HEATHER ANN was born in Boston, MA on 8 October 1973.

iii.   LAUREN ALYSSA was born in Berkeley, CA on 24 November 1976.

iv.   WALTER COACHMAN III was born in Berkeley, CA on 2 March 1981.

49. MINOT WELD TRIPP, JR. (H'61) was born in Cambridge, MA on 18 June 1939 and died in San Francisco, CA on 13 July, 1996. Married in Orinda, CA on 3 October 1964 MALLORY ANN PENFIELD who was born in Los Angeles, CA on 30 July 1943, daughter of Raymond Cozenove Penfield and Thelma Hanson.

Two children:

i.   STEPHEN MINOT was born in Walnut Creek, CA on 6 February 1969.

ii.   JOHN PENFIELD was born in Walnut Creek, CA on 2 December 1972.

50. SUSAN VINCENT TRIPP was born in Newton, MA on 4 August 1947. Married in Swathmore, PA on 24 March 1968 LYLE BYRON SNIDER who was born in Chicago, IL on 18 May 1947, son of Byron Snider and Helen Frances Griffith.

Two children:

i.   NATHAN PETER was born in Meadowbrook, PA on 21 June 1971.

ii.   JEREMY DAVID was born in 16 May 1977 Durham, NC.

51. GWENDOLYN STEARNS TURNBULL was born in Boston, MA on 2 December 1940, married in Boston, MA on 18 June 1965 to PETER LAURENCE FENNINGER, who was born in Quincy, MA on 26 June 1942, son of Laurence Fenninger, Jr. and Mary Farmhoff.

Two children:

i.   MICHAEL TURNBULL was born in Chambersburg, PA on 24 November 1967.

ii.   HILARY HOBART was born in Chambersburg, PA on 19 May 1970.

52. HERBERT RICHARD ALCORN was born in St Louis, MO on 24 October 1933. Married (1) in E. St. Louis, IL on 31 October 1954 (divorced 1977) JOANNE KELLER who was born in St. Louis, MO on 26 December 1937, daughter of Ray Keller and Marion Roeser. Married (2) in Ft. Lauderdale, FL on 1 June 1980 (divorced 1981) ROSETTA ELIZABETH FALKENRATH (KREISEL) who was born in Rolla, MO on 10 December 1944. Married (3) in Naples, FL on 23 September 1983, PATRICIA GEDOS (BERLY) who was born in Barberton, OH on 18 November 1942, daughter of Alex Gedos and Edith Gilly.

Four children by Joanne Keller:

94.   i.   MARION, born in Kirkwood, MO on 1 June 1955. Married (1) CHARLES PENNIMAN DANIELS, Jr. Married (2) JOSEPH CARMEL STITES.

95.   ii.   HERBERT RICHARD, JR., born in Kirkwood, MO on 27 April 1958. Married DONNA HELGE (BROWN).

96.   iii. JOHN WELD, born in Rolla, MO on 11 August 1960. Married (1) TRACIA R. WAFE. Married (2) LISA GAYE HOLT (LONG).

97.   iv.   JANE WRIGHT, born in Rolla, MO on 8 October 1965. Married TROY WALKER.

53. WILLIAM WRIGHT ALCORN was born in St. Louis, MO on 2 February 1936. Married (1) in St. Louis, MO on 27 November 1957 (divorced 1971), MARY ELIZABETH JONES, who was born in St. Louis, MO on 16 September 1935, daughter of

Robert McKittrick Jones and Ann Fitzgerald. Married (2) in Eagle Island, ME on 11 September 1977 (divorced 1977) SUSAN WHITE who was born in Columbus, OH on 23 June 1947, daughter of Richard White and Dorothy Swendel.

Four children by Mary Elizabeth Jones:

98.   i.   WILLIAM WRIGHT, JR. born in Cincinnati, OH on 9 January, 1959. Married BETH LOUISE HIPPE.

    ii.   PETER WELLINGTON was born in New Haven, CT on 25 December 1961.

    iii.   ETHAN was born in Portland, ME on 19 September 1964.

    iv.   MATTHEW was born in Portland, ME on 26 July 1966. Married in Tivoli, NY on 12 August 1989 ELLEN SIFF, who was born in New York, NY on 9 December 1964.

54. LUCIEN WELD MINOR was born in Charlottesville, VA on 6 November 1926. Married in Heathsville, VA on 24 November 1950 (divorced) BARBARA MASON BRENT, who was born in Hampton, VA on 24 January 1927, daughter of John Harper Brent and Mary Olive Scruggs.

Two children:

    i.   ALISON WELD was born in St. Louis, MO on 31 May 1951. Married (1) in St. Louis, MO on 6 April 1972 (divorced 1978) WARREN HUMMERT who was born in St. Louis, MO on 22 November 1947, son of Henry Hummert. Married (2) in Denver, CO on 30 October 1986 RAYMOND ENZENAUER who was born in St. Louis, MO on 25 November 1953, son of Robert Enzenauer and Dorothy Oberfeld.

    ii.   PATIENCE HARPER was born in Newton, MA on 10 February 1954.

55. PATRICIA JEANNE MINOR was born in Covington, KY on 21 November 1928. Married in Webster Grove, MO on 13 June 1953 WALTER JACKSON TAYLOR, JR. who was born in St. Louis, MO on 1 August 1924, son of Walter Jackson Taylor and Evelyn Stearns.

Three children:

    i.   JANE LLOYD was born in St. Louis, MO on 15 March 1956. Married in Crystal

Lake, MI on 19 August 1989 MARK BRAUN, who was born in Flint, MI in March   1955, son of Philip Jackson Braun.

ii.   THOMAS WELD was born in St. Louis, MO on 13 November 1960.

iii.   ANN ELIZABETH was born in St. Louis, MO on 15 October 1964.

56. JOHN WELD PECK MINOR was born in Cincinnati, OH on 29 June 1935. Married (1) in Mexico, MO on 11 April 1963 (divorced) VIRGINIA GREENE who was born in Mexico, MO on 10 September 1943, daughter of Grantland Greene and Mildred Willingham. Married (2) in Coeur D'Alene, ID on 14 July 1987 SUSAN LYNN KUEHL, who was born in Clarkfield, MI on 17 June 1953, daughter of Leo Kuehl and Mavis _____.

Child of Virginia Greene:

i.   LAURA JANE was born in Mexico, MO on 25 July 1969.

Child of Susan Lynn Kuehl:

ii.   GRANT MATTHEW WELD was born in Mexico, MO on 25 March 1986.

57. DAVID WINCHESTER PECK was born in Wyoming, OH on 1 June 1936. Married in Cincinnati, OH on 8 July 1961 BEVERLY JEAN AYERS who was born in Richmond, VA on 1 July 1938, daughter of Roy Mormon Ayers and Audrey Viar.

Three children:

i.   MICHAEL WINCHESTER was born in Cincinnati, OH on 7 April 1962. Married in Birmingham, MI on 30 July 1989 SUSAN BETH ZWEIG who was born in Birmingham, MI on 3 January 1963, daughter of Ray Xavier Zweig and Judith _____.

ii.   ANDREW WELD was born in Cincinnati, OH on 1 March 1964. Married in Sevierville, TN on 5 January 1990, LISA RILEY.

iii.   AMY AYERS was born in Cincinnati, OH on 3 March 1970.

58. MARY ELLEN PECK was born in Wyoming, OH. Married (divorced) JOHN THOMAS STONE.

One child:

i.   Thomas Peck was born in 1974.

59. JOHN WELD PECK, III was born in Cincinnati, OH on 29 January 1944. Married (1) in Cincinnati, OH on 26 August 1967 (divorced 1986) SUSAN BELT who was born on 3 March 1944 Cincinnati, OH. Married (2) in 1986 to SUE ANN BLOCKER.

One child of Susan Belt:

i.   JOHN WELD IV was born in 1972.

Two children by Sue Ann Blocker:

i.   CHRISTOPHER WEBSTER.

ii.   STEPHEN BRADLEY.

60. JAMES HIRAM PECK was born in Cincinnati, OH in 1945. Married in 1968 (divorced) BARBARA TROMBLY.

Two children:

i.   MELISSA MINOT was born in 1970.

ii.   SARAH was born in 1972.

61. CHARLES EDWIN PECK was born in Cincinnati, OH in 1948. Married in 1972 MARY ELLEN HAGEN.

One child:

i.   CHED HAGEN was born in 1973.

62. NANCY MINOT PECK was born in Cincinnati, OH on 1 March 1948. Married in Wyoming, OH on 28 December 1968 (divorced) JOHN AMOS LONG, JR. who was born in PA on 27 October 1946, son of John Amos Long and Ruth _____.

Two children:

i.   AMY ELIZABETH was born in Oscoda, MI on 5 March 1971.

ii.   ABIGAIL MINOT was born in Columbus, OH on 20 March 1974.

63. ELIZABETH GRAVES PECK was born in Cincinnati, OH on 27 August 1949. Married in Wyoming, OH on 26 December 1970 (divorced) TERRY ALAN DUNLAP, who was born in Flint, MI on 21 March 1946, son of Francis T. Dunlap and Florence E. Owen.

Two children:

i.   STEPHANIE PECK was born in Cincinnati, OH on 19 July 1977.

ii.   JENNIFER OWEN was born in Cincinnati, OH on 19 March 1981.

64. CHRISTINE WELD PECK was born in Cincinnati, OH on 9 November 1951. Married in Wyoming, OH on 25 August 1973 (divorced 1988) CARL HINZ MARGRAF, JR. who was born in Cincinnati, OH on 14 September 1950, son of Carl Hinz Margraf and Marion Knagge.

Two children:

i.   CARL HINZ III was born in Spokane, WA on 3 April 1978.

ii.   MEREDITH WELD was born in Spokane, WA on 9 March 1980.

SIXTH GENERATION

65. CHARLES ST. CLAIR BROWN (H'67) was born in Boston, MA on 10 December 1944. Married in Ladysmith, WI on 30 August 1969 JACQUELINE ANN STONE who was born in Ladysmith, WI on 26 May 1946, daughter of Richard Rueban Stone and Gundella Clara Olsen.

Two children:

i.   RICHARD STONE was born in Washington, D.C. on 14 June 1974.

ii.   STEPHEN ST. CLAIR was born in Washington D.C. on 18 December 1978.

66. JAMES SOUTHWICK BROWN was born in Boston, MA on 24 April 1948. Married in Greenwich, CT on 2 June 1972 (divorced 1985) CYNTHIA CONWAY GROSS (EICHEN) who was born in Greenwich, CT on 31 March 1945 daughter of Walter Gross and Eileen _____ .

One stepson:

i.   JOHN PIERRE EICHEN.

67. CHRISTOPHER STRAWBRIDGE CLEWS (twin) was born in Bryn Mawr, PA on 16 November 1944. Married on Isle of Shoals, NH on 11 September 1971 NOELE DOYLE (MACKENZIE) who was born in Red Bank, NJ on 1 December 1942, daughter of Harold Doyle and Florence Hughes.

Two children:

i.   NATASHA ELIZABETH STRAWBRIDGE was born in Exeter, NH on 26 December 1974.

ii.   CHRISTINA VENESSA MADISON was born in Exeter, NH on 26 November 1978.

68. HENRY MADISON CLEWS (twin) was born in Bryn Mawr, PA on 16 November 1944. Married in Hancock, ME on 20 August 1966 (divorced 1975) HENRIETTA BOOTH THOMPSON who was born in Elgin AFB, FL on 2 June 1943, daughter of Henry Swift Thompson and Henrietta Booth Wise.

Four children:

i.   HENRY ALEXANDER was born in Raleigh, NC on 12 November 1967.

ii.   MARGARET THOMPSON was born in Brunswick, ME on 14 May 1969.

iii.   LETA HENRIETTA (twin) was born in Ellsworth, ME on 16 February 1975.

iv.   CHARLOTTE LOUISE (twin) was born in Ellsworth, ME on 16 February 1975.

69. FREDERIC STRAWBRIDGE WRIGHT was born in Philadelphia, PA on 25 November 1949. Married in Monessen, PA on 22 September 1979 DIANNE MARIE DIMASCIO, who was born in Monessen, PA on 26 May 1956, daughter of Cataldo DiMascio and Angeline Scirotto.

One child:

i.   JOHN CATALDO was born in Philadelphia, PA on 4 August 1980.

70. ALEXANDRA MARIE (WRIGHT) SMITH was born in Philadelphia, PA on 17 August 1954. Married in Coudersport, PA on 11 January 1978 KURT WENZEL.

One child:

i.   MEGAN was born in Tulsa, OK on 17 June 1979.

71. TIMOTHY JAMES (WRIGHT) SMITH was born in Philadelphia, PA on September 1955. Married in Emporium, PA on 26 February 1980 (divorced) CATHERINE MCFALL, daughter of Rodney McFall and Vivian _____.

One child:

i.   TIMOTHY JAMES, JR. ("TJ") was born in 1984.

72. GREGORY GIRARD (WRIGHT) SMITH was born in Philadelphia, PA on 12 March 1957. Married in Coudersport, PA on 3 July 1982 PAMELA RAE SNYDER who was born in Coudersport, PA on 3 July 1963, daughter of Allen Dale Snyder and Marilyn Stilson.

Three children:

i.   EMILY RAE was born in Coudersport, PA on 9 January 1983.

ii.   STEPHEN GERARD was born in Bradford, PA on 9 April 1984.

iii.   LUKE ALLEN was born in Coudersport, PA on 10 July 1988.

73. ELIZABETH ANN (WRIGHT) SMITH was born in Philadelphia, PA on 26 February 1964. Married in Tulsa, OK on 25 March 1983 KENNETH RUTER, was born in Coudersport, PA on 3 May 1960, son of Chester Ruter and Leona McGraw.

Two children:

i.　　JESSICA MAE was born in Tulsa, OK on 6 November 1983.

ii.　　CHRISTOPHER CLOTHIER was born in Coudersport, PA on 1986.

74. ANNE CLAGHORN LONGSTRETCH was born in Philadelphia, PA on 13 May 1942. Married (1) in Philadelphia, PA on 11 April 1964 (divorced 1980) JAY ALLEN ANDERSON who was born in Syracuse, NY on 13 June 1940, son of Joseph Allen Anderson and Joyce Muriel Snyder. Married (2) ROBERT PAUL DELAY who was born in Cedar Rapids, IA on 24 March 1934, son of Earl DeLay and Marie Mulhern.

Three children by Jay Allen Anderson:

i.　　IAIN ALLEN was born in Kampala, Uganda on 3 February 1965.

ii.　　ANNA LONGSTRETH was born in Des Moines, IA on 12 July 1968.

iii.　　COLL MCFARLAND was born in Philadelphia, PA on 25 May 1970.

75. PETER STRAWBRIDGE LONGSTRETH was born in Philadelphia, PA on 15 October 1944. Married in Philadelphia, PA on 16 June 1967 ELIZABETH ERICKSON STEEL who was born in Philadelphia, PA on 31 May 1945, daughter of Alfred Steel and Nancy McLellen Boyd.

Three children:

i.　　HADLEY HOWE was born in Panama City, Panama on 7 December 1973.

ii.　　AMANDA CLAGHORN was born in Panama City, Panama on 18 June 1975.

iii.　　JOHN STRAWBRIDGE was born in Philadelphia, PA on 6 January 1978.

76. ELLEN KINCAID LONGSTRETH was born in Philadelphia, PA on 28 November 1945. Married in Philadelphia, PA on 26 November 1966 EDWARD HOWARD GOODWIN, JR.

who was born in Norfolk, VA on 27 February 1944, son of Edward Howard Goodwin and Alice Cocke.

Four children:

i.   FREDERICK DEAN was born in Chestnut Hill, PA in 1972 and died a day later.

ii.   EDWARD HOWARD III was born in Chestnut Hill, PA on 3 January 1972.

iii.   CARY was born in Chestnut Hill, PA on 25 July 1974.

iv.   THACHER was born in Chestnut Hill, PA on 2 August 1976.

77. WILLIAM THACHER LONGSTRETH, JR. was born in Detroit, MI on 13 April 1949. Married in Philadelphia, PA on 11 June 1974, ALICE BRECKINRIDGE GOODWIN, who was born in Philadelphia, PA on 9 June 1952, daughter of Edward Howard Goodwin and Alice Cocke.

Three children:

i.   COURTNEY was born in Philadelphia, PA on 19 January 1975.

ii.   GALEN LANGSTON was born in Seattle, WA on 11 August 1976.

iii.   ALEC BRANDSON was born in Seattle, WA on 4 October 1979.

78. ALAN MCILVAIN JR. was born in Philadelphia, PA on 28 June 1948. Married in Philadelphia, PA on 2 February 1974 ANN HAVENS who was born in Bryn Mawr, PA on 17 February 1949, daughter of Richard Woodruff Havens and Carolyn Louise Jameson.

Three children:

i.   ELIZABETH CORYELL was born in Wynnewood, PA on 19 October 1975.

ii.   ALAN III was born in Wynnewood, PA on 8 May 1978.

iii.   JOHN WICK HAVENS was born in Wynnewood, PA on 30 January 1981.

79. GORDON WELD MCILVAIN was born in Philadelphia, PA on 4 February 1951. Married in Valley Forge, PA on 30 March 1979 MARCIA H. JORDAN who was born in Valley Forge, PA circa 1958, daughter of Frederick Peter Jordan and Beatrice L. Renwick.

Three children:

i.   GORDON WELD, JR. was born in Philadelphia, PA.

ii.   JORDAN STRAWBRIDGE was born in Philadelphia, PA.

iii.   ALIDA FELL was born in Philadelphia, PA on 12 October 1985.

80. JANET LIVINGSTON MCILVAIN was born in Philadelphia, PA on 21 April 1954. Married in Villanova, PA on 14 May 1976 DAVID OAKES O'HARA who was born in Stamford, CT on 12 November 1950, son of Charles Edward O'Hara and Theodora Pomeroy Oakes.

Two Children:

i.   ELIZABETH LIVINGSTON was born in Boston, MA on 14 May 1980.

ii.   CAROLYN BURDETT was born in Boston, MA on 1 August 1983.

81. MARGERY RICHARDSON CLAGHORN was born in Philadelphia, PA on 4 May 1947. Married in Princeton, NJ on 13 July 1985 RANDALL WARREN ROBERTSON who was born in South Gate, CA on 11 January 1948, son of Thomas Robertson and Rosemary Hunter.

One child:

i.   CHEYNEY ELIZABETH was born in Orange, CA on 29 August 1989.

82. JOHN WINTHROP CLAGHORN, III was born in Philadelphia, PA on 24 August 1950. Married in Port Washington, NY on 26 May 1979 MARGARET ELLEN JUMP, who was born in New York, NY on 4 December 1949, daughter of William A. Jump, Jr. and Mrs. Dudley B. Tenney.

Three children:

i.   JOHN WINTHROP, IV was born in New York, NY on 15 March 1981.

ii.   LILA STRAWBRIDGE was born in New York, NY on 11 September 1984.

iii.   WILLIAM MCKAY JUMP was born in New York, NY on 3 May 1989.

83. DAVID TOWNSEND CLAGHORN was born in Boston, MA on 15 May 1953. Married in Princeton, NJ on 29 October 1983 ELIZABETH VAN TASSEL WEISBECKER, who was born in Princeton, NJ on 12 November 1955, daughter of Burton Franklin Weisbecker and Elizabeth Gordon Dannehower.

Three children:

i.   LANE RICHARDSON was born in Baltimore, MD on 2 July 1985.

ii.   DAVID TOWNSEND, JR. was born in Haddonfield, NJ on 17 November 1986.

iii.   ELIZABETH ANNE was born in Philadelphia, PA on 17 May 1989.

84. SUSAN STRAWBRIDGE CLAGHORN was born in Princeton, NJ on 2 July 1957. Married in Princeton, NJ on 10 September 1983 STUART WILLIAM FERGUSON, who was born in Newton, IA on 12 February 1946, son of Stuart Woodrow Ferguson.

Adopted child:

i.   MCADIE STRAWBRIDGE WAS born in Philadelphia, PA on 20 November 1985.

85. FREDERICK STRAWBRIDGE CLAGHORN, JR. was born in Philadelphia, PA on 8 March 1950. Married in Whitemarsh, PA on 30 December 1972 MARY HOLT SCOTT who was born in Pimehurst, NC on 22 May 1951, daughter of Watson Guerrant Scott and Mary Helen Stewart.

Four children:

i.   MARY CATHERINE was born in Phoenixville, PA on 30 August 1974.

ii.   TARA TAWS was born in Phoenixville, PA on 7 March 1977.

iii.   ANNE SCOTT was born in Phoenixville, PA on 5 June 1978.

iv.   FREDERICK STRAWBRIDGE III was born in Phoenixville, PA on 11 November

1979.

86. EDWARD TAWS CLAGHORN was born in Philadelphia, PA on 29 May 1952. Married in Walton, NY on 19 July 1975 KATRINA ELIZABETH VAN BUREN who was born in Montclair, NJ on 18 April 1954, daughter of James Martin Van Buren and Mary Ellen White.

Two children:

i. EDWARD TAWS, JR. was born in Phoenixville, PA on 6 March 1980.

ii. JUSTUS VAN BUREN was born in Phoenixville, PA on 8 September 1982.

87.. LESLIE ELIZABETH MAGNESON was born in Sacramento, CA on 6 June 1948. Married in Ballico, CA on 5 May 1973 RONALD PETER CHILDS who was born in New Orleans, LA on 7 October 1946, son of Robert Childs and Ernestine Benchel.

One child:

i. ROBERT MAGNESON was born in Sacramento, CA on 30 September 1978.

88. NANCY LYNN MAGNESON was born in Turlock, CA on 7 May 1950. Married in Ballico, CA on 12 November 1983 JOHN BRADLEY CASSIDY, who was born in Summit, NJ on 5 December 1949, son of Donald James Cassidy and Anna Marie Bradley.

Two children:

i. CODY STRAWBRIDGE was born in Palo Alto, CA on 14 April 1984.

ii. SCOTT FORREST was born in Palo Alto, CA on 20 April 1987.

89. ROBIN MOSCHEL MAGNESON was born in Turlock, CA on 23 December 1951. Married in Coloma, CA on 24 April 1977 WILLIAM NORMAN CENTER who was born in Berkeley, CA on 9 July 1949, son of Norman Robert Center and Emily McDermid Minton.

Two children:

i. REBECCA EMILY was born in Placerville, CA on 28 January 1978.

ii.   CHARLES MAGNESON was born in Placerville, CA on 18 August 1981.

90. SCOTT STRAWBRIDGE MAGNESON was born in Turlock, CA on 1 May 1953. Married in Carson City, NV on 25 October 1980 PAMELA ANN GREENSTREET, who was born in Modesto, CA on 22 September 1954, daughter of John Russell Greenstreet and Dora Bouchard.

Two children:

i.   CLAY MCKINLEY was born in Modesto, CA on 17 March 1981.

ii.   KATE LOUISE was born in Merced, CA on 4 February 1983.

91. JOHN FORREST MAGNESON was born in Ceres, CA on 18 March 1955. Married in Merced, CA on 13 December 1985 PATRICIA LYNN GOOCH (MCCORMICK) who was born in Gavelson Island, TX on 6 December 1954, daughter of Billy Allen Gooch and Jennie Sue Linn.

One child:

i.   SARAH HAZEL was born in Bellico, CA on 28 April 1987.

92. MARK DOWNING MAGNESON was born in Modesto, CA on 25 August 1956. Married in Beverly Hills, CA on 23 July 1983 JAN MCKELVEY who was born in San Rafael, CA on 2 July 1956, daughter of Alden Day McKelvey and Joanne Clare.

Two children:

i.   CLARE ROSE was born in Turlock, CA on 25 August 1985.

ii.   VERONICA STRAWBRIDGE was born in Bakersfield, CA on 20 March 1988.

93. LAURA WOODBURY BIRD was born in Chicago, IL on 6 June 1957. Married in Granite City, IL on 18 August 1974 TERRY WAYNE BERNAIX, who was born in Granite City, IL on 18 August 1954, son of James Arthur Bernaix and Patricia Ellenwood.

Two children:

i.   KELLY NICOLE was born in Granite City, IL on 28 December 1980.

ii.   LINDSEY KAYE was born in Granite City, IL on 13 August 1982.

94. MARION ALCORN was born in Kirkwood, MO on 1 June 1955. Married (1) in Rolla, MO on 23 August 1975 (divorced) CHARLES PENNIMAN DANIELS, JR. who was born on 16 June 1951, son of Charles Penniman Daniels and Lucy Dewing. Married (2) in Rolla, MO on 16 April 1977 (divorced) JOSEPH CARMEL STITES who was born in 1950, son of Carmel Lyle Stites and Dorothy _____.

Child of Joseph Carmel Stites:

i.   JASON LYLE was born in Hamilton, OH on 6 August 1978.

95. HERBERT RICHARD ALCORN, JR. was born in Kirkwood, MO on 27 April 1958. Married in Rolla, MO on 8 July 1989 DONNA HELGE (BROWN) who was born in Los Angeles, CA on 2 May 1963, daughter of Gerald Helge and Dorothy May Turner.

Child of Herbert Richard Alcorn, Jr.

i.   TANYA SOUTHARD was born in Columbia, MO on 8 February 1978.

96. JOHN WELD ALCORN was born in Rolla, MO on 11 August 1960. Married (1) in Wentzville, MO on 25 January 1983 (divorced) TRACIA R. WAFE who was born in Wentzville, MO on 7 August 1960. Married (2) in Troy, MO on 20 October 1990 LISA GAYE HOLT (LONG) who was born in Hereford, TX on 12 June 1962, daughter of Norvert Holt and Grace Moore.

Two children:

i.   TABATHA RENE was born in St. Louis, MO on 7 March 1984.

ii.   JOHN WELD, JR. was born in St. Louis, MO on 29 March 1985.

Two stepchildren:

i.   MISTY DAWN LONG was born in Des Peres, MO on 22 March 1981.

ii.   COLEMAN DAVID LONG was born in Des Peres, MO on 22 November 1986.

97. JANE WRIGHT ALCORN was born in Rolla, MO on 8 October 1965. Married in

Moscow Mills, MO on 15 August 1987 TROY WALKER who was born in Henryetta, OK on 27 September 1957, son of Charles Ray Walker and Shirley Golightly.

Two children:

i.   DUSTIN RAY was born in Lake St. Louis, MO on 21 December 1987.

ii.   JOSHUA DEAN was born in Troy, MO on 30 June 1989.

Two Stepchildren:

i.   TANYA was born in Troy, MO on 29 June 1978.

ii.   APRIL was born in Troy, MO on 22 April 1982.

98. WILLIAM WRIGHT ALCORN, JR. born in Cincinnati, OH on 9 January 1959. Married in Cape Elizabeth, ME on 8 August 1987 BETH LOUISE HIPPE, who was born in Madison, WI on 28 April 1962, daughter of Kenneth Duane Hippe and Arline Meister.

One child:

i.   ANNA BERIT was born in Portland, ME on 19 July 1989.

The Third Weld Brother
STEPHEN MINOT WELD
and his descendants

FIRST GENERATION

1. STEPHEN MINOT WELD (H'1826) was born in Roxbury, MA on 29 September 1806 and died in West Roxbury, MA on 13 December 1867, son of William Gordon Weld and Hannah Minot. Married (1) in Roxbury, MA on 6 June 1839 SARAH BARTLETT BALCH, who was born in Roxbury, MA on 26 November 1817 and died in Jamaica Plain, MA on 7 June 1854, daughter of Joseph Balch and Caroline Ann Buckminster Williams. Married (2) in West Roxbury, MA on 17 September 1856 GEORGIANA HALLET, who was born in Boston, MA on 8 October 1823 and died in West Roxbury, MA on 21 December 1867, daughter of George Hallet and Eliza Gordon.

Five children by Sarah Bartlett Balch:

     i.   HANNAH MINOT was born in Jamaica Plain, MA on 17 May 1840 and died in Boston, MA on 5 March 1923. (Unmarried).

2.   ii.   STEPHEN MINOT, JR. born in Jamaica Plain, MA on 4 January 1842. Married (1) ELOISE RODMAN. Married (2) SUSAN EDITH WATERBURY.

    iii.   ALICE BALCH was born in Roxbury, MA on 28 February 1844 and died in Boston, MA on 8 December 1902. (Unmarried).

3.   iv.   CAROLINE BALCH, born in Boston, MA on 15 January 1846. Married SAMUEL SHOBER GRAY.

    v.   EDITH was born in Roxbury, MA on 4 August 1848 and died in Brookline, MA on 7 March 1938. (Unmarried).

Two children by Georgiana Hallet:

    i.   HENRY HALLET was born in West Roxbury, MA on 19 January 1861 and died in West Roxbury, MA on 5 March 1868.

4.   ii.   ARTHUR CYRIL GORDON was born in West Roxbury, MA on 4 March 1862. Married (1) KATE DE ROSSET WOODBURY. Married (2) HELWIG WAHL. Married (3) JENNIE VAN NORMAN. Married (4) CLAUDIA CLARKE.

SECOND GENERATION

2. STEPHEN MINOT WELD, JR. (H'1860) was born in Jamaica Plain, MA on 4 January 1842 and died in Boca Grande, FL on 16 March 1920, son of Stephen Minot Weld and Sarah Bartlett Balch. Married (1) in Dedham, MA on 1 June 1869 ELOISE RODMAN, who was born in Milton, MA on 1 January 1850 and died in Dedham, MA on 14 January 1898, daughter of Alfred Rodman and Anna Lothrop Motley. Married (2) in Boston, MA on 26 May 1904 SUSAN EDITH WATERBURY, who was born in Winona, MN on 31 July 1866 and died in Boston, MA on 24 September 1960, daughter of Julius Henry Waterbury and Jane Rebecca Bradford.

Seven children by Eloise Rodman:

i.   STEPHEN MINOT, III was born in Dedham, MA on 2 September 1870 (twin) and died in Dedham, MA on 17 September 1887.

5.   ii.   ALFRED RODMAN, born in Dedham, MA on 2 September 1870 (twin). Married ADELAIDE WATSON LADD.

6.   iii.   EDWARD MOTLEY, born in Dedham, MA on 4 September 1872. Married SARAH LOTHROP KING.

iv.   LOTHROP MOTLEY was born in Dedham, MA on 26 July 1874 and died in Wareham, MA on 18 August 1882 (drowned).

v.   ELOISE MINOT was born in Boston, MA on 24 January 1879 and died in Malmsbury, England on 5 January 1908. (Unmarried).

7.   vi.   RUDOLPH, born in Canton, MA on 22 August 1883. Married SYLVIA CAROLINE PARSONS.

8.   vii.   PHILIP BALCH, born in Dedham, MA on 4 January 1887. Married KATHARINE LEVERETT SALTONSTALL.

3. CAROLINE BALCH WELD was born in Boston, MA on 15 January 1846 and died in Boston, MA on 16 June 1912. Married in Boston, MA on 15 January 1879 SAMUEL SHOBER GRAY, who was born in Boston, MA on 20 December 1849 and died in Boston, MA on 6 November 1926, son of Francis H. Gray and Hedwiga R. Shober.

Three children:

i.   RALPH WELD (H'01), born in Boston, MA on 19 January 1880 and died in Tucson, AZ on 28 March 1944. Married in Weston, MA on 26 December 1921 GEORGINA C. HEMMINGWAY (MERRIAM) who was born in Holyoke, MA on 6 May 1881 and died in Boston, MA in April 1971, daughter of Charles Samuel Hemmingway and Alice Higginbotham. (No children).

ii.   HOPE was born in Boston, MA on 29 March 1882 and died in Boston, MA on 7 February 1979. (Unmarried).

iii.   STEPHEN MINOT WELD was born in Boston, MA on 9 February 1883 and died in Sudbury, MA on 25 December 1974. Married in Cambridge, MA on 2 December 1922 MARJORIE ELIZABETH WHITING who was born in Pottsville, PA on 28 July 1898 and died in Wayland, MA on 12 May 1987, daughter of Walter S. Whiting and Maude Clinton. (No children).

4. ARTHUR CYRIL GORDON WELD was born in Jamaica Plain, MA on 4 March 1862 and died near West Point, NY (Stricken while driving) on 11 October 1914. Married (1) in Far Rockaway, NY in 1883 (divorced in 1892)) KATE DE ROSSET WOODBURY, born 30 November 1859 in Tortugas, FL, and died 26 December 1937 in Rome, Italy, daughter of Gen. Daniel Phineas Woodbury (1812-1864) and Catharine Rachel Childs (1819-1896). Married (2) in Milwaukee, WI in 1893 (divorced 1896) HELWIG WAHL, who was born in Milwaukee, WI and died probably in Milwaukee, WI. Married (3) JENNIE VAN NORMAN (a.k.a. Jane Payton, she appeared in *The Woman* by Wm. C. DeMille and produced by David Belasco) born in Milwaukee, WI and died after 1912, daughter of George B. Van Norman. Married (4) in Jersey City, NJ on 20 February 1908 CLAUDIA CLARKE (a musical comedy actress) born in Milwaukee, WI and died after 1914.

Two children by Kate de Rosset Woodbury:

9.   i.   RENÉE born in Boston, MA on 6 August 1884. Married (1) COUNT WILLIAM J. MORETTI DEI BARATTI. Married (2) BARON FEDERIGO DURINI DI BOLOGNANO.

10.   ii.   ALICE GORDON born in Munich, Germany on 22 May 1887. Married DON RICCARDO ASTUTO DEI DUCHI DI LUCCHESI.

Child by Helwig Wahl:

i.   CHRISTOPHER WELD was born in Milwaukee, WI in 1896 and died in New York, NY on 13 January 1936. (Legally changed his name to CYRIL GORDON WELD. Died while acting in first Broadway role in *Dead End*.) Buried in Milwaukee, WI. He was a nephew of Mrs. Agnes Wahl Nieman. (Unmarried).

THIRD GENERATION

5. ALFRED RODMAN WELD (H'1891) was born in Dedham, MA on 3 September 1870 and died in Dedham, Ma on 27 August 1902. Married in Milton, MA on 2 June 1900 ADELAIDE WATSON LADD, who was born in Milton, MA on 28 September 1870 and died in Milton, MA on 31 August 1942, daughter of William Jones Ladd (H'63) and Annie Russell Watson.

One child:

11.   i.   STEPHEN MINOT, born in Milton, MA on 19 December 1901. Married ELIZABETH STEVENS EATON.

6. EDWARD MOTLEY WELD (H'1893) was born in Dedham, MA on 4 September 1872 and died in New York, NY on 27 December 1929. Married in Boston, MA on 22 April 1897 SARAH LOTHROP KING, who was born in Boston, MA on 21 February 1874 and died in Tuxedo Park, NY on 21 March 1959, daughter of George Parsons King and Sarah Williams Bishop.

Three children:

12.   i.   LOTHROP MOTLEY, born in Boston, MA on 16 February 1898. Married (1) DOROTHY LIVERMORE WELLS. Married (2) GERALDINE FITZGERALD ADEE (BRADLEY). Married (3) DONNA BELL SMITH. Married (4) YOSENE BALFOUR KER.

13.   ii.   EDWARD MOTLEY, JR. born in New York, NY on 24 May 1906. Married ELIZABETH BARBARA MERRIMAN.

14.   iii.   ANNE KING, born in New York, NY on 4 April 1910. Married (1) WILLIAM CRAWFORD, JR.. Married (2) ALLAN MCLANE, JR.. Married (3) SAMUEL SLOAN COLT.

7. RUDOLPH WELD (H'05) was born in Canton, MA on 22 August 1883 and died in Brockton, MA on 27 August 1941. Married in New York, NY on 7 November 1908 SYLVIA CAROLINE PARSONS, who was born in New York, NY on 19 November 1885 and died in New York, NY on 19 December 1962, daughter of William Barclay Parsons and Anna DeWitt Reed.

Three children:

15.   i.   SYLVIA, born in New York, NY on 16 September 1909. Married ALBERT SMITH BIGELOW.

16.   ii.   ELOISE RODMAN, born in New York, NY on 18 April 1911. Married (1) WILLIAM LUKENS ELKINS. Married (2) WILLIAM THOMAS FLEMING, JR.. Married (3) ARTHUR OSGOOD CHOATE, JR.

17.   iii.   PRISCILLA ALDEN, born in Boston, MA on 22 February 1917. Married CHARLES ADOLPHE GROSJEAN.

8. PHILIP BALCH WELD (H'08) was born in Dedham, MA on 4 January 1887 and died in Manchester, MA on 14 May 1964. Married in Milton, MA on 12 November 1912 KATHARINE LEVERETT SALTONSTALL, who was born in Milton, MA on 10 April 1891 and died in Manchester, MA on 29 February 1987, daughter of Philip Leverett Saltonstall (H'89) and Frances Anna Fitch Sherwood.

Six children:

18.   i.   MARY ELIZABETH, born in New York, NY on 8 September 1913. Married SAMUEL HUNTINGTON WOLCOTT, JR.

19.   ii.   PHILIP SALTSONSTALL, born in New York, NY on 11 December 1914. Married ANNE WARREN.

20.   iii.   ROSE, born in Tuxedo Park, NY on 18 August, 1917. Married IAN BALDWIN.

21.   iv.   ADELAIDE, born in Islip, NY on 8 November 1919 (twin). Married (1) ROBERT BACON WHITNEY. Married (2) JAMES KNOTT. Married (3) WILLIAM BRADEN.

22.   v.   KATHERINE WELD, born in Islip, NY on 8 November 1919 (twin). Married WILLIAM BENJAMIN BACON.

23.   vi.   FRANCES, born in Boston, MA on 12 March 1922. Married (1) ROBERT HALLOWELL GARDINER. Married (2) WILLIAM VINCENT MCDERMONTT.

9. RENÉE WELD was born in Munich, Germany on 6 August 1884 and died in Pescara, Italy on 27 May 1967. Married (1) COUNT WILLIAM J. MORETTI DEI BARATTI who was born in _____ on _____ and died in _____ on _____, son

of _____ and _____. Married (2) in _____ on _____ Baron
Federigo Durini di Bolognano who was born in Chieta, Italy on 4 December 1882
and died in San Silvestro, Pescara, Italy on 18 April 1942, son of _____ and
_____.

Three children by Count Moretti:

24.   i.   Rennell Gordon Moretti born in _____ on _____. Married
Eddie Benigold.

         ii.   Mafalda Giuliana Moretti was born in _____ on _____ and
died in _____ on _____. No children.

         iii.   Carlo Borromeo Moretti was born in _____ on _____.
Married (1) Leonie _____ who was born in _____ on
_____ and died in Italy before 1986. Married (2) _____. No
children.

One child by Baron Federigo Durini:

25.   i.   Giuseppe Durini born in Merano, Italy on 16 November 1924. Married (1)
Concetta Tozzi Fontana. Married (2) Lucrezia De Domizio.

10. Alice Gordon Weld was born in Munich, Germany on 22 May 1887 and died in
Rome, Italy on 9 May 1957. Married in Rome, Italy on 25 April 1911 Riccardo
Astuto dei Duchi di Lucchesi, born in Naples, Italy on 1 January 1882 and died in
Francavilla by the Sea, Italy on 25 August 1952, son of Giuseppe Astuto (d.1919) and
Maria Laura Castrone (d.1938).

Two children:

26.   i.   Caterina (Kitty) Astuto born in Rome, Italy on 30 March 1913. Married
George Gleason.

27.   ii.   Maria Bianca Astuto born in Rome, Italy on 9 February 1927. Married
Raymond John Eyre.

FOURTH GENERATION

11. Stephen Minot Weld (H'23) was born in Milton, MA on 19 December 1901
and died in Milton, MA on 16 October 1982. Married in Boston, MA on 19

September 1945 ELIZABETH STEVENS EATON, who was born in Iron Belt, WI on 15 February 1908 and died in Milton, MA on 11 July 1964, daughter of Lucien Eaton (H'00) and Eleanor Archibald.

One child:

28.   i.   STEPHEN MINOT, JR. born in Milton, MA on 11 December 1947. Married LINDA RUTH BANK.

12. LOTHROP MOTLEY WELD (H'20) was born in Boston, MA on 16 February 1898 and died in New York, NY on 6 June 1947. Married (1) in Boston, MA on 20 June 1921 (divorced 1929) DOROTHY LIVERMORE WELLS, who was born in Boston, MA on 15 January 1900 and died in Dedham, MA on 9 November 1963 daughter of Bulkley Wells (H'94) and Grace Daniels Livermore. Married (2) in New York, NY on 3 October 1929 GERALDINE FITZGERALD ADEE (BRADLEY), who was born in Seabright, NJ on 31 August 1897 and died in Southampton, NY on 16 August 1931, daughter of Ernest Rufus Adee (Y'85) and Geraldine Fitzgerald. Married (3) in Texarkana, AR on 1 September 1932 (divorced 1933) DONNA BELL SMITH who was born in Texarkana, AR poss. Sept.-Dec. 1913. Married (4) in New York, NY on 27 January 1934 YOSENE BALFOUR KER, who was born in London, England on 21 April 1910 daughter of William Balfour Ker and Josephine Philips.

Two children by Dorothy Livermore Wells:

29.   i.   LOTHROP MOTLEY, JR. born in Boston, MA on 12 May 1922. Married (1) HOPE MAYNARD. Married (2) VIRGINIA GAY CROSS (GUILD). Married (3) PRISCILLA QUINCY PETERS (LOBURG).

       ii.   THOMAS LIVERMORE (H'50) was born in Westbury, NY on 4 March 1926 and died in Eureka, NV on 3 August 1994 (mining accident).

Three children by Yosene Balfour Ker:

30.   i.   SARAH KING, born in Boston, MA on 27 May 1935. Married (1) JOHN GARSIDE ROBBINS. Married (2) ANDREW RAPHAEL MORRIS, JR.. Married (3) HOWARD MORTON COOPER. Married (4) ROBERT GILSON HARBAUGH, JR.

31.   ii.   DAVID BALFOUR, born in Boston, MA on 5 February 1937. Married (1) PATRICIA LENTZ (MARTIN). Married (2) SUSAN GRAY.

32.   iii.   SUSAN KER (a.k.a. Tuesday Weld), born in New York, NY on 27 August 1943. Married (1) CLAUDE JOHN HARZ. Married (2) DUDLEY STUART JOHN MOORE. Married (3) PINCAS ZUCKERMAN.

13. EDWARD MOTLEY WELD, JR. (H'27) was born in New York, NY on 24 May 1906 and died in New York, NY on 9 June 1969. Married in Bushkill, PA on 21 October 1932 ELIZABETH BARBARA MERRIMAN, who was born in Warwick, RI on 15 August 1904 and died in New York, NY on 10 October 1984, daughter of Edward Bruce Merriman and Helen Abbe Pearce.

Two children:

33.   i.   BARBARA BRUCE, born in New York, NY on 4 March 1936. Married (1) WILLIAM GOODMAN CLARK. Married (2) AUGUSTUS BRADHURST FIELD III.

34.   ii.   HELEN MERRIMAN, born in New York, NY on 28 March 1938. Married GUY PASCHAL.

14. ANNE KING WELD was born in New York, NY on 4 April 1910 and died in Port Jefferson, NY on 29 July 1982. Married (1) in New York, NY on 21 March 1931 (divorced 1934) WILLIAM CRAWFORD, JR. who was born in Bedford, NY on 10 July 1908 and died in Waltham, MA on 12 November 1972, son of William Crawford and Adele MacMillan. Married (2) in Tuxedo Park, NY on 28 August 1935 (divorced 1944) ALLAN MCLANE, JR. who was born in Baltimore, MD on 26 October 1894 and died in Santa Monica, CA on 7 August 1948, son of Judge Alan McLane and Augusta James. Married (3) in New York, NY on 10 September 1945 SAMUEL SLOAN COLT, who was born in New York, NY on 13 July 1892 and died in Westhampton Beach, NY on 2 May 1975, son of Richard Collins Colt and Mary Sloan.

One child by William Crawford, Jr.:

i.   WILLIAM CRAWFORD III was born in New York, NY on 18 August 1932.

One child by Allan McLane, Jr.:

ii.   NEIL MCLANE was born in Tuxedo Park, NY on 14 March 1937 and died on 2 April 1995 in Puerto Rico.

15. SYLVIA WELD was born in New York, NY on 16 September 1909 and died in

Cambridge, MA on 2 December 2002. Married in Wareham, MA on 10 September 1931 ALBERT SMITH BIGELOW (H'29), who was born in Brookline, MA on 1 May 1906 and died in Walpole, MA on 6 October 1993, son of Albert Francis Bigelow and Gwladys Williams.

Three children:

35.   i.   LISA BARCLAY, born in Cambridge, MA on 27 August 1932. Married (1) LOYALL HOWARD EDGE. Married (2) ALFRED LESLIE. Married (3) MARTIN HUGH ROBERTS. Married (4) FRANK RODRIGUEZ.

36.   ii.   KATE, born in Cambridge, MA on 29 March 1935. Married NICHOLAS BENTON.

        iii.   MARY DEFORD BIGELOW was born in Boston, MA on 20 September 1946 and died in Hanover, MA on 25 April 1947.

16. ELOISE RODMAN WELD was born in New York, NY on 18 April 1911 and died in Haverford, PA on 12 November 2001. Married (1) in Brookline, MA on 22 June 1931 WILLIAM LUKENS ELKINS (H'29), who was born in Abington, PA on 8 May 1906 and died in Penllyn, PA on 3 September 1933, son of William McIntire Elkins and Elizabeth Wolcott Tuckerman. Married (2) in Ambler, PA on 28 January 1936 (divorced 1947) WILLIAM THOMAS FLEMING, JR. who was born in Philadelphia, PA on 18 October 1899 and died in Chestnut Hill, PA on 31 January 1977, son of William Thomas Fleming and Bertha Christie. Married (3) in Boston, MA on 8 December 1951 ARTHUR OSGOOD CHOATE, JR.(H'34) who was born in New York, NY on 15 November 1911 and died in Jupiter, FL on 19 April 1987, son of Arthur Osgood Choate and Anne Hyde Clark.

Two children:

37.   i.   WILLIAM LUKENS, JR. born in Boston, MA on 2 August 1932. Married HELEN TORBERT MACLEOD.

38.   ii.   CAROL, born in Philadelphia, PA on 17 November 1933. Married ANDREW VARICK STOUT, JR.

17. PRISCILLA ALDEN WELD was born in Boston, MA on 22 February 1917. Married in Boston, MA on 27 June 1939 CHARLES ADOLPHE GROSJEAN, who was born in Woluwe St. Pierre, Belgium and died in Uccle, Belgium on 9 July 1986, son of Paul Grosjean and Mabel Beatrice Lahr.

Three children:

39.   i.   CLAIRE WELD, born in New York, NY on 1 November 1940. Married MARC DE VILLERS GRANDCHAMPS.

40.   ii.   MICHELLE, born in New York, NY on 1 May 1943. Married RICHARD WARREN BREWSTER.

41.   iii.   DAPHNE, born in New York, NY on 2 October 1949. Married THIERRY DE LA HAMAIDE.

18. MARY ELIZABETH WELD was born in New York, NY on 8 September 1913 and died in Beverly, MA on 30 March 1990. Married in Wareham, MA on 8 September 1934 SAMUEL HUNTINGTON WOLCOTT, JR.(H'33) who was born in Milton, MA on 31 August 1910 and died in Westwood, MA on 7 November 2000, son of Samuel Huntington Wolcott (H'03) and Hannah Stevenson.

Four children:

42.   i.   SAMUEL HUNTINGTON, III, born in Boston, MA on 1 June 1935. Married NORA BRADLEY.

43.   ii.   PHILIP WELD, born in Boston, MA on 24 September 1936. Married BARBARA FLYNN.

44.   iii.   PAMELA, born in Boston, MA on 10 October 1941. Married ANTHONY JAMES FINGLETON.

45.   iv.   WILLIAM PRESCOTT, born in Boston, MA on 10 December 1944. Married SANDRA CRAIN LAMB.

19. PHILIP SALTONSTALL WELD (H'35) was born in New York, NY on 11 December 1914 and died in Cambridge, MA on 6 November 1984. Married in Boston, MA on 6 February 1937 ANNE WARREN, who was born in Essex, MA on 11 April 1912 and died in Gloucester, MA on 19 October 1992, daughter of Samuel Dennis Warren (H'08) and Helen Thomas. (He endowed a Chair in Atmospheric Chemistry at Harvard c.1980.)

Five children:

46.   i.   PHILIP SALTONSTALL, JR., born in Chicago, IL on 6 July 1938. Married (1) ELIZABETH STAYER NEW. Married (2) ANITA DAGMARA BIRNBAUMS (LICIS).

47.   ii.   ELOISE, born in Chicago, IL on 6 May 1940. Married ARTHUR CARLISE HODGES.

48.   iii.   KATHERINE, born in Boston, MA on 24 June 1947. Married GOODWIN WARNER HARDING, JR.

49.   iv.   ANNE, born in Boston, MA on 30 November 1948. Married MORRIS MAC STEWART BELL.

50.   v.   HELEN WARREN, born in Boston, MA on 20 April 1954. Married (1) CRAIG MERWIN STEWART. Married (2) ROBERT KIRK STRACHAN.

20. ROSE WELD was born in Tuxedo Park, NY on 18 August 1917. Married in Wareham, MA on 18 September 1937 IAN BALDWIN (H'33), who was born in Mt. Kisco, NY on 21 September 1912 and died in Wareham, MA on 6 June 2001, son of Joseph Clark Baldwin, Jr. and Fanny Taylor.

Four children:

51.   i.   IAN, JR. born in New York, NY on 18 December 1938. Married (1) SYBIL KANE JAY KINNICUTT. Married (2) MARGARET WEEKS PRESTON.

52.   ii.   MICHAEL, born in New York, NY on 28 November 1940. Married MARGHERITA BAILEY.

53.   iii.   HOWARD LAPSLEY, born in New York, NY on 14 May 1942. Married (1) ANNE LOUISE REDDY (FOSTER). Married (2) KAREN ELISE MULVIHILL.

54.   iv.   PHILIP WELD, born in New York, NY on 24 March 1947. Married (1) VICTORIA MONROE CUNNINGHAM. Married (2) MONICA GUGGISBERG.

21. ADELAIDE WELD was born in Islip, NY on 8 November 1919. Married (1) in Wareham, MA on 16 September 1939 ROBERT BACON WHITNEY (H'39), who was born in New York, NY on 16 December 1916 and died in Old Westbury, NY on 24 December 1952, son of George Whitney (H'07) and Martha Beatrice Bacon. Married (2) in Old Westbury, NY on 24 October 1954 JAMES KNOTT (Y'32), who was born in New York, NY on 7 August 1909 and died in New York, NY on 21 April 1989, son of David Hurst Knott and Agnes Geekie. Married (3) in Cold Spring, NY on 3 March 2001 WILLIAM BRADEN who was born in Santiago, Chile on 2 April 1919, son of Spruille Braden and Maria Humeres.

Four children by Robert Bacon Whitney:

55.   i.   HOPE, born in New York, NY on 13 December 1940. Married JOHN WILLARD LAPSLEY.

56.   ii.   ROBERT BACON, JR, born in New York, NY on 12 January 1943. Married LOUISE PURCELL GRASSI.

      iii.   STEPHEN WELD was born in New York, NY on 11 September 1944 and died in Tahiti, French Polynesia on 24 September 1965.

      iv.   WILLIAM MICHAEL was born in New York, NY on 23 October 1948 and died in Old Westbury, NY on 1 March 1955.

Child by James Knott:

57.   v.   JAMES KNOTT, JR, born in New York, NY on 3 June 1955. Married SUSAN FRANCIS GORDON.

22. KATHERINE WELD was born in Islip, NY on 8 November 1919. Married in Riverdale, NY on 2 March 1940 WILLIAM BENJAMIN BACON (H'33), who was born in Jamaica Plain, PA on 15 May 1911 and died in Beverly, MA on 3 April 1991, son of Gaspar Griswold Bacon and Priscilla Toland.

Four children:

58.   i.   WILLIAM BENJAMIN, JR., born in Boston, MA on 22 November 1940. Married PENELOPE SHAW CRITTENDEN.

59.   ii.   PRISCILLA, born in Boston, MA on 26 September 1942. Married WARD WILSON WOODS, JR.

60.   iii.   DANIEL CARPENTER, born in Boston, MA on 3 September 1944. Married SUSAN MORELAND MAKRIANES.

61.   iv.   MARTHA, born in Boston, MA on 24 April 1947. Married DAVID BRITON HADDEN MARTIN, JR.

23. FRANCES WELD was born in Boston, MA on 12 March 1922 and died in Boston, MA on 15 December 1993. Married (1) in Riverdale, NY on 7 June 1941 ROBERT

HALLOWELL GARDINER (H'37), who was born in Needham, MA on 29 Septebmer 1914 and died in Cambridge, MA on 18 November 1984, son of Robert Hallowell Gardiner (H'04) and Elizabeth Denny. Married (2) in Dedham, MA on 16 June 1989 WILLIAM VINCENT MCDERMOTT, JR (H'38), who was born in Salem, MA on 7 March 1917, son of William Vincent McDermott (H.Med'96) and Mary A. Feenan.

Five children by Robert Hallowell Gardiner:

	i.	ALISON was born in New York, NY on 28 September 1942. Married in Gardner ME on 16 September 1975 (divorced 1988) ARTHUR CAMPBELL PIERSON who was born in New York, NY on 27 August 1941, son of Henry Lowrey Pierson and Cornelia Waldo Blagden.
62.	ii.	ROBERT HALLOWELL, JR., born in Portsmouth, VA on 27 June 1944. Married ANNE BRANDON MCILHENNY.
63.	iii.	HOLLY, born in Boston, MA on 13 February 1948. Married DANIEL CARNEY BURNES.
64.	iv.	NATHANIEL SALTONSTALL, born in Boston, MA on 16 June 1953. Married NANCY ELLEN BADER.
65.	v.	PHYLLIS, born in Boston, MA on 8 August 1955. Married ROBERT LAWRENCE JOHNSTON.

24. RENNELL GORDON MORETTI was born in _____ on _____ and died in Geneva, Switzerland before 1967 (predeceased his mother). Married in _____ on _____ EDIE BENIGOLD who was born in _____ on _____, daughter of _____ and _____.

One child:

i.   DANIELLE was born in _____ on _____. Married _____.

25. GIUSEPPE DURINI was born in Merano, Italy on 16 November 1924. Married (1) in Chieti, Italy on 15 October 1945 CONCETTA TOZZI FONTANA daughter of _____ and _____. Married (2) in _____ on _____ LUCREZIA DE DOMIZIO who was born in _____ on _____, daughter of _____ and _____.

Two children by Concetta Tozzi Fontana:

i.   ARCANGELA was born in Pescara, Italy on 13 July 1946. Married in _____ on _____ BRUNO MARINI who was born in _____ on _____ son of _____ and _____. One daughter born 1979.

ii.   FEDERIGO was born in Pescara, Italy on 15 July 1950. Married in _____ on _____ IVANA FUSCHI who was born in _____ on _____ and was killed in a road accident in _____ in 1996. (No children).

26. CATERINA (KITTY) ASTUTO was born in Rome, Italy on 30 March 1913and died in Albany, NY on 22 November 1981. Married in Rome, Italy on 29 April 1946 GEORGE GLEASON born in Endicott, NY on 11 February 1914 and died in Albany, NY on 3 March 1994, son of James Joseph Gleason and Mary Bridget Sheehan.

Three children:

i.   FRANCESCA ROMANA was born in Rome, Italy on 14 February 1947.

ii.   RICHARD ASTUTO was born in Albany, NY on 8 September 1949. Married in Virginia on _____ (divorced 1991)Nancy Dale Sherman born in _____ on 6 February 1943, daughter of _____ and _____. (No children).

66.   iii.   DANIEL WOODBURY born in Binghamton, NY on 24 February 1953. Married KAREN CRISTIANO.

27. MARIA BIANCA ASTUTO DI LUCCHESI was born in Rome, Italy 9 February 1927. Married in Rome, Italy on 28 April 1951 RAYMOND JOHN EYRE born in Paris, France on 15 September 1929, son of William Joseph Eyre (b. 18 January 1887 in Lima, Peru) and Margarita Serrano Pellé (b. in Santiago, Chile on 2 May 1900).

Three children:

i.   WILLIAM RICHARD was born in Geneva, Switzerland on 23 May 1952.

67.   ii.   ALEXANDRA MARGARET born in Geneva, Switzerland on 13 February 1955. Married GILES FITZHERBERT.

68.   iii.   ANTHONY JOHN STRATFORD who was born in Geneva, Switzerland on 12 May 1956. Married PHILLIPA MARY KATHERINE (KATE) ROUS.

FIFTH GENERATION

28. STEPHEN MINOT WELD, JR. was born in Milton, MA on 11 December 1947. Married in Milton, MA on 15 August 1987 LINDA RUTH BANK, who was born in Chicago, IL on 16 April 1947, daughter of Thor G. Bank and Ruth Wagner.

One child:

i.   RUTH EATON (adopted) was born in Boston, MA on 3 May 1992.

29. LOTHROP MOTLEY WELD, JR. (H'50) was born in Boston, MA on 12 May 1922. Married (1) in Dedham, MA on 3 October 1953 (divorced 1958) HOPE MAYNARD, who was born in Boston, MA on 26 February 1933, daughter of David Howell Maynard and Susan Elizabeth Rogers. Married (2) in Boston, MA on 9 June 1959 VIRGINIA GAY CROSS (GUILD) who was born in Cambridge, MA on 19 August 1934 and died in Duxbury, MA on 29 January 1978, daughter of John Cross and Barbara Ballantine. Married (3) in Milton, MA on 12 June 1986 PRISCILLA QUINCY PETERS (LOBURG) who was born in Tisbury, MA on 18 July 1923, daughter of Richard Dudley Peters and Ruth Sumner Draper.

Two children by Virginia Gay Cross (Guild):

i.   THOMAS LIVERMORE, II was born in Waltham, MA on 8 March 1960.

ii.   JOHN SARGENT was born in Boston, MA on 23 May 1961.

30. SARAH KING WELD was born in Boston, MA on 27 May 1935. Married (1) in New York, NY on 8 May 1952 (divorced 1956) JOHN GARSIDE ROBBINS, who was born in Hartford, CT on 8 May 1918 and died in New York, NY on 15 August 1970, son of John Wolcott Robbins and Marion Ames Garside. Married (2) in New York, NY on 5 January 1957 (divorced 1964) ANDREW RAPHAEL MORRIS, JR. who was born in New York, NY on 18 December 1935, son of Andrew Raphael Morris and Agnes Bosche. Married (3) in New York, NY on 14 November 1964 (divorced 1986) HOWARD MORTON COOPER, who was born in Mt. Vernon, NY on 21 August 1926, son of Samuel Cooper and Clara Levine. Married (4) in Miami, FL on 7 June 1997 ROBERT GILSON HARBAUGH, JR. son of Robert Gilson Harbaugh and Martha Rita McAlister.

Child by John Garside Robbins:

69.   i.   JENNIFER WELD, born in New York, NY on 11 April 1953. Married MICHAEL ROBERT HORSBURGH.

Child by Andrew Raphael Morris, Jr.:

70.   i.   SARAH ANN, born in New York, NY on 31 October 1957. Married LOUIS ELI ROUSSO.

Child by Howard Morton Cooper:

i.   NEAL STUYVESANT was born in Queens, NY on 8 January 1966. Married on 14 June 1998 in the N.Y. Botanical Gardens, Bronx, NY to JODY ELIZABETH HANDLER who was born in New York, NY on 4 August 1969, adopted daughter of Mark Handler and Barbara Justin.

31. DAVID BALFOUR WELD was born in Boston, MA on 5 February 1937 and died in California on 9 December 1999. Married (1) in Las Vegas, NV on 30 June 1962 (divorced) PATRICIA LENTZ (MARTIN) who was born in Alhambra, CA on 3 May 1939, daughter of Walter Paul Lentz and Marjory Faye Barber. Married (2) in Santa Clara, CA on 12 July 1969 (divorced) SUSAN GRAY, who was born in Columbus, OH on 26 August 1945, daughter of William Anderson Gray and Anna Peters.

Two children by Patricia Lentz (Martin):

i.   DANA was born in Newport Beach, CA on 25 October 1963.

ii.   DAVID BALFOUR, JR. was born in Newport Beach, CA on 28 October 1964.

Three children by Susan Gray:

i.   WILLIAM MATTHEW was born in Santa Clara, CA on 26 November 1972.

ii.   PAUL JOSEPH was born in Santa Clara, CA on 27 November 1975.

iii.   SARAH MARY was born in Santa Clara, CA on 3 May 1978.

32. SUSAN KER WELD (a.k.a. Tuesday Weld) was born in New York, NY on 27 August 1943. Married (1) in New York, NY on 23 October 1965 (divorced 1971) CLAUDE JOHN HARZ, who was born in Jersey City, NJ on 29 February 1936, son of Claude J. Harz and Julia Sullivan. Married (2) in Las Vegas, NV on 20 September 1975 (divorced 1983) DUDLEY STUART JOHN MOORE, who was born in Dagenham, Essex, England on 19 April 1935, son of John Moore and Ada Francis. Married (3) in Los Angeles, CA on 18 October 1985 PINCAS ZUCKERMAN, who was born in Tel Aviv, Israel on 16 July 1948, son of Yehuda Zuckerman and Miriam Lieberman.

Child by Claude John Harz:

i.   NATASHA HARZ was born in Los Angeles, CA on 26 August 1966.

Child by Dudley Stuart John Moore:

ii.   PATRICK HAVILAND MOORE was born in Los Angeles, CA on 20 February 1976.

33. BARBARA BRUCE WELD was born in New York, NY on 4 March 1936 and died in Tuxedo Park, NY on 14 January 1998. Married (1) in Tuxedo Park, NY on 13 April 1957 (divorced 1968) WILLIAM GOODMAN CLARK, who was born in Englewood, NJ on 14 January 1933 son of Watson Gerould Clark and Helen Mary Goodman. Married (2) in Tuxedo Park, NY on 26 November 1977 (divorced 1993) AUGUSTUS BRADHURST FIELD, III (H'55) who was born in New York, NY on 2 January 1934, son of Augustus Bradhurst Field, Jr. and Helen G. Hackett.

Four children by William Goodman Clark:

71.   i.   WILLIAM GOODMAN, JR., born in Tacoma, WA on 1 November 1957. Married SARAH JEAN HLAVKA.

72.   ii.   MICHAEL WELD, born in New York, NY on 23 November 1959. Married PAMELA RYDER VAN HOVEN.

73.   iii.   JONATHAN BRUCE was born in New York, NY on 18 August 1963. Married ALICE VAN B. SMITH.

        iv.   TIMOTHY ADAMS was born in New York, NY on 17 January 1966.

34. HELEN MERRIMAN WELD was born in New York, NY on 28 March 1939. Married in Tuxedo Park, NY on 21 June 1958 GUY PASCHAL (H'55) who was born in Mt, Kisco, NY on 11 December 1933, son of Guy Sherman Paschal and Dorothy Iselin.

Five children:

74.   i.   ELEANOR MERRIMAN, born in Boston, MA on 17 July 1959. Married CHRISTOPHER VERRILL REICH.

75.   ii.   CECILY JAY, born in Albany, NY on 7 June 1961. Married TIMOTHY JAMES CASEY.

iii.   ELIZABETH WELD (H'86) was born in New York, NY on 15 September 1963.

iv.   DOROTHY ISELIN was born in New York, NY on 15 September 1963.

v.   EMILIE BOURNE was born in December 1981 in Greenwich, CT.

35. LISA BARCLAY BIGELOW was born in Cambridge, MA on 27 August 1932. Married (1) in Milton, MA on 16 June 1951 (divorced 1958) LOYALL HOWARD EDGE, who was born in Washington D.C. on 25 April 1929 and died in Tallahassee, FL on 6 June 1978, son of Walter Evans Edge and Camilla Loyall Ashe Sewall. Married (2) in Greenwich, CT on 31 May 1960 (divorced 1969) ALFRED LESLIE (born LIPPITZ) who was born in Bronx, NY on 29 October 1927, son of Irving Lippitz and Jeanette Wolff. Married (3) in New York, NY on 3 April 1975 (divorced 1979) MARTIN HUGH ROBERTS, who was born in New York, NY on 22 November 1949, son of David Roberts and Irene Liebowitz. Married (4) in New York, NY on 15 December 1984 (vows made at Immanuel Lutheran Church) FRANK RODRIGUEZ, who was born in New York, NY on 28 June 1950 and died in New York, NY on 26 August 1989, son of Frank Rodriguez and Juanita Ubiera Nunez.

Three children by Loyall Howard Edge:

76.   i.   WALTER EVANS, II born in Boston, MA on 19 January 1952. Married (1) KIMBERLY ANNE SMITH. Married (2) NANCY JEAN KEENEY.

77.   ii.   ALBERT SMITH BIGELOW, born in Boston, MA on 17 April 1953. Married DENA SUE GEWANTER.

78   iii.   LISA HOWARD, born in New Haven, CT on 13 October 1955. Married JACK MARTIN SCHRAETER.

One child by Alfred Leslie:

i.   JOSEPH was born in New York, NY on 28 December 1961.

36. KATE BIGELOW was born in Cambridge, MA on 29 March 1935. Married in Chestnut Hill, MA on 5 June 1954 NICHOLAS BENTON (H'51), who was born in Boston, MA on 18 October 1926, son of Jay Rogers Benton (H'08) and Frances Hill.

Four children:

79. i. FRANCES HILL born in New York, NY on 12 September 1955. Married DAVID EDWARD NALLETT.

80. ii. KATE, born in New York, NY on 14 October 1958. Married JAMES FRANCIS DOUGHAN.

81. iii. EMILY WELD (H'84) born in New York, NY on 18 February 1962. Married JOHN FRANCIS MORGAN.

  iv. LOUISA BARCLAY (H'86) was born in New York, NY on 12 April 1964.

37. WILLIAM LUKENS ELKINS, JR. (H MED'58) was born in Boston, MA on 2 August 1932. Married in Bryn Mawr, PA on 11 June 1966 HELEN TORBERT MACLEOD, who was born in Bryn Mawr, PA on 24 May 1941, daughter of George Inglis Macleod and Elizabeth Torbert McMullin.

Two children:

  i. SHEILA MACLEOD was born in Philadelphia, PA on 25 March 1968. Married in East Fallowfield, PA on 14 September 2002 to WILLIAM HEWSON BALTZELL, V who was born in Philadelphia, PA in 1959, son of William Hewson Baltzell, IV and Sarah H. Edwards.

82. ii. JACOB STEPHEN BROOMALL (H Med.'98) born in Philadelphia, PA on 16 March 1970. Married HILLARY LEWIS.

38. CAROL ELKINS was born in Philadelphia, PA on 17 November 1933. Married in Wilmington, DE on 21 September 1957 (divorced 1982) ANDREW VARICK STOUT, JR. who was born in New York, NY on 2 August 1930, son of Andrew Varick Stout and Juliet Carleton.

Six children:

83. i. ELOISE RODMAN, born in Greenwich, CT on 25 October 1958. Married (1) ALEXANDER FREDERICK MACDONALD III. Married (2) PETER JOHN GINTY.

  ii. ANDREW VARICK, III was born in Greenwich, CT on 9 September 1959 and died in New Canaan, CT on 28 September 1959.

84. iii. SUZANNA CARLETON, born in Greenwich, CT on 16 December 1960. Married PETER STOUT BANWELL.

85.   iv.   ETHEL DOMINICK was born in Greenwich, CT on 11 April 1963. Married STEVEN ALAN MCLAUGHLIN.

        v.   HENRY WINSLOW was born in Greenwich, CT on 4 August 1966. Married in Thetford, VT on 19 August 1995 JENNIFER LEE SMITH, born in Chicago, IL on 17 May 1967, daughter of Timothy Dawn Smith and Laurel Susan Davis.

86.   vi.   ARTHUR ELKINS STOUT, born in Greenwich, CT on 3 February 1969. Married BARBARA SARGENT.

39. CLAIRE WELD GROSJEAN was born in New York, NY on 1 November 1940. Married in Notre Dame Au Bois, Belgium on 26 July 1963 MARC DE VILLERS GRANDCHAMPS, who was born in Brussels, Belgium on 6 April 1933, son of Charles de Villers Grandchamps and Elizabeth Le Hodey.

One child:

87.   i.   ERIC DE VILLERS, born in Brussels, Belgium on 5 December 1964. Married VERONIQUE DIERCKX.

40. MICHELLE GROSJEAN was born in New York, NY on 1 May 1943. Married in Overijse, Belgium on 1 September 1965 (divorced 1987) RICHARD WARREN BREWSTER (H'Law 67) who was born in New York, NY on 15 November 1941, son of Warren Dwight Brewster and Marion Maxell Darrah.

Two children:

        i.   SYLVIA WELD was born in New York, NY on 28 October 1969. Married in Brooklyn, NY on 10 July 1993 (divorced 2001) DALE O'CONNOR, born in Listowell, County Kary, Ireland on 11 January 1969, son of Timothy Pascal O'Connor and Elizabeth Ann Murphy.

        ii.   CHARLES ERSKINE SCOTT was born in New York, NY on 19 July 1971. Married in Inserhagen, Germany on 7 June 2003 AMELIE GRIMM who was born in Hanover, Germany on 13 February 1978, daughter of Arno Grimm and Milfer Stedt.

41. DAPHNE GROSJEAN was born in New York, NY on 2 October 1949. Married in Overijse, Belgium on 18 May 1968 THIERRY DE LA HAMAIDE, who was born in Brussels, Belgium on 16 April 1949, son of Adalbert de La Hamaide and Martha Everhard de Harzir.

Two children:

i.　　JEAN-CHARLES was born in Brussels, Belgium on 5 September 1969.

ii.　　SYBILLE was born in Brussels, Belgium on 13 February 1972.

42. SAMUEL HUNTINGTON WOLCOTT III (H'57) was born in Boston, MA on 1 June 1935. Married in San Mateo, CA on 29 December 1960 NORA BRADLEY, who was born in San Francisco, CA on 21 February 1938, daughter of John Lockwood Bradley and Gabrielle Wright.

One child:

88.　　i.　　NATALIE, born in San Francisco, CA on 18 June 1963. Married HUGO ANDREW YOUNGER WILLIAMS.

43. PHILIP WELD WOLCOTT was born in Boston, MA on 24 September 1936. Married in Weston, MA on 29 September 1962 BARBARA FLYNN, who was born in Fall River, MA on 24 October 1939, daughter of John Doyle Flynn and Catharine Coughlin.

One child:

89　　i.　　STEPHEN WELD (adopted) born in Westwood, CA on 27 February 1968. Married AMY JOINER ALVAREZ.

44. PAMELA WOLCOTT was born in Boston, MA on 10 October 1941. Married in Milton, MA on 16 June 1967 ANTHONY JAMES FINGLETON (H'67), who was born in Brisbane, Australia on 13 April 1940, son of Harold William Fingleton and Dora Milner.

Two children:

i.　　SAMANTHA was born in New York, NY on 12 January 1969.

ii.　　PRISCILLA was born in New York, NY on 24 September 1971. Married in New York, NY on 23 October 1998 J. Laurence Sheerin, Jr who was born in San Antonio, TX in 1971, son of J. Laurence Sheerin and Betty Lou Burton.

45. WILLIAM PRESCOTT WOLCOTT (H'67) was born in Boston, MA on 10 December 1944 and died in Sun Valley, ID on 6 July 1989. Married in Oyster Bay, NY on 3 June 1967 SANDRA CRAIN LAMB, who was born in Oyster Bay, NY on 21 July 1945, daughter of Stephen Burnham Lamb and Carol Miner Hill.

Two children:

i.   WILLIAM PRESCOTT, JR. was born in Boston, MA on 25 June 1968. Married in Sun Valley, ID on 19 July 1997 KRISTINE ELLEN WEILER who was born in Jacksonville, FL on 30 October 1968, daughter of G. William Weiler and Ellen Anne Weston.

ii. JESSICA LAMB was born in Boston, MA on 29 January 1971.

46. PHILIP SALTONSTALL WELD, JR. (H'60) was born in Chicago, IL on 6 July 1938 and died in Glendale, CA on 13 June 1988. Married (1) in Gloucester, MA on 21 September 1963 (divorced 1981) ELIZABETH STAYER NEW, who was born in Macon, GA on 18 August 1939, daughter of Frederick Winburn New and Elizabeth S. Stayer. Married (2) in Malibu, CA on 7 November 1981 ANITA DAGMARA BIRNBAUMS (LICIS), who was born in Riga, Latvia on 1 June 1943, daughter of Karlis Peteris Birnbaums and Erika Cielava.

Two children by Elizabeth Stayer New:

90.   i.   SARAH WINBURN (H'87) born in Boston, MA on 13 November 1965. Married WAYNE KESSLER SNODGRASS.

      ii. ROSE SALTONSTALL (H'90) was born in Beverly, MA on 3 February 1968. Married in Boston, MA on 5 September 1998 MICHAEL ANTHONY DORRINGTON (H'90) who was born in Truro, Nova Scotia on 5 January 1968, son of Gary Dorrington and Carole Thompson.

47. ELOISE WELD (Rad'62) was born in Chicago, IL on 6 May 1940. Married in Ipswich, MA on 29 March 1961 ARTHUR CARLISLE HODGES (H'57), who was born in Indianapolis, IN on 10 September 1935, son of Fletcher Hodges Jr. (H'28) and Sarah Margaret Moore.

Three children:

91.   i.   ARTHUR CARLISLE, JR. was born in Boston, MA on 14 February 1963. Married SUNHEE JUHON.

92.   ii.   SUSANNA was born in Boston, MA on 20 July 1964. Married ERIC DAVID SALK.

93.   iii. ALEXANDER WELD was born in Beverly, MA on 16 September 1968. Married MARY ELIZABETH KLUG.

48. KATHERINE WELD was born in Boston, MA on 24 June 1947. Married in Gloucester, MA on 22 January 1972 GOODWIN WARNER HARDING, JR. (H'69), who was born in Boston, MA on 20 February 1947, son of Goodwin Warner Harding and Mary Louise Rice.

Three children:

i.   JOHANNA was born in Portland, OR on 3 September 1973.

ii.   MEGAN was born in Portland, OR on 25 March 1975.

iii.   SEAN GOODWIN was born in Portland, OR on 6 October 1980.

49. ANNE WELD was born in Boston, MA on 30 November 1948. Married in Gloucester, MA on 18 August 1979 MORRIS MAC STEWART BELL, who was born in Beverly, MA on 30 April 1952, son of Richard Samuel Bell and Winnie Fay Lumpkin.

Four children:

i.   PHILIP FRANKLIN MORRIS was born in Stoneham, MA on 6 April 1981.

ii.   WINNIE FAY LUMPKIN was born in Malden, MA on 16 October 1982.

iii.   SAMUEL THOMAS WARREN was born in Stoneham, MA on 1 April 1985.

iv.   SYLVIE ANNE KATHERINE CROCKETT was born in Malden, MA on 10 April 1987.

50. HELEN WARREN WELD was born in Boston, MA on 20 April 1954. Married (1) in Gloucester, MA on 14 June 1975 (divorced 1982) CRAIG MERWIN STEWART, who was born in Salem, OR on 21 June 1954, son of Bruce Stewart and Ruth Barnett. Married (2) in Edgecomb, ME on 13 September 1985 ROBERT KIRK STRACHAN, born in San Francisco, CA on 30 November 1950, son of James Strachan and Mary Louise Forde.

Three children by Robert Kirk Strachan:

i.   IAN JAMES was born in Bath, ME on 28 April 1986.

ii.   ANNE LOUISE was born in Bath, ME on 29 June 1987.

iii.   WILLIAM was born in Bath, ME on 6 February 1991.

51. IAN BALDWIN, JR. was born in New York, NY on 18 December 1938. Married (1) in Cambridge, MA on 2 June 1962 (divorced 1976) SYBIL KANE JAY KINNICUTT, who was born in New York, NY on 25 April 1938, daughter of Francis Parker Kinnicutt (H'30) and Sybil Kane Jay. Married (2) in Woodbury, CT on 21 June 1980 MARGARET WEEKS PRESTON, who was born in Berkeley, CA on 21 March 1950, daughter of William Payne Thompson Preston and Nora Oliver Weeks.

Two children by Sybil Kane Jay Kinnicutt:

i.   ELIZABETH SARAH was born in New Haven, CT on 5 October 1964.

ii.   BENJAMIN was born in New York, NY on 30 May 1967. Married RACHEL HOPE TOBIAS who was born in Washington, D.C. on 11 August 1969, daughter of Susan Meader and Robert Sweeney. (Adoptive father: Robert Tobias.)

Two children by Margaret Weeks Preston:

i.   ANGUS WEEKS was born in Randolph, VT on 24 May 1983.

ii.   ROSE PRESTON was born in Randolph, VT on 20 August 1987.

52. MICHAEL BALDWIN (H'62) was born in New York, NY on 28 November 1940. Married in Bedford, NY on 3 March 1973 MARGHERITA BAILEY, who was born in Westwood, MA on 1 September 1947, daughter of Horace Converse Bailey and Elizabeth Ware.

Three children:

i.   HELENA-MARGHERITA was born in Wareham, MA on 27 February 1975.

ii.   TAYLOR CONVERSE was born in Wareham, MA on 21 January 1977.

iii.   NATHANIEL KINSMAN was born in Wareham, MA on 19 September 1980.

53. HOWARD LAPSLEY BALDWIN was born in New York, NY on 14 May 1942. Married (1) in New York, NY on 22 December 1967 (divorced 1982) ANNE LOUISE REDDY (FOSTER), who was born in Sewickley, PA on 14 January 1946, daughter of Michael James Reddy and Elizabeth Hoyt Tener. Married (2) in Farmington, CT on 17 October 1987 KAREN ELISE MULVIHILL, who was born in Boston, MA on 16 June 1964, daughter of James Edward Mulvihill and Mary Jane Forino.

Son of Anne Louise Reddy (Foster) and adopted by Howard Lapsley Baldwin:

94.   i.   ROBERT PRESCOTT, born in New Haven, CT on 18 September 1964. Married PATRICIA ANN SULLIVAN.

Two children by Anne Louise Reddy (Foster):

95.   ii.   REBECCA ANNE, born in New Haven, CT on 12 January 1964. Married (1) BRADFORD RICHARD SILVA. Married (2) JON ARTHUR FAULKNER.

       iii.   HOWARD LAPSLEY, JR. was born in Wareham, MA on 26 June 1971. Married in Davidsville, PA in June 1999 NICOLE KASCHALK born in Johnstown, PA on 12 June 1975, daughter of Harry Kaschalk and Mary Lee Polosky.

54. PHILIP WELD BALDWIN was born in New York, NY on 24 March 1947. Married (1) in Gladwyne, PA on 6 September 1969 (divorced 1973) VICTORIA MONROE CUNNINGHAM, who was born in Brooklyn, NY on 8 March 1948, daughter of Donald Monroe Cunningham and Madelon Wicks. Married (2) in Venice, Italy on 19 December 1986 MONICA GUGGISBERG, who was born in Bern, Switzerland on 29 June 1955, daughter of Armin Frederich Guggisberg and Alda Rosa Angelina Malossini.

Two children by Monica Guggisberg:

       i.   NAJA was born in Lausanne, Switzerland on 15 January 1987.

       ii.   IAN MARCO was born in Yverdon, Switzerland on 23 March 1990.

55. HOPE WHITNEY was born in New York, NY on 13 December 1940. Married in Old Westbury, NY on 24 September 1960 JOHN WILLARD LAPSLEY (H'57), who was born in New York, NY on 22 June 1935 and died in Oyster Bay, NY on 26 January 2002, son of Howard Lapsley (H'33) and Eleanor H. Hallowell.

Three children:

96.   i.   ADELAIDE WELD, born in Oyster Bay, NY on 29 September 1962. Married SEAN FRANCIS MULRY.

97.   ii.   HOWARD (H'87) (twin) was born in Oyster Bay, NY on 18 August 1965. Married KAREN LYNN CANAVAN.

98.   iii.   ROBERT WHITNEY, (H'87) (twin) born in Oyster Bay, NY on 18 August 1965.

Married ELIZABETH THORNE DEKKER.

56. ROBERT BACON WHITNEY, Jr. (H'65) was born in New York, NY on 12 January 1943. Married in Baltimore, MD on 16 November 1968 (divorced 1987) LOUISE PURCELL GRASSI, who was born in Glen Cove, NY on 3 March 1944, daughter of Ettore Howard Anthony Grassi and Edith Shepard Gwathmey.

Three children:

i.   STEPHEN WELD was born in New York, NY on 4 November 1970.

ii.   JASON was born in New York, NY on 18 September 1972.

iii.   ELI was born in Stanford, CA on 25 August 1980.

57. JAMES KNOTT, JR. was born in New York, NY on 3 June 1955 and died in Andrew's Bridge, NY on 5 June 1995. Married in Vail, CO on 12 February 1988 SUSAN FRANCIS GORDON, who was born in Featherston, New Zealand, daughter of Peter Michael Gordon and Ann Cecilia Tree.

Two children:

i.   ADELAIDE WELD was born in Edinburgh, Scotland on 7 October 1988.

ii.   IAIN GORDON was born in Christiana, DE on 8 November 1991.

58. WILLIAM BENJAMIN BACON, JR (H'63) was born in Boston, MA on 22 November 1940 and died in Charleston, SC on 8 February 1989. Married in Dedham, MA on 11 June 1966 (divorced 1980) PENELOPE SHAW CRITTENDEN, who was born in Boston, MA on 21 January 1946, daughter of Gazaway Lamar Crittenden and Gertrude Bramwell Shaw.

Two children:

i.   JENNIFER CRITTENDEN was born in Chicago, IL on 8 January 1969.

ii.   WILLIAM BENJAMIN, III was born in Lake Forest, IL on 4 June 1971.

59. PRISCILLA BACON (Rad'64) was born in Boston, MA on 26 September 1942. Married in Manchester, MA on 4 November 1967 WARD WILSON WOODS, JR, who was born in Ann Arbor, MI on 27 June 1942, son of Word Wilson Woods and Patricia Fay.

Two children:

99.   i.   KATHERINE born in New York, NY on 12 February 1970. Married BRIAN KELLY EMERICK.

100.   ii.   ALEXANDRA born in New York, NY on 6 June 1972.

60. DANIEL CARPENTER BACON was born in Boston, MA on 3 September 1944. Married in East Hampton, NY on 11 September 1982 (divorced 1994) SUSAN MORELAND MAKRIANES, who was born in Springfield, MA on 18 March 1956, daughter of James Konstantine Makrianes and Susan Moreland Mantz.

Three children:

i.   NATHANIEL was born in Boston, MA on 28 September 1984 and died in Boston, MA on 12 March 1987.

ii.   ISABEL MAKRIANES was born in Boston, MA on 15 October 1987.

iii.   ANTHONY WELD was born in Boston, MA on 24 March 1989.

61. MARTHA BACON was born in Boston, MA on 24 April 1947. Married in South Hamilton, MA on 21 June 1969 DAVID BRITON HADDEN MARTIN, JR. who was born in Beverly, MA on 9 December 1946, son of David Briton Hadden Martin and Mary Louise Ward.

Three children:

i.   CHARLOTTE was born in Charlottesville, VA on 16 April 1975.

ii.   JESSICA was born in Alexandria, VA on 30 July 1978.

iii.   BENJAMIN WARD was born in Alexandria, VA on 2 July 1981.

62. ROBERT HALLOWELL GARDINER, JR. (H'66) was born in Portsmouth, VA on 27 June 1944. Married in Avery Island, New Iberia, LA on 4 April 1970 ANNE BRANDON MCILHENNY, who was born in New Orleans, LA on 30 December 1946, daughter of Edward McIlhenny and Virginia Smart.

Four children:

i.   ANDREW MARSH was born in Lewiston, ME on 19 April 1972.

ii.   AVERY WELD (H'97) was born in Lewiston, ME on 18 May 1975.

iii.   KATHARINE MCILHENNY was born in Portland, ME on 6 May 1978.

iv.   ELIZABETH HALLOWELL was born in Augusta, ME on 17 March 1988.

63. HOLLY GARDINER was born in Boston, MA on 13 February 1948. Married in Gardiner, ME on 12 September 1970 DANIEL CARNEY BURNES (H'68), who was born in Boston, MA on 24 June 1946, son of Richard Mellier Burnes (H'39) and Ruth Patricia Carney.

Three children:

i.   IAN GARDINER was born Hanover, NH on 22 March 1975.

ii.   LAURA GARDINER was born in Hanover, NH on 31 January 1978.

iii.   ADELE GARDINER was born in Hartford, CT on 18 September 1981.

64. NATHANIEL SALTONSTALL GARDINER (H'76) was born in Boston, MA on 16 June 1953. Married in New York, NY on 28 April 1984 NANCY ELLEN BADER (H'78), who was born in New York, NY on 23 October 1956, daughter of Richard Arthur Bader and Elizabeth Oppenheimer.

Two children:

i.   ELIZA WELD was born in Boston, MA on 24 February 1986.

ii.   CHARLOTTE was born in Boston, MA on 27 June 1990.

65. PHYLLIS GARDINER (H'78) was born in Boston, MA on 8 August 1955. Married in Gardiner, ME on 26 August 1979 ROBERT LAWRENCE JOHNSTON (H'75), who was born in Los Angeles, CA on 19 September 1952, son of Robert Kirk Johnson and Joan Doebbler.

One child:

i.   PHILIP was born in Gardiner, ME on 18 June 1990.

66. DANIEL WOODBURY GLEASON was born in Binghampton, NY on 24 February 1953. Married in Naples, Italy on 27 April 1991 KAREN CRISTIANO who was born in Somerville, NJ on 1 November 1961, daughter of Domenico Cristiano and Rosa Borgese.

One child:

i.   SEAN WOODBURY was born in Rome, Italy on 14 April 1994.

67. ALEXANDRA MARGARET EYRE was born in Geneva, Switzerland on 13 February 1955. Married in Roncengo, Trentino, Italy in June 1988 GILES FITZHERBERT, born in County Meath, Ireland on 8 March 1935, son of Harry FitzHerbert and Sheelagh Murphy. (Note: *FitzHerbert's first wife, Margaret Waugh, daughter of the noted British author, Evelyn Waugh, was tragically killed in a street accident in the spring of 1986. They had five children.*)

Four children of Alexandra Margaret Eyre and Giles FitzHerbert:

i.   WILLIAM ORINOCO was born in Caracas, Venezuela on 7 June 1989.

ii.   ALLEGRA RORAIMA was born in Caracas, Venezuela on 20 January 1991.

iii.   OCTAVIAN COLUMBUS was born in Caracas, Venezuela on 22 September 1992.

iv.   LUKE ROTHWELL was born in Kilkenny, Ireland on 28 October 1993.

68. ANTHONY JOHN STRATFORD EYRE was born in Geneva, Switzerland on 12 May 1956. Married in Roncengo, Trentino, Italy on July 1986 PHILLIPA MARY KATHERINE (KATE) ROUS who was born in Salisbury, Southern Rhodesia in 1960, daughter of Peter

James Mowbray Rous (1914-1997) and Elizabeth Alice Mary Fraser (d. 1968).

Four children:

i.   EDMUND ANTHONY was born in Swindon, England on 25 February 1988.

ii.   GILES PETER DUSMET was born in Swindon, England on 5 May 1989.

iii.   HUW RAYMOND BUNDU was born in Swindon, England on 18 September 1991.

iv.   ELENA ALICE was born in Poppy Cottage, Driffield, Gloucestershire, England on 8 March 1993.

SIXTH GENERATION

69. JENNIFER WELD ROBBINS was born in New York, NY on 11 April 1953. Married in East Hampton, NY on 10 September 1977 (divorced 1989) MICHAEL ROBERT HORSBURGH, who was born in Beckenham, Kent, England on 18 April 1945, son of Ian Hepburn Horsburgh and Ann Owen.

Two children:

i.   EMILY ROBBINS was born in New York, NY on 9 June 1980.

ii.   NICHOLAS IAN WELD was born in New York, NY on 14 June 1984.

70. SARAH ANN MORRIS was born in New York, NY on 31 October 1957. Married in New York, NY on 20 May 1984 LOUIS ELI ROUSSO, who was born in Brooklyn, NY on 31 December 1951, son of Eli Louis Rousso and Julia Saporta.

One child:

i.   ELI was born in New York, NY on 8 June 1987.

71. WILLIAM GOODMAN CLARK, JR. was born in Tacoma, WA on 1 November 1957. Married in Tuxedo Park, NY on 20 August 1983 SARAH JEAN HLAVKA, who was born in Tuxedo Park, NY on 30 April 1958, daughter of Dr. Joseph Hlavka and Lois Marie Dolan.

Four children:

i.   WILLIAM GOODMAN, III was born in Summit, NJ on 3 May 1985.

ii.   AMANDA ADAMS was born in Livingston, NJ on 15 May 1987.

iii   NICHOLAS BOWNE was born in Summit, NJ on 15 May 1990.

iv.   PERIN was born in Summit, NJ on 19 January 1996.

72. MICHAEL WELD CLARK was born in New York, NY on 23 November 1959. Married in Greenwich, CT on 24 August 1985 PAMELA RYDER VAN HOVEN, who was born in Williamsport, PA on 11 November 1959, daughter of John Emerson Van Hoven and Sandra Elizabeth Johnson.

Two children:

i.   AVERY EMERSON was born in Stamford, CT on 25 August 1987.

ii.   CAITLIN RYDER was born in Stamford, CT on 6 December 1988.

73. JONATHAN BRUCE CLARK was born in New York, NY on 18 August 1963. Married in Darien, CT on 28 April 1990 ALICE VAN B. SMITH, who was born on _____ in _____, daughter of _____ and _____.

Two children:

i.   CAROLINE was born in _____ on _____.

ii.   JACK was born in _____ on _____.

74. ELEANOR MERRIMAN PASCHAL was born in Boston, MA on 17 July 1959. Married in Bedford, NY on 18 May 1991 CHRISTOPHER VERRILL REICH who was born in New York, NY on 6 August 1958, son of R. Donald Reich and Constance Verrill.

Two children:

i.   GEORGE SCOVILLE was born in New York, NY on 5 February 1994.

ii.   ELEANOR VERRILL was born in New York, NY on 25 July 1996.

75. CECILY JAY PASCHAL was born in Albany, NY on 7 June 1961. Married in Rye, NY on 18 July 1987 TIMOTHY JAMES CASEY, who was born in Evanston, IL on 16 May 1960, son of Robert Dillon Casey and Rosemary O'Riley.

Three children:

i.   LUCY JAY was born in Lake Forest, IL on 25 December 1987.

ii.   QUINLIN PASCHAL was born in Grayslake, IL on 1 November 1990.

iii.   AIDEN KING was born in Grayslake, IL on 14 July 1998.

76. WALTER EVANS EDGE II was born in Boston, MA on 19 January 1952. Married (1) in Annandale-on Hudson, NY on 25 August 1975 (divorced 1985) KIMBERLY ANNE SMITH, who was born in Brooklyn, NY on 23 May 1953, daughter of Roger Smith and Lois Detweiler. Married (2) in Mattapoisett, MA on 3 July 1988 NANCY JEAN KEENEY, who was born in Seattle, WA on 13 July 1960, daughter of Frank William Kenney and Carol Merrihew.

Child by Kimberly Anne Smith:

i.   MATTHEW LOYALL was born in Albany, NY on 7 December 1981. Married in New Rochelle, NY on 12 May 2001 LIZETTE CASTILLO who was born in Bogota, Columbia on 5 July 1982, daughter of Sandra Roman.

Two children by Nancy Jean Keeney:

i.   ELIZA LIVINGSTON was born in Albany, NY on 8 November 1990.

ii.   SARA BUSHNELL was born in Albany, NY on 22 September1992.

77. ALBERT SMITH BIGELOW EDGE was born in Boston, MA on 17 April 1953. Married in Crescent, NY on 22 June 1975 (divorced 1999) DENA SUE GEWANTER, who was born in New York, NY on 9 February 1953, daughter of Aaron Philip Gewanter and Ruth Leah Bleishewitz.

Two children:

i.   DANIEL ALBERT was born in Schenectady, NY on 26 September 1979 and died in Cambridge, MA on 4 November 2000.

ii.   JOSHUA PARIS was born in Boston, MA on 2 April 1982.

78. LISA HOWARD EDGE was born in New Haven, CT on 13 October 1955. Married in Wareham, MA on 27 August 1978 (divorced 2003) JACK MARTIN SCHRAETER, who was born in Springfield, MA on 21 March 1949, son of Rabbi Arnold Hirch Schraeter and Louise Belle Shankman.

Two children:

i.   HANNAH LAKE was born in Portland, ME on 16 August 1984.

ii.   SOPHIE LOYALL was born in Portland, ME on 12 December 1991.

79. FRANCES HILL BENTON was born in New York, NY on 12 September 1955. Married in Virgin Gorda, BWI on 27 February 2002 DAVID EDWARD NALLETT who was born in Keene, NH on 21 August 1948, son of Edward Joseph Nallett and Clara Ellis.

Two stepchildren (by Nallett's first marriage):

i.   WILLIAM NALLETT was born in Keene, NH on 24 December 1983.

ii.   HANNA NALLETT was born in Keene, NH on 24 June 1986.

80. KATE BENTON was born in New York, NY on 14 October 1958. Married in Wareham, MA on 27 August 1988 JAMES FRANCIS DOUGHAN, who was born in Ravenswood, IL on 2 August 1959, son of Leo Francis Doughan and Nancy Jane Berry.

Two children:

i.   CHARLES BENTON was born in Los Angeles, CA on 22 April 1991.

ii.   HENRY LEO BIGELOW was born in Los Angeles, CA on 1 December 1993.

81. EMILY WELD BENTON was born In New York, NY on 18 February 1962. Married in Wareham, MA on 29 August 1998 JOHN FRANCIS MORGAN who

was born in St. Paul, MN on 17 January 1961, son of James Paul Morgan and Joan Margaret Fitzgerald.

One child (adopted):

i.   AUGUST YONG KEE was born in Taegu, Korea on 24 May 2002.

82. JACOB STEPHEN BROOMALL ELKINS was born in Philadelphia, PA on 16 March 1970. Married in Stowe, VT on 12 July 1997 HILLARY LEWIS born in New York, NY on 7 December 1969, daughter of Wright Lewis and Joyce Nichols.

One child:

i.   MAISIE was born in San Francisco, CA on 22 January 2001.

83. ELOISE RODMAN STOUT was born in Greenwich, CT on 25 October 1958. Married (1) in Etna, NH on 15 December 1980 (divorced 1984) ALEXANDER FREDERICK MACDONALD III, who was born in Portsmouth, NH on 2 March 1959, son of Alexander Frederick MacDonald, Jr. and Linda Barton. Married (2) in Norwich, VT on 20 December 1985 PETER JOHN GINTY, who was born in Hanover, NH on 13 February 1957, son of John Joseph Ginty and Dorothy Sayre.

Two children by Alexander Frederick MacDonald III:

i.   ALEXANDER FREDERICK IV was born in Hanover, NH on 23 May 1981.

ii.   BAYARD TUCKERMAN was born in Hanover, NH on 23 May 1981.

Child by Peter John Ginty:

i.   EMMA SAYRE was born in Lebanon, NH on 26 March 1986.

84. SUZANNA CARLETON STOUT was born in Greenwich, CT on 16 December 1960. Married in Corinth, NH on 12 September 1987 PETER STOUT BANWELL, who was born in Hanover, NH on 4 October 1961, son of Roy Wendell Banwell and Nina Kelly.

Two children:

i.   OTIS LIVINGSTON was born in Newburyport, MA on 21 Novmeber 1991.

ii.   ROY WILLIAM was born in Newburyport, MA on 23 April 1994.

85. ETHEL DOMINICK STOUT was born in Greenwich, CT on 11 April 1963. Married In Post Mills, VT on 12 October 1991 STEVEN ALAN MCLAUGHLIN, who was born in Spokane, WA on 27 August 1962, son of Dennis Steven McLaughlin and Claire Caldwell.

Four children:

i.   MOLLY MABEL was born in Wheatland, WY on 13 November 1994.

ii.   TIMOTHY ANDREW, was born in Wheatland, WY on 17 February 1996.

iii.   MARY ALICE was born in Carnation, WA on 5 February 1999.

Iv.   GRACE ELKINS was born in Kirkland, WA on 8 May 2001.

86. ARTHUR ELKINS STOUT was born in Greenwich, CT on 3 February 1969. Married in Pittsburg, NH on 26 October 1996 BARBARA SARGENT who was born in Lebabon, NH on 8 September 1961, daughter of Talbert Hill Sargent and Barbara Brown.

Two children:

i.   TAYLOR MAY was born in Lebanon, NH on 16 March 1997.

ii.   LILLIAN BARBARA was born in Lebanon, NH on 21 May 1999.

87. ERIC DE VILLERS GRANCHAMPS was born in Brussels, Belgium on 5 December 1964. Married in Oud-Turnhout, Belgium on 30 June 1990 VERONIQUE DIERCKX, who was born in Brussels, Belgium on 27 December 1965, daughter of Francois Dierckx and Ghislaine Simonis.

Five children:

i.   CORALIE was born in Dallas, TX on 19 December 1991.

ii.   NICOLAS was born in Brussels, Belgium on 26 November 1993.

iii.   GREGOIRE was born in Brussels, Belgium on 15 March 1996

iv.   VALENTINE (twin) was born in Brussels, Belgium on 14 November 2000.

The Seven Weld Brothers

v.   GUILLAUME (twin) was born in Brussels, Belgium on 14 November 2000.

88. NATALIE WOLCOTT (H'83) was born in San Francisco, CA on 18 June 1963. Married in Locust Valley, NY on 10 June 1993 HUGO ANDREW YOUNGER WILLIAMS who was born in London, England on 18 March 1965, son of David Malcolm Younger Williams and Felicia Marjorie Bennett.

Two children:

i.   GEORGIA BRADLEY was born in London, England on 5 December 1995.

ii.   DAISY WOLCOTT was born in London, England on 8 March 1999.

89. STEPHEN WELD WOLCOTT (adopted) was born in Westwood, CA on 27 February 1968. Married in La Cañada, CA on 25 June 1994 AMY JOINER ALVAREZ who was born in Burbank, CA on 1 January 1972, daughter of Raymond Alvarez and Linda Joiner.

Two children:

i.   JACK JOINER was born in Laguna Hills, CA on 20 February 1999.

ii.   NICHOLAS JOINER was born in Laguna Hills, CA on 16 August 2001.

90. SARAH WINBURN WELD (H'87) was born in Boston, MA on 13 November 1965. Married in San Francisco, CA on 2 July 1994 WAYNE KESSLER SNODGRASS (H'86) who was born in Boston MA on 19 July 1964, son of Samuel Robert Snodgrass and Kay Bolgen Kessler. (She retains her Weld maiden name and gives it to her children..)

Two children:

i.   COLIN KINNEY WELD was born in San Francisco, CA on 27 November 1997.

ii.   NAOMI KESSLER WELD was born in San Francisco, CA on 21 December 1999.

91. ARTHUR CARLISLE HODGES, JR (H'85). was born in Boston, MA on 14 February 1963. Married SUNHEE JUHON (H'85), born in Seoul, Korea on 12 May 1963, daughter of Hongkyoo Juhon and Nansoo Lee (of Denver, CO).

Three children:

i.   ALEXANDER HONGKYOO JUHON was born in Denver, CO on 8 June 1995.

ii.   NATALIE WELD JUHON was born in Denver CO in 1996.

iii.   ELOISE NANSOO JUHON was born in Denver, CO on 28 January 1999.

92. SUSANNA HODGES was born in Boston MA on 20 July 1964. Married in Ipswich, MA on 2 November 1991 ERIC DAVID SALK, who was born in New York, NY 14 August 1961, son of Dr. Lee Salk and Kerstin Anderson.

One child:

i.   OLIVER LEE WARREN was born in Los Angeles, CA on 13 May 1995.

93. ALEXANDER WELD HODGES was born in Beverly, MA on 16 September 1968. Married in Pittsburgh, PA on 1 June 1996 MARY ELIZABETH KLUG born in Pittsburgh, PA on 2 October 1967, daughter of William F. Klug IV and Mary Elizabeth DeMatt.

One child:

i.   MIA ALESII was born in Miami, FL on 28 August 1999.

94. ROBERT PRESCOTT BALDWIN was born in New Haven, CT on 18 September 1964. Married in Hartford, CT on 28 December 1987 (divorced 1991) PATRICIA ANN SULLIVAN, who was born in Enfield, CT on 27 June 1968, daughter of James Sullivan and Mary Arquiarro.

One child:

i.   CHELSIE ANNE was born in Adelanto, CA on 29 November 1988.

95. REBECCA ANNE BALDWIN was born in New Haven, CT on 12 January 1964. Married (1) in Wareham, MA on 18 August 1990 (divorced 1994.) BRADFORD RICHARD SILVA, who was born in New Bedford, MA on 11 November 1966, son of Frank Joseph Silva and Betty Lois Parker. Married (2) in Jacksonville, NC on 3 February 1996 JON ARTHUR FAULKNER, who was born in New Bedford, MA on 18 December 1968, son of Richard Arthur Faulkner and Mary Antoinette Morse.

One child by Bradford Silva:

i.   GAGE HOWARD was born in Wareham, MA on 7 October 1991.

Two children by Jon Arthur Faulkner:

i.   TAYLOR ANNE was born in Wareham, MA on 17 September 1997.

ii.   GABRIELLE ANNE was born in Wareham, MA on 24 July 1999.

96. ADELAIDE WELD LAPSLEY was born in Oyster Bay, NY on 29 September 1962. Married in Westbury, NY on 24 September 1988 SEAN FRANCIS MULRY who was born in New York, NY on 27 September 1963, son of Thomas Carroll Mulry and Margaret Mary Power.

Two children:

i.   HOPE WHITNEY was born in Plainview, NY on 29 January 1993.

ii.   CECILIA FOX was born in Mineola, NY on 5 July 1995.

97. HOWARD LAPSLEY (twin) (H'87) was born in Oyster Bay, NY on 18 August 1965. Married in New Haven, CT on 6 September 1997 KAREN LYNN CANAVAN who was born in New Haven, CT on 15 July 1968, daughter of Michael Joseph Canavan and Mary Beth Harkins.

One child:

i.   TIMOTHY JOSEPH was born in Boston, MA on 4 June 1999.

98. ROBERT WHITNEY LAPSLEY (twin) (H' 87) was born in Oyster Bay, NY on 18 August 1965. Married in Springwater, MN on 30 December 1995 ELIZABETH THORNE DEKKER, daughter of Hans Dekker and Lynne Crouter.

Two children:

i.   WALLIS DEKKER was born in Seattle, WA on 14 April 1997.

ii.   SUSANNA HALLOWELL was born in Seattle, WA on 18 May 1999.

99. KATHARINE WOODS was born in Boston, MA on 12 February 1970. Married in Hailey, ID on 18 June 1994 (divorced) BRIAN KELLY EMERICK, who was born in Tacoma, WA on 20 May 1965, son of Brian Herbert Emerick and Kathleen Rust.

One child:

i.   INDIA TESS was born in Sun Valley, ID on 13 June 1993.

100. ALEXANDRA WOODS was born in New York, NY on 6 June 1972. She has a son by RANDALL EDIGER.

One child:

i.   ROWAN EDIGER was born in Aubury, CA on 2 August 1995.

The Fourth Weld brother
THOMAS SWAN WELD
and his descendants

FIRST GENERATION

1. THOMAS SWAN WELD was born in Boston, MA on 23 October 1810 and died in Jamaica Plain, MA on 4 June 1848 son of William Gordon Weld and Hannah Minot. Married in Charlestown, NH on 5 March 1838 SARAH FITCH SUMNER who was born in Charlestown, NH on 8 April 1819 and died on 25 April 1901, daughter of Judge Frederick Augustus Sumner and Abigail Little Bailey. (She married in 1851, Donald Thane.)

Two Children:

2. i. SARAH SWAN, born in Roxbury, MA on 16 December 1839. Married JOSÉ FRANCISCO CARRET.

3. ii. FRANCIS MINOT, born in Dalton, NH on 17 January 1840. Married FANNY ELIZABETH BARTHOLOMEW.

SECOND GENERATION

2. SARAH SWAN WELD was born in Roxbury, MA on 16 December 1839 and died in Cambridge, MA on 27 February 1927. Married in West Roxbury, MA on 6 October 1864 JOSÉ FRANCISCO CARRET (H'1856) who was born in Trinidad de Cuba on 3 April 1834 and died in Cambridge, MA on 8 December 1897, son of Joseph Francis Carret and Eliza Henchman Tidd.

Four children:

4. i. ANNA WELD, born in Cincinnati, OH on 13 July 1865. Married CHARLES BATES DUNLAP.

5. ii. MARGARET MINOT, born in Cincinnati, OH on 10 November 1869. Married CHARLES GARRISON.

iii. FRANCES WELD was born in Cincinnati, OH on 30 August 1871 and died in Santa Barbara, CA on 19 October 1954. (Unmarried).

6.   iv.   JAMES WELD, born in Cambridge, MA on 16 May 1876. Married ELIZABETH HAMMILL CALKINS.

3. FRANCIS MINOT WELD was born in Dalton, NH on 17 January 1840 and died in Jamaica Plain, MA on 31 December 1893. Married in Hartford, CT on 11 April 1872 FANNY ELIZABETH BARTHOLEMEW who was born in New York, NY on 22 February 1851 and died in New York, NY on 27 February 1923, daughter of George Medad Bartholomew and Fanny Griswold Fowler.

Three children:

    i.   SARAH SWAN was born in New York, NY on 20 August 1873 and died in Kittery, ME after 1926. Married in Jamaica Plain, MA on 28 October 1905 CHARLES CHANDLER BLAKE who was born in Portsmouth, NH on 31 October 1872 and died in Kittery Pt. ME, after 1926, son of Charles F. Blake and Mary T.H. Ladd. (No children.)

7.   ii.   FRANCIS MINOT, JR. born in New York, NY on 18 February 1875. Married (1) MARGARET LOW WHITE. Married (2) JULIA DEFOREST TIFFANY (Parker).

8.   iii.   CHRISTOPHER MINOT, born in New York, NY on 30 March 1876. Married (1) SERENA GILMAN MARSHALL. Married (2) GRACE L. VAN WINKLE.

THIRD GENERATION

4. ANNA WELD CARRET was born in Cincinnati, OH on 13 July 1865 and died in Scarsdale, NY on 26 July 1956. Married in Cambridge, MA on 23 September 1902 DR. CHARLES BATES DUNLAP (H'89) who was born in Cambridge, MA on 24 August 1863 and died in New York, NY on 6 June 1926 son of Charles Henry Dunlap and Martha Smart Bates (of Hans Creek, WV).

Three children:

9.   i.   MARTHA WELD, born in Waltham, MA on 5 September 1904. Married KING HIRAM GREEN.

10.   ii.   RUTH WELD, born in New York, NY on 2 July 1906. Married JOHN WATSON MACDOWELL.

11. iii. CHARLES EDWARD, born in New York, NY on 8 June 1908. Married LORNA MARGARET ALFRED.

5. MARGARET MINOT CARRET was born in Cincinnati, OH on 10 November 1869 and died in Santa Barbara, CA on 25 December 1946. Married in Wianno, MA on 14 September 1895 CHARLES GARRISON (H'1892) who was born in Roxbury, MA on 19 June 1868 and died in Port Angeles, WA on 14 April 1951, son of William Lloyd Garrison, Jr. and Ellen Wright.

Two children:

12. i. ROBERT HALE, born in Belmont, MA on 16 June 1896. Married (1) CATHERINE ELIZABETH COOPER. Married (2) GRACE LOUISE WHITEFORD.

     ii. MARGARET (R'19) was born in Lexington, MA on 18 October 1898 and died in Berkeley, CA on 28 February 1959. Married in Wianno, MA on 9 April 1921 ARISTIDES EVANGELUS PHOUTRIDES (H'11) who was born in Icaria, Greece on 17 April 1887 and died in Chebeague Island, ME on 26 August 1923, son of Evangelus Phoutrides and Aspasia Puolianos. (No children.)

6. JAMES WELD CARRET (H'97) was born in Cambridge, MA on 16 May 1876 and died in Brookline, MA on 10 November 1929. Married in Kenilworth, IL on 6 October 1906 ELIZABETH HAMMIL CALKINS who was born in Chicago, IL circa 1880 and died prob. Brookline, MA after 1947.

One child:

13. i. ELIZABETH, born in Brookline, MA on 24 September 1908. Married KILBY PAGE SMITH, JR.

7. FRANCIS MINOT WELD, JR. (H'1897) was born in New York, NY on 18 February 1875 and died in New York, NY on 1 November 1949. Married (1) in New York, NY on 7 November 1903 (divorced 1922) MARGARET LOW WHITE who was born in Brooklyn, NY on 2 March 1883 and died in Greenwich, CT on 30 July 1948 (as Mrs. Hugh Marshall) daughter of William August White and Harriet Hilliard. Married (2) in New York, NY on 17 August 1930 JULIA DEFOREST TIFFANY (PARKER) who was born in New York, NY on 24 September 1887 and died in New York, NY on 22 November 1973, daughter of Louis Comfort Tiffany and Louise Wakeman Knox.

Four children by Margaret Low White:

14.   i.   MARJORY LOW, born in New York, NY on 4 December 1904. Married WILLIAM MASON AUSTIN.

15.   ii.   ALFRED WHITE, born in New York, NY on 23 January 1908. Married SARAH ANN DUGGAN.

        iii.   FRANCIS MINOT (H'32) was born in New York, NY on 16 December 1909 and died in Palm Beach, FL on 25 October 1967. (Unmarried).

16.   iv.   DAVID, born in New York, NY on 10 January 1911. Married MARY BLAKE NICHOLS.

8. CHRISTOPHER MINOT WELD (H'1897) was born in New York, NY on 30 March 1876 and died in New York, NY on 9 January 1936. Married (1) in New York, NY on 12 December 1910 SERENA GILMAN MARSHALL who was born in New York, NY on 24 March 1882 and died in New York, NY on 4 October 1921, daughter of Henry Rutgers Marshall and Julia Robbins Gilman. Married (2) in New York, NY on 24 May 1924 GRACE L. VAN WINKLE who was born in New York, NY on 21 December 1881 and died in New York, NY on 7 February 1976, daughter of Edgar Beach Van Winkle and Elizabeth Mitchell.

Five children by Serena Gilman Marshall:

17.   i.   SERENA MARSHALL, born in Washington, D.C. on 10 November 1911. Married HOWARD ALDEN BLYTH.

18.   ii.   ELIZABETH MINOT, born in Low Moor, VA on 29 June 1913. Married (1) PHILIP MILLEDOLER BRETT, JR. Married (2) JOSEPH FARRELL HASKELL.

19.   iii.   CHRISTOPHER MINOT JR., born in Dongan Hills, Staten Island, NY on 3 November 1914. Married MARGUERITE WALKER ROGERS (GIBSON).

20.   iv.   JULIA WINTHROP (twin), born in Dongan Hills, Staten Island, NY on 12 August 1916. Married JOHN GRANBERY.

21.   v.   PENELOPE (twin), born in Dongan Hills, Staten Island, NY on 12 August 1916. Married HAROLD TREDWAY WHITE, JR.

FOURTH GENERATION

9. MARTHA WELD DUNLAP was born in Waltham, MA on 5 September 1904 and died in Trout, WV on 22 December 1974. Married in Lewisburg, WV on 23 December 1936 KING HIRAM GREEN who was born in McDowell County, WV on 8 February 1906 son of Stephen Green and Julianna Estep.

Three children:

22.　　i.　　HIRAM STEPHEN, born in Boston, MA on 17 December 1938. Married LOIS MARIE MULLINS.

23.　　ii.　　MARTHA ELLEN, (adopted) born in Charleston, WV on 13 June 1940. Married (1) DANIEL L. MAYER. Married (2) DONALD MACK FREEMAN.

24.　　iii.　　CHARLES WILLIAM, born in Charleston, WV on 23 July 1942. Married ALMA LEE PAULIN.

10. RUTH WELD DUNLAP was born in New York, NY on 2 July 1906. Married in Scarsdale, NY on 22 September 1928 JOHN WATSON MACDOWELL who was born in Yonkers, NY on 1 April 1886 and died in Scarsdale, NY on 15 March 1969, son of John Shannon MacDowell and Evelyn Parke.

Five children:

25.　　i.　　JOHN WATSON, JR., born in Bronxville, NY on 16 August 1929. Married AUDREY JEANETTE D'HEEDENE.

26.　　ii.　　WILLIAM DUNLAP, born in Bronxville, NY on 2 December 1931. Married JANE MOLLIE KEMMERER.

27.　　iii.　　EDWARD PARKE, born in Bronxville, NY on 15 February 1934. Married ELEANOR VIRGINIA MAIER.

28.　　iv.　　ANNE FRANCES, born in Bronxville, NY on 18 October 1937. Married HEINZ JASTER.

　　　　v.　　THEODORE WELD was born in Bronxville, NY on 26 February 1941. Married in Oneonta, NY on 4 January 1997 JUDITH ZURBRICK who was born in _____ on 26 January 1955, daughter of _____ Zurbrich and _____ Bell.

11. CHARLES EDWARD DUNLAP was born in New York, NY on 8 June 1908 and died

in New Orleans, LA on 21 February 1990. Married in Chicago, IL on 29 September 1937 LORNA MARGARET ALFRED who was born in Genoa, NE on 2 February 1909 and died in New Orleans, LA on 29 October 1988, daughter of Olaf Alfred and Sigrid Alfred.

Four Children:

i.   ELIZABETH NASON was born in Boston, MA on 7 July 1939 and died in Alamosa, CO on 3 June 1985.

29. ii.   WILLIAM PETRIE, born in Boston, MA on 14 March 1941. Married JANICE LUNDY (BUSH).

30. iii.   CHARLES DAWES, born in Boston, MA on 25 April 1942. Married RUTH LORENE JONES.

31. iv.   JOHN ALFRED, born in New Orleans, LA on 1 June 1944. Married MARIE LOVATO.

12. ROBERT HALE GARRISON (H'18) was born in Belmont, MA on 16 June 1896 and died in Upland, CA on 4 January 1988. Married (1) in Ventura, CA on 25 March 1927 CATHERINE ELIZABETH COOPER who was born in Merrimac, WI on 4 February 1903 and died in Claremont, CA on 11 July 1967, daughter of William Edward Cooper and Ora Linnie Utter. Married (2) in Los Angeles, CA on 13 December 1968 GRACE LOUISE WHITEFORD who was born in Reno, NV on 21 September 1904, daughter of Gustavus Adolphus Whiteford and Grace Kepler.

Two children by Catherine Elizabeth Cooper:

32. i.   ROBERT LINN, born in Santa Barbara, CA on 18 July 1928. Married JOYCE CLARKE.

33. ii.   ANNE WRIGHT, born in Pasadena, CA on 5 June 1930. Married JAMES WARREN GOULD.

13. ELIZABETH CARRET was born in Brookline, MA on 24 September 1908 and died in Greenville, SC on 23 October 1984. Married in Brookline, MA on 20 May 1932 KILBY PAGE SMITH, JR. who was born in Waltham, MA on 25 February 1904 and died in Boston, MA on 13 May 1980, son of Kilby Page Smith and Alice Slade Milton.

Four children:

34.   i.   SANDRA CARRET, born in Weymouth, MA on 12 January 1933. Married LEONARD VICTOR SHORT, JR.

35.   ii.   KILBY PAGE Jr., born in Waltham, MA on 28 December 1933. Married (1) PATRICIA ALDEN. Married (2) JANE M. McCRARY (ROHRBAUGH). Married (3) PAMPANIDA SRIARJBUAPAN.

       iii.   MARGOT WELD was born in Nantucket, MA on 23 August 1938 and died in San Francisco, CA in 1987. Married (1) in Nantucket, MA on 9 September 1962 (divorced 1973) HARRY BISHOP HAMBLY, III who was born in San Francisco, CA in 1933, son of Harry Bishop Hambly, Jr. and Lillian Blackman. Married (2) in San Francisco, CA on 10 September 1981 RICHARD S. COLE who was born in 1928. No children.

       iv.   JENNIFER HAYNES who was born in Boston, MA on 18 July 1945. Married in Boston, MA on 6 December 1969 RICHARD E. STIEFEL who was born in Baltimore, MD in 1941, son of Earl R. Stiefel and Gertrude Rea Meeks. No children.

14. MARJORY LOW WELD was born in New York, NY on 4 December 1904 and died in Certreville, MD in May 1950. Married in New York, NY on 12 February 1927 (divorced 1934) WILLIAM MASON AUSTIN (H'25) who was born in Jamaica Plain on 7 September 1902 and died in Blue Hill, ME on 28 June 1977, son of Francis Boylston Austin (H'86) and Mary Lydia Fisher.

Two children:

36.   i.   MARJORY WELD, born in New York, NY on 22 November 1927. Married RICHARD IRWIN JOHNSON.

37.   ii.   FRANCIS REED, born in Boston, MA on 21 December 1929. Married BARBARA KNOX HALL.

15. ALFRED WHITE WELD (H'30) was born in New York, NY on 23 January 1908 and died in Greenwich, CT on 8 September 1957. Married in New York, NY on 21 January 1938 SARAH ANN DUGGAN who was born in New York, NY on 12 February 1914, daughter of Stephen Pierce Duggan and Sarah Elsesser.

Three children:

38.   i.   SALLY ANN, born in New York, NY on 13 June 1939. Married JEROME PIERCE

WEBSTER, JR.

39.   ii.   JONATHAN MINOT, born in Greenwich, CT on 25 February 1941. Married JANE CATHARINE PAIGE.

        iii.   ALFRED MATTHEW (H'64) was born in Greenwich, CT on 21 July 1942. Married in Fairfax, VA on 30 October 1978 (divorced) JACQUELINE BOGARD who was born in New York, NY on 25 June 1946, daughter of Miguel Bogard and Juana Beatriz Sheppard Idarte-Borda. (No children.)

16. DAVID WELD (H'34) was born in New York, NY on 10 January 1911 and died in St. James, NY on 21 July 1972. Married in New York, NY on 4 January 1936 MARY BLAKE NICHOLS who was born in Garden City, NY on 13 April 1913 and died in St. James, NY on 10 February 1986, daughter of John Treadwell Nichols (H'05) and Cornelia Dubois Floyd.

Four children:

40.   i.   DAVID LOW, born in New York, NY on 6 July 1938. Married (1) LOUISE PARSONS. Married (2) SHERLEY SHELVIN.

41.   ii.   FRANCIS MINOT, born in New York, NY on 22 November 1939. Married HELENE SINGLETON MUELLER.

42.   iii.   ANNE FLOYD, born in New York, NY on 27 April 1941. Married (1) GEORGE CRAWFORD, JR. Married (2) DANIEL GERARD COLLINS.

43.   iv.   WILLIAM FLOYD, born in New York, NY on 31 July 1945. Married (1) SUSAN ROOSEVELT. Married (2) Leslie Marshall (Bradlee).

17. SERENA MARSHALL WELD was born in Washington, D.C. on 10 November 1911. Married in Bedford, NY on 23 June 1934 HOWARD ALDEN BLYTH who was born in Dongan Hills, Staten Island, NY on 27 May 1911 and died in Old Greenwich, CT on 21 June 1987, son of Bertham Dukes Blyth and Bertha_____.

Two children:

44.   i.   HOWARD ALDEN, JR., born in Arlington, NJ on 19 April 1938. Married LINDA MORGAN.

45.　ii.　SERENA GILMAN, born on 14 January 1941. Married (1) ROBERT MINER. Married (2) HARRY PALIN.

18. ELIZABETH MINOT WELD was born in Low Moor, VA on 29 June 1913 and died in New York, NY on 29 June 1982. Married (1) in Bedford, NY on 20 September 1935 (divorced 1962) PHILIP MILLEDOLER BRETT, JR. who was born in New York, NY on 2 September 1908 and died in New York, NY in Jan./Feb. 1988, son of Philip Milledoler Brett and A. Margaret Strong. Married (2) in New York, NY on 20 December 1962 JOSEPH FARRELL HASKELL who was born in Ft. Omaha, NE on 1 July 1908 and died in New York, NY on 10 October 1983, son of William Nafew Haskell and Winifred A. Farrell.

Three children by Philip Milledoler Brett, Jr.:

46.　i.　PHILIP MILLEDOLER III, born in New York, NY on 7 August 1937. Married ANNE LENOX ALEXANDRE.

47.　ii.　KATRYNA ROMBOUT, born in New York, NY on 6 November 1940. Married (1) GEORGE GARDNER HERRICK. Married (2) NEIL CAROTHERS, III.

48.　iii.　ELIZABETH WELD, born in New York, NY on 6 November 1940. Married ROBERT DAVID WEBSTER.

19. CHRISTOPHER MINOT WELD JR. (H'36) was born in Dongan Hills, Staten Island, NY on 3 November 1914. Married in Garrison, NY on 1 August 1942 MARGUERITE WALKER ROGERS (Gibson) who was born in New York, NY on 13 January 1914 daughter of Ray Rogers and Marguerite Elmendorf.

Two children:

49.　i.　MARGUERITE VAN WINKLE, born in New York, NY on 14 May 1944. Married (1) MICHAEL O'BRIEN. Married (2) WILLIAM WILLIAMS, JR. Married (3) WILLIAM COSTEN.

50.　ii.　CHRISTOPHER MINOT III, born in Evanston, IL on 6 April 1949. Married CATHERINE JOHNSON.

Two stepchildren:

51.　i.　WILLIAM SLOAN (GIBSON), born in New York, NY on 9 October 1938. Married BARBARA WILLETT LOWE.

52.   ii.   ELLEN WALKER (GIBSON), born in New York, NY on 30 May 1940. Married ROBERT HENRY PERLITZ, JR.

20. JULIA WINTHROP WELD was born in Dongan Hills, Staten Is. NY on 12 August 1916. Married in Bedford, NY on 17 June 1939 (divorced 1972) JOHN GRANBERY who was born in Brooklyn, NY on 30 May 1911, son of Edwin Carleton Granbery and Julia Kinport Barr.

Four children:

53.   i.   BARBARA KINPORT, born in New York, NY on 22 January 1942. Married ANDREW DOUGLASS HALL, JR.

54.   ii.   WILLIAM PRESTON, born in New York, NY on 15 March 1944. Married ANN RUTH HOFFMAN.

55.   iii.   SERENA WELD, born in Stamford, CT on 8 May 1948. Married (1) STEPHEN MICHAEL DWORETZ. Married (2) CHARLES WEBSTER CARLETON, JR.

56.   iv.   CHRISTOPHER MINOT, born in Stamford, CT on 7 January 1954. Married NOREEN CLARE DUFFY.

21. PENELOPE WELD was was born in Dongan Hills, Staten Island NY on 12 August 1916. Married in Bedford, NY on 3 May 1941 HAROLD TREDWAY WHITE, JR. (H'37) who was born in Atlantic City, NJ on 26 June 1914, son of Harold Tredway White (H'1897) and Ruth Underhill.

Five children:

        i.   CHARLES DANA was born in Washington, D.C. on 30 March 1942.

57.   ii.   ALEXANDER WELD, born in New York, NY on 14 August 1944. Married ANNE HYDE MEISSNER.

        iii.   HAROLD TREDWAY III was born in Darien, CT on 3 November 1947. Married in Post Mills, VT on 12 August 1978 ELIZABETH WHITE (PHILLIPS) who was born in 1944, daughter of C. Spencer White.

58.   iv.   CHRISTOPHER MINOT, born in New Canaan, CT on 22 January 1951. Married MELINDA HARLY SAXTON.

v.   FRANCIS WELD was born in New Canaan, CT on 23 May 1955. Married in Helena, MT on 26 November 1981 REBECCA LEA HARPER who was born in Kansas on 23 November 1957, daughter of Jack Harper and Mary Francis.

FIFTH GENERATION

22. HIRAM STEPHEN GREEN was born in Boston, MA on 17 December 1938. Married in Charleston, WV on 5 August 1961 LOIS MARIE MULLINS who was born in Chelyan, WV on 2 September 1931, daughter of Blanch Harvey Mullins and Sadie Reffelt.

Three children:

i.   LEAH MARIE was born in Frankfurt, Germany on 23 August 1963.

ii.   LAURA ELAINE was born in Charleston, WV on 3 June 1965.

iii.   AMY LOUISE was born in Charleston, WV on 15 April 1969.

23. MARTHA ELLEN GREEN was born in Charleston, WV on 13 June 1940. Married (1) on 24 June 1961 DANIEL L. MAYER. Married (2) in York, SC on 26 March 1967 DONALD MACK FREEMAN who was born in Charlotte, NC on 21 July 1945, son of Ronald Mack Freeman and Mary Jewell Price.

Two children by Daniel L. Mayer:

i.   TINA MARIE was born on 8 December 1961.

ii.   MARTHA ANNE was born on November 1963 and died on 12 August 1965.

Child of Donald Mack Freeman:

i.   JULIE TABITHA was born in Charlotte, NC on 26 March 1977.

24. CHARLES WILLIAM GREEN was born in Charleston, WV on 23 July 1942. Married in Frankfort, WV on 23 December 1962 (divorced 1990) ALMA LEE PAULIN who was born in Renick, WV on 25 June 1943, daughter of Victor Emmanuel Paulin and May Whittaker.

Three children:

i.   CHARLES DAVID was born in Clifton Forge, VA on 2 January 1965.

ii.   ANDREA ELIZABETH was born in Charlottesville, VA on 24 March 1967.

iii.   STEPHEN WILLIAM was born in Clifton Forge, VA on 19 March 1971.

25. JOHN WATSON MCDOWELL, JR. was born in Bronxville, NY on 16 August 1929. Married in Morristown, NJ on 1 September 1951 AUDREY JEANETTE D'HEEDENE who was born in Lynbrook, NYon 8 February 1931, daughter of Albert d'Heedene and Thelma Loser.

Four children:

59.   i.   ROGER PARKE, born in Mt. Vernon, NY on 14 September 1953. Married (1) DALE EVELYN FIELD. Married (2) BARBARA LANE.

60.   ii.   CHARLES EDWARD, born Bronxville, NY on 24 August 1955. Married DONNA FINCHIARO.

61.   iii.   CYNTHIA JEANETTE, born in Bronxville, NY on 7 June 1957. Married HAROLD WAYNE SANBORN.

62.   iv.   ELIZABETH RUTH, born in Bronxville, NY on 3 February 1959. Married CHRISTOPHER BRUCE LEVITT.

26. WILLIAM DUNLAP MACDOWELL was born in Bronxville, NY on 2 December 1931. Married in Palmerton, PA on 3 July 1954 JANE MOLLIE KEMMERER who was born in Palmerton, PA on 10 December 1929, daughter of LeRoy Joseph Kemmerer and Lillian May Pennel (of Laurel, DE).

Three children:

63.   i.   ANNE KATHERINE, born in Boston, MA on 28 October 1956. Married MARTIN RAE QUIGLEY.

64.   ii.   WILLIAM DOUGLAS, born in Baltimore, MD on 13 July 1961. Married LISA MARCIONE.

65.   iii.   EDWARD WATSON ("NED") born in White Plains, NY on 14 August 1968. Married MARIANNE ELIZABETH JOHNSON.

27. EDWARD PARKE MACDOWELL was born in Bronxville, NY on 15 February

1934. Married in Dobbs Ferry, NY on 21 June 1958 ELEANOR VIRGINIA MAIER who was born in Hastings, NY on 6 December 1935, daughter of Frederick John Maier.

Four children:

66.   i.   DAVID FREDERICK, born in Dobbs Ferry, NY on 25 August 1959. Married BETH HAMER WHITE.

67.   ii.   JEAN CAROLYN (H'84), born in Port Chester, NY on 12 January 1962. Married WILLIAM QUINCY JEFFRIES (H'82).

       iii.   JAMES EDWARD was born in Port Chester, NY on 30 December 1965. Married in Johnson, VT in August 1999 KRISTEN _____.

       iv.   NANCY ANNE was born in Port Chester, NY on 8 November 1969.

28. ANNE FRANCES MACDOWELL was born in Bronxville, NY on 18 October 1937. Married in San Francisco, CA on 21 November 1962 HEINZ JASTER who was born in Berlin, Germany on 23 August 1938, son of Otto Jaster and Alice Kampe.

Two children:

68.   i.   JOHN THOMAS, born in El Paso, TX on 20 December 1964. Married JANET MARIE PARTINGTON.

       ii.   THEODORA was born in White Plains, NY on 25 February 1967. Married in Evergreen, CO on 21 June 1999 JEFFREY ALLEN COOK who was born in Boston, MA on 31 May 1967, son of Peter Cook and Cynthia Cornwell.

29. WILLIAM PETRIE DUNLAP was born in Boston, MA on 14 March 1941 and died in New Orleans, LA on 28 February 2002. Married in Palmerton, PA on 11 August 1968 (divorced 1984) JANICE LUNDY KEMMERER (BUSH) born in Palmerton, Pa on 10 December 1929, daughter of Leroy Kemmerer and Lillian Penrel.

Two children:

       i.   SUSAN ELIZABETH was born in New Orleans, LA on 21 July 1970.

       ii.   ANNE MARGARET was born in New Orleans, LA on 20 June 1974.

Adopted son:

i.   STEPHEN JEFFREY BUSH was born in New Orleans, LA on 14 December 1965,and died c.1996, son of Vance R. Bush and Janice Lundy.

30. CHARLES DAWES DUNLAP was born in Boston, MA on 25 April 1942. Married in Shreveport, LA on 4 June 1966 RUTH LORENE JONES who was born in Shreveport, LA on 28 July 1946, daughter of John Edward Jones and Ruth Ozelle Benefield.

Two children:

i.   CHARLES EDWARD was born in Ruston, LA on 19 January 1967.

ii.   REBECCA ANNE was born in New Orleans, LA on 7 December 1974.

31. JOHN ALFRED DUNLAP was born in New Orleans, LA on 1 June 1944. Married in Albuquerque, NM on 22 June 1982 MARIE CALABAZA (LOVATO) who was born in Santo Domingo Pueblo, NM on 16 February 1947, daughter of Jose Cruz Lovato and Vincentita Calabaza.

One child:

i.   RUTH LORNA was born in Albuquerque, NM on 18 March 1983.

Stepchild of John Alfred Dunlap:

i.   JOSEPHINE LOVATO was born in Santa Fe, NM on 16 April 1966.

32. ROBERT LINN GARRISON was born in Santa Barbara, CA on 18 July 1928 and died in Long Beach, CA on 11 June 1982. Married in Pasadena, CA on 14 February 1955 JOYCE CLARKE who was born in Iowa City, IA on 16 May 1926, daughter of Dr. Benjamin Earl Clarke and Gail Harris.

Three children:

i.   ROBERT EARL was born in Pasadena, CA on 6 August 1957.

69.   ii.   MARGARET ANNE, born in Pasadena, CA on 20 April 1959. Married JAMES EDWARD PARKER.

  iii. CHARLES LLOYD was born in Pasadena, CA on 13 June 1961.

33. ANNE WRIGHT GARRISON was born in Pasadena, CA on 5 June 1930. Married in Glendora, CA on 6 January 1951 JAMES WARREN GOULD who was born in Boulder, CO on 14 May 1924, son of Douglas Warren Gould and Elsa Henrietta Dohne.

Five children:

  i. ROBERT DOUGLAS was born in Medan, Sumatra (Indonesia) on 1 April 1952.

70. ii. STEVEN COOPER, born in Glendora, CA on 2 October 1953. Married JANET ELIZABETH SAWICKI.

71. iii. CHRISTOPHER WELD, born in Washington, D.C. on 5 May 1955. Married JOAN DINEEN.

  iv. CATHERINE LINN was born in Upland, CA on 11 October 1958.

72. v. ELIZABETH ANNE, born in Upland, CA on 28 January 1960. Married JAMES PHILIP SOLIMANO.

34. SANDRA CARRET SMITH was born in Weymouth, MA on 12 January 1933 and died in New Ipswich, NH on 2 October 1981. Married in Waltham, MA on 28 January 1956 LEONARD VICTOR SHORT, JR. who was born in Tewksbury, MA on 11 April 1932, son of Leonard Victor Short and Winifred Hurley.

Four children:

73. i. LEONARD VICTOR, III, born in Woburn, MA on 24 August 1959. Married CHRISTINE MARY CALAGNA.

74. ii. ELIZABETH HAYNES, born in Woburn, MA on 16 May 1961. Married TOBEY J. RUSS.

  iii. THOMAS PAGE was born in Peterborough, NH on 7 May 1967.

  iv. JAMES GARRISON was born in Peterborough, NH on 3 May 1968.

35. KILBY PAGE SMITH, JR. was born in Waltham, MA on 28 December 1933.

Married (1) in New Orleans, LA on 11 February 1962 (divorced) PATRICIA ALDEN. Married (2) in New Ipswich, NH on 27 December 1980 (divorced 1981) JANE M. MCCRARY (ROHRBAUGH) who was born in South Carolina on 22 November 1950, daughter of John M. McCrary and Mildred Burnette.Marrird (3) on 11 December 1998 PAMPANIDA SRIARJBUAPAN.

Two children by Priscilla Alden:

i.   KILBY PAGE, III was born in Bethpage, Long Island, NY on 26 May 1967.

ii.   STACY ALDEN was born in Greenville, SC on 4 May 1970.

36. MARJORY WELD AUSTIN was born in New York, NY on 22 November 1927 and died in Boston, MA on 30 November 1988. Married in New York, NY on 27 March 1954 (divorced 1982) RICHARD IRWIN JOHNSON (H'51), who was born in Everett, MA on 17 March 1925, son of Karl H. Johnson and Louise Irwin.

Three children:

i.   SALLY WELD was born in Boston, MA on 19 January 1955. Married in Boston, MA on 9 June 1993 DAVID VICTOR LURIE who was born in St.Louis, MO on 18 November 1939, son of George Lurie and Marie Hogan. He has two daughters by a previous marriage, Renee C. and Katherine C. Lurie.

ii.   MARJORY WELD was born in Boston, MA on 28 July 1956.

75.   iii.   RICHARD MINOT WELD was born in Boston, MA on 23 December 1965. Married KAREN KATHLEEN O'LEARY.

37. FRANCIS REED AUSTIN was born in Boston, MA on 21 December 1929. Married in Wellesley, MA on 21 December 1950 BARBARA KNOX HALL who was born in Boston, MA on 29 January 1930, daughter of Roger Eastman Hall and Isabel Cobb Knox.

Four children:

76.   i.   CAROLYN HALL born in Boston, MA on 10 December 1951. Married ANDREW SHEPARD.

77.   ii.   FRANCIS REED, JR. born in Boston, MA on 17 March 1953. Married MARGARET GORDON HALL WASLEY.

78. iii. WILLIAM FISHER born in Boston, MA on 25 May 1955. Married BRENDA LOUISE ALVERSON.

iv. RICHARD WALKER was born in Boston, MA on 27 November 1959.

38. SALLY ANN WELD was born in New York, NY on 13 June 1939 and died in New York, NY on 3 March 1967. Married in Stamford, CT on 8 August 1962 JEROME PIERCE WEBSTER, JR. who was born in New York, NY on 30 October 1968, son of Jerome Pierce Webster and Geraldine McAlpin.

Two children:

i. PENELOPE WELD was born in Virginia Beach, VA in 1963.

ii. JEROME PIERCE, III was born in Bethesda, MD in 1964 and died in Mt. Orizapa, Mexico on 13 January 1986 (Climbing accident).

39. JONATHAN MINOT WELD (H'63) was born in Greenwich, CT on 25 February 1941. Married in Larchmont, NY on 19 June 1965 JANE CATHARINE PAIGE who was born in Brooklyn, NY on 2 January 1942, daughter of Raymond North Paige and Mary ____.

Two children:

i. ELIZABETH PAIGE was born in Greenwich, CT on 11 June 1971.

ii. ERIC MINOT was born in Greenwich, CT on 3 July 1974.

40. DAVID LOW WELD was born in New York, NY on 6 July 1938. Married (1) in New York, NY on 9 September 1960 (divorced 1988) LOUISE PARSONS, who was born in New York, NY on 17 April 1940, daughter of William Parsons and Louise Bigelow. Married (2) in Mt. Kisco, NY on 14 August 1989 SHERLEY SHEVLIN, who was born in New York, NY on 25 February 1955, daughter of Thomas Henry Shevlin and Durie Malcolm.

Three children by Louise Parsons:

i. DAVID LOW, JR. was born in New York, NY on 10 March 1963.

ii.   CHRISTOPHER PARSONS was born in New York, NY on 24 May 1965. Married in Locust Valley, NY on 17 July 1993 TYLER INGHAM, daughter of Jonathan Ingham and Shawn McWeeney (now Baroness Dimitri de Gunzburg).

iii.   ASHLEY NICHOLS was born in Mt. Kisco, NY on 7 November 1969.

Child by Sherley Shevlin:

i.   WILLIAM SHELVIN was born in Greenwich, CT on 17 February 1990.

41. FRANCIS MINOT WELD (H'61) was born in New York, NY on 22 November 1939. Married in New York, NY on 26 September 1970 HELENE SINGLETON MUELLER who was born in New York, NY on 2 December 1945, daughter of George Christopher Mueller and Frances McGrath.

Three children:

i.   FRANCIS MINOT, JR. was born in New York, NY on 21 October 1972.

ii.   ALEXANDRA SINGLETON was born in New York, NY on 15 March 1975.

iii.   MARGARET DUBOIS was born in New York, NY on 27 December 1978.

42. ANNE FLOYD WELD was born in New York, NY on 27 April 1941. Married (1) in New York, NY on 11 September 1965 (divorced 1979) GEORGE CRAWFORD, JR. (H'60) who was born in New York, NY on 13 December 1937, son of George Crawford (H'27) and Beatrice Iselin. Married (2) in New York, NY on 4 January 1983 DANIEL GERARD COLLINS, who was born in Brooklyn, NY on 29 March 1930, son of David Aloysius Collins and Mary Elizabeth Mahoney.

Four children by George Crawford, Jr.:

i.   ALEXANDER ISELIN (H'88) was born in New York, NY on 12 September 1966. Married in Wellesley, MA on 1 June 1991 DEBORAH CLAIRE BANDANZA, daughter of Santo Bandanza.

ii.   WILLIAM BLAKE was born in New York, NY on 28 October 1968.

iii.   SERENA WELD was born in New York, NY on 28 April 1970.

iv.   EVELYN FLOYD was born in New York, NY on 8 June 1974.

43. WILLIAM FLOYD WELD (H'70) was born in New York, NY on 31 July 1945 (Governor of MA). Married (1) in Oyster Bay, NY on 7 June 1975 (divorced 2002) SUSAN ROOSEVELT (H'70) who was born in Glen Cove, NY on 11 April 1948, daughter of Quentin Roosevelt (H'41) and Frances Blanche Webb. Married (2) in Bellport NY on 14 June 2003 LESLIE M. MARSHALL (BRADLEE)

Five children by Susan Roosevelt:

i.   DAVID MINOT (H'9?) was born in Boston, MA on 26 August 1976.

ii.   ETHEL DERBY was born in Boston, MA on 26 October 1977.

iii.   MARY BLAKE was born in Boston, MA on 21 January 1979.

iv.   QUENTIN ROOSEVELT was born in Boston, MA on 9 July 1981.

v.   FRANCES WYLIE was born in Boston, MA on 18 September 1983.

44. HOWARD ALDEN BLYTH, JR. was born in Arlington, NJ on 19 April 1938. Married LINDA MORGAN.

Two children:

i.   JENNIFER was born in 1967.

ii.   CHRISTOPHER was born in 1970.

45. SERENA GILMAN BLYTH was born on 14 January 1941. Married circa 1961 ROBERT MINER. Married (2) HARRY PALIN.

Three children by Robert Miner:

i.   LYNN was born in 1962.

ii.   LAURA was born in 1964.

iii.   ELIZABETH was born in 1967.

46. PHILIP MILLEDOLER BRETT, III was born in New York, NY on 7 August 1937. Married in Bernardsville, NJ on 18 October 1969 ANNE LENOX ALEXANDRE, who was born in Far Hills, NJ circa 1942, daughter of DeWitt Alexandre and Winifred Farrell.

Two children:

i.   PETER MILLEDOLER was born in 1972.

ii.   JAMES LENOX.

47. KATRYNA ROMBOUT BRETT was born in New York, NY on 6 November 1940. Married (1) in Paris, France on 31 December 1966 (divorced 1984) GEORGE GARDNER HERRICK (H'60) who was born in New York, NY on 8 April 1938, son of Parmely Webb Herrick (H'34) and Katherine Peabody Gardner. Married (2) in Washington, D.C. on 18 May 1989 NEIL CAROTHERS, III who was born in Fayetteville, AR on 11 October 1919, son of Neil Carothers, Jr. and Eileen Hamilton.

Three children by George Gardner Herrick:

i.   JASON NICHOLAS ROQUE was born in Brussels, Belgium on 15 September 1970.

ii.   ADAM GARDNER FISHKILL was born in New York, NY on 22 December 1973.

iii.   TIMOTHY BRETT GODWIT was born in Washington, D.C. on 28 January 1977.

48. ELIZABETH WELD BRETT was born in New York, NY on 6 November 1940. Married in New York, NY on 4 April 1964 ROBERT DAVID WEBSTER who was born in New York, NY on 14 March 1937, son of Louis Webster and Thelma Alcott.

Three children:

i.   ELIZABETH ALCOTT was born in New York, NY on 25 October 1965.

ii.   HOPE BRETT was born in New York, NY on 13 November 1967.

iii.   CHRISTOPHER WELD was born in New York, NY on 24 February 1971.

49. MARGUERITE VAN WINKLE WELD, born in New York, NY on 14 May 1944. Married (1) in Evanston, IL on 25 January 1964 (divorced 1970) MICHAEL O'BRIEN,

who was born in IL, son of Richard O'Brien and Beatrice _____. Married (2) in Key Biscayne, FL on 2 September 1972 (divorced 1977) WILLIAM WILLIAMS, JR. who was born in New York, NY on 24 August 1944, son of William Williams and Thushalda Pell. Married (3) in Stone Mountain, PA on 29 September 1984 (divorced 1986) WILLIAM COSTEN, who was born in Alabama on 14 November 1935 son of Wallace Costen and Lois Posten.

Two children by Michael O'Brien:

i.   WILLIAM MICHAEL O'BRIEN WELD (legally changed his surname to Weld prior to his marriage) was born in Evanston, IL on 13 February 1964. Married in Hephzibah, GA on 14 November 1988 DENISE TURNER who was born in Hephzibah, GA on 19 February 1969, daughter of James Turner and Mary_____.

ii.   JAMES ANDREW O'BRIEN (subsequently adopted by William Williams, Jr.) was born in Highland Park, IL on 20 August 1966.

Child of William Willams, Jr:

i.   CHRISTINE MARIE was born in Atlanta, GA on 9 May 1975.

50. CHRISTOPHER MINOT WELD, III was born in Evanston, IL on 6 April 1949. Married in Gambier, OH on 29 July 1972 CATHERINE JOHNSON who was born in Long Beach, CA on 28 December 1950, daughter of Walter Franklin Johnson and Annie Loyce Petrey.

Two children:

i.   AMANDA CAITLIN was born in Baltimore, MD on 10 September 1975.

ii.   MATTHEW CHRISTOPHER was born in Nashua, NH on 3 May 1978.

51. WILLIAM SLOAN (GIBSON) WELD was born in New York, NY on 9 October 1938. Married in Glencoe, IL on 5 July 1957 (divorced 1967) BARBARA WILLETT LOWE who was born in Chicago, IL on 13 December 1938, daughter of Ward Lowe and Evelyn_____.

Two children:

i.   MICHAEL WILLIAM was born in Evanston, IL on 19 October 1961.

ii.   LAURA MARGUERITE was born in Evanston, IL (poss. Savannah, GA) on 28 September 1963.

52. ELLEN WALKER (GIBSON) WELD was born in New York, NY on 30 May 1940. Married in Winnetka, IL on 12 May 1961 ROBERT HENRY PERLITZ, JR who was born in Houston, TX on 20 May 1938, son of Robert Henry Perlitz and Noel Cremin.

Two children:

i.   NANCY ELIZABETH was born in Oak Park, IL on 17 March 1965.

ii.   ROBERT HENRY, III WAS born in Highland Park, IL on 3 April 1967 and died in Highland Park, IL on 5 April 1967.

53. BARBARA KINPORT GRANBERY was born in New York, NY on 22 January 1942. Married in Bedford, NY on 22 June 1963 ANDREW DOUGLAS HALL, JR. who was born in New York, NY on 9 June 1940, son of Andrew Douglas Hall and Marie LeMoyne Noyes.

Two children:

i.   ELIZABETH WELD was born in Morristown, NJ on 23 February 1968.

ii.   JONATHAN DOUGLAS was born in Morristown, NJ on 30 September 1970.

54. WILLIAM PRESTON GRANBERY was born in New York, NY on 15 March 1944. Married in Bryn Mawr, PA on 19 July 1969 ANN RUTH HOFFMAN who born in Philadelphia, PA on 1 August 1945, daughter of Corbit Strickland Hoffman and Dorothy Roberts.

Three children:

i.   JOHN HASTINGS was born in Philadelphia, PA on 30 May 1977.

ii.   CORBIT WELD was born in Philadelphia, PA on 19 January 1979.

iii.   ABIGAIL SHREVE was born in Morristown, NJ on 20 October 1987.

55. SERENA WELD GRANBERY was born in Stamford, CT on 8 May 1948. Married (1) in Newton, MA on 7 Apirl 1969 (divorced) STEPHEN MICHAEL DWORETZ who was born in New York, NY on 13 April 1947 son of Philip L. Dworetz and Mildred Shure. Married (2) in Salisbury, CT on 29 September 1984 CHARLES WEBSTER CARLETON, JR. who was born in Minneapolis, MN on 25 June 1956, son of Charles Webster Carleton and Ardis Emelia Voeglin.

Child by Charles Webster Carleton:

i.   ADRIAN GRANBERY was born in Sharon, CT on 22 February 1987.

56. CHRISTOPHER MINOT GRANBERY was born in Stamford, CT on 7 January 1954. Married in Brooklyn, NY on 12 February 1979 NOREEN CLARE DUFFY who was born in Brooklyn, NY on 12 August 1955, daughter of Michael Duffy and Agnes McHugh.

Two children:

i.   LIAM was born in Danbury, CT on 25 September 1985.

ii.   ERIN JULIA was born in Danbury, CT on 23 July 1987.

57. ALEXANDER WELD WHITE was born in New York, NY on 14 August 1944. Married in Falmouth, MA on 18 June 1972 ANNE HYDE MEISSNER who was born in Boston, MA on 22 December 1943, daughter of John Nimeyer Meissner and Katherine Hyde Wormelle.

Two children:

i.   CYNTHIA NIMEYER was born in Boston, MA on 16 December 1974.

ii.   ALEXANDER WELD, JR. was born in Beverly, MA on 18 May 1978.

58. CHRISTOPHER MINOT WHITE was born in New Canaan, CT on 22 January 1951. Married in Cambridge, MA on 31 December 1971 (divorced 1990) MELINDA HARLY SAXTON who was born in Rochester, MN on 29 June 1950, daughter of George Albert Saxton and Anne Kemble.

Three children:

i.   NATHANIEL TUCKER was born in Brattleboro, VT on 28 November 1974.

ii.   GAVIN WELD was born in Middlebury, VT on 2 April 1978.

iii.   HENRY MOSS was born in Burlington, VT on 25 April 1988.

SIXTH GENERATION

59. ROGER PARKE MACDOWELL was born in Mt. Vernon, NY on 14 September 1953. Married (1) in Sag Harbor, NY on 4 October 1978 (divorced 1988) DALE EVELYN FIELD who was born in Brooklyn, NY on 24 May 1957, daughter of Marshall Field and Evelyn _____. Married (2) BARBARA LANE was born in Portland, ME on 11 September 1958, daughter of Arnold Lane and Mary Corliss.

Two children by Field:

i.   JESSICA LEE was born in Ellsworth, ME on 27 November 1981.

ii.   STACY RUTH who was born in Ellsworth, ME on 14 April 1985.

Two children by Lane:

i.   MORGAN CORLISS was born in Blue Hill, ME on 12 January 1985.

ii.   CHASE STERLING was born in Blue Hill, ME on 18 July 1986.

60. CHARLES EDWARD MACDOWELL was born in Bronxville, NY on 24 August 1955. Married on 25 October 1986 DONNA FINCHIARO who was born on 28 May 1964.

Two children:

i.   DIANE MARIE was born in Middletown, NY on 13 December 1990.

ii.   CHARLES ROBERT was born in Middletown, NY on 5 April 1993.

61. CYNTHIA JEANETTE MACDOWELL was born in Bronxville, NY on 7 June 1957. Married in Blauvelt, NY on 28 June 1980 HAROLD WAYNE SANBORN who was born in New Hampshire on 16 May 1957, son of _____ Sanborn and _____ Warren.

Two children:

i.   MEGHAN ELIZABETH was born in Concord, NH on 22 January 1987.

ii   JARED WELD was born Raleigh, NC on 18 December 1990.

62. ELIZABETH RUTH MacDOWELL was born in Bronxville, NY on 3 February 1959. Married in Blauvelt, NY on 3 June 1978 CHRISTOPHER BRUCE LEVITT who was born on 7 December 1954, son of _____ Levitt and _____ Coldwell.

Two children:

i.   CASSANDRA LEE WAS born in Nyack, NY on 1 October 1980.

ii.   TYLER JOHN was born in Nyack, NY on 23 May 1984.

63. ANNE KATHERINE MacDOWELL was born in Boston, MA on 28 October 1956. Married in Solebury, PA on 2 July 1988 MARTIN RAE QUIGLEY who was born in Aberdeen, Scotland on 25 November 1957, son of John Spears Quigley and Minnie Cecelia Bennett.

Two children:

i.   KATHARINE ANNE was born in White Plains, NY on 2 March 1990.

ii.   CHARLES BENNETT was born in Little Kingshill, Buckinghamshire, England on 30 October 1992.

64. WILLIAM DOUGLAS MacDOWELL was born in Baltimore, MD on 13 July 1961. Married in Solebury, PA on _____ LISA MARCHIONE born in Philadelphia, PA on 29 March 1966, daughter of Joseph Marchione and Janet Kelly.

Two children

i.   JOHN WATSON who was born in Doylestown, PA on 10 April 2000.

ii.   WILLIAM KELLY who was born in Doylestown, PA on 13 October 2001.

65. EDWARD WATSON ("NED") MacDOWELL was born in White Plains, NY on 14 August 1968. Married in Stockton, NJ on 11 October 1992 MARIANNE JOHNSON who

was born in Philadelphia, PA on 18 June 1968, daughter of Alexander Johnson and Mary Koehr.

Two children

i.   KIRSTEN ELIZABETH was born in Doylestown, PA on 8 February 1999.

ii.   COLLIN EDWARD was born in Doylestown, PA on 31 January 2000.

66. DAVID FREDERICK MACDOWELL was born in Dobbs Ferry, NY on 25 August 1959. Married in Galia, OH on 11 September 1982 ELIZABETH HAMER WHITE who was born in Galia, OH on 5 June 1959, daughter of _____ White and _____.

Four children:

i.   FREDERICK PARKE was born in Cleveland, OH on 18 November 1984.

ii.   SHANNON CARRET was born in Anchorage, AK on 17 January 1987.

iii.   BRANDON ROSS was born in Cleveland, OH on 23 February 1989.

iv.   CAMDEN JOHN was born in Anchorage, AK on 12 October 1992.

67. JEAN CAROLYN MACDOWELL (H'84) was born in Port Chester, NY on 12 January 1962. Married in New Marlborough, MA on 12 August 1989 WILLIAM QUINCY JEFFRIES (H'82) who was born in Boston, MA on 18 August 1960, Son of David Jeffries and Marjorie Shaw.

Two children:

i.   NATHANIEL MAIER who was born in Northampton, MA on 23 January 1993.

ii.   THOMAS EDWARD was born in Chilton, Oxfordshire, England on 22 February 1995.

68. JOHN THOMAS JASTER was born in El Paso, TX on 20 December 1964. Married in Schenectady, NY on 4 September 1991 JANET MARIE PARTINGTON who was born in Schenectady, NY on 20 January 1964, daughter of _____ Partington and _____.

Three children:

i.   JOHN HENRY was born in Schenectady, NY on 30 July 1992.

ii.   JAMES PATRICK was born in Schenectady, NY on 7 March 1995.

iii.   JULIA FRANCES was born in Schenectady, NY on 22 August 1997.

69. MARGARET ANNE GARRISON was born in Pasadena, CA on 20 April 1959. Married in Fullerton, CA on 6 August 1988 JAMES EDWARD PARKER.

One child:

i.   CHRISTINE ANNE was born in Fullerton, CA on 28 April 1989.

70. STEPHEN COOPER GOULD was born in Glendora, CA on 2 October 1953. Married in Waltham, MA on 1 August 1982 JANET ELIZABETH SAWICKI who was born in Gardner, MA on 22 April 1957, daughter of Joseph Adam Sawicki and Arlene Virginia Teir.

Two children:

i.   LLOYD TIMMINS was born in Boston, MA on 28 May 1988.

ii.   GARRAN COOPER was born in Hyannis, MA on 18 March 1991.

71. CHRISTOPHER WELD GOULD was born in Washington, D.C. on 5 May 1955. Married in Chappaqua, NY on 26 June 1983 JOAN DINEEN who was born in New York, NY on 19 April 1957, daughter of Capt. James Joseph Dineen and Margaret Irene Reilly.

Three children:

i.   AIDAN JAMES DINEEN was born in New York, NY on 16 March 1989.

ii.   DEVIN DINEEN was born in New York, NY on 8 April 1988.

iii.   BLYTHE MAIREAD GOULD DINEEN was born in New York, NY on 9 August 2001.

72. ELIZABETH ANNE GOULD was born in Upland, CA on 28 January 1960. Married in Cotuit, MA on 15 June 1986 (divorced 1997) JAMES PHILIP SOLIMANO who was born in Brooklyn, NY on 26 September 1957, son of James Philip Solimano and Eileen Joan Nolan.

Three children:

i.   TIMOTHY DOUGLAS GOULD was born in Seattle, WA on 23 June 1987.

ii.   MATTHEW GOULD was born in Seattle, WA on 14 February 1989.

iii.   NICHOLAS GOULD was born in Seattle, WA 28 June 1992.

73. LEONARD VICTOR SHORT, III was born in Woburn, MA on 24 August 1959. Married in Smithtown, NY on 10 November 1985 CHRISTINE MARY CALAGNA who was born on 15 September 1961, daughter of Arthur Calagna and Katherine _____.

Three children:

i.   SANDRA CARRET SHORT was born in Weymouth, MA on 15 September 1988.

ii.   ALEC ROSSI (twin) was born in Birmingham, MI on 20 August 1990.

iii.   COLE HURLEY (twin) was born in Birmingham, MI on 20 August 1990.

74. ELIZABETH HAYNES SHORT was born in Woburn, MA on 16 May 1961. Married in New Ipswich, NH on 6 August 1983 TOBEY J. RUSS who was born in Portsmouth, NH on 10 June 1958, son of Jon R. Russ and Gloria Boisvert.

Two children:

i.   MARGOT WELD was born in Palo Alto, CA on 26 September 1989.

ii.   Child expected in Palo Alto, CA in the latter part of 1991.

75. RICHARD MINOT WELD JOHNSON was born in Boston, MA on 23 December 1965. Married in Coos Bay, OR on 16 October 1993 KAREN KATHLEEN O'LEARY who was born in Boston, MA on 9 July 1959, daughter of Jay Francis O'Leary (H'54) and Eleth Adele Cook.

Two children:

i.   RICHARD MASON WELD was born in Boston, MA on 22 October 1996.

ii.   WILLIAM ALDEN WELD was born in Boston, MA on 17 January 1999.

76. CAROLYN HALL AUSTIN was born in Boston, MA on 10 December 1952. Married in South Dartmouth, MA on 19 June 1982 ANDREW SHEPARD who was born in Boston, MA on 27 February 1953, son of Wentworth Dutton Shepard and Constance Chick.

Two children:

i.   DAVID LORING was born in Newton, MA on 7 November 1985.

ii.   LAURA HALL was born in Newton, MA on 15 May 1988.

77. FRANCIS REED AUSTIN, JR. was born in Boston, MA on 17 March 1953. Married in Old Lyme, CT on 18 June 1983 MARGARET GORDON HALL WASLEY, who was born in New York, NY on 27 March 1956, daughter of John Sechrist Warwick Wasley (H'44) and Margaret Gordon McCall.

Three children:

i.   KIAMECHE MASON was born in Newton, MA on 11 May 1985.

ii.   KATHARINE WHEELER was born in Newton, MA on 3 September 1987.

iii.   FRANCIS REED III was born in Newton, MA on 14 March 1990.

78. WILLIAM FISHER AUSTIN was born in Boston, MA on 25 May 1955. Married in South Dartmouth, MA on 23 August 1986 BRENDA LOUISE ALVERSON who was born in Pine Bluff, AK on 30 July 1955, daughter of Bobbie Gene Alverson and Luta B. Young.

One child:

i.   CHAD FRANCIS was born in Concord, MA on 11 October 1989.

The Fifth Weld Brother
CHRISTOPHER MINOT WELD
A brother without direct descendants

FIRST GENERATION

1. CHRISTOPHER MINOT WELD (H'33) was born in Boston, MA 19 January 1812 and died in Jamaica Plain, MA 14 March 1878, son of William Gordon Weld and Hannah Minot. Married in Boston, MA 20 May 1841 MARY JANE JARVIS who was born in Boston, MA 21 July 1815 and died in Boston, MA 21 November 1898, daughter of William Benjamin Jarvis and Mary Porter.

No children. However, as the Index shows he was the original Christopher Minot Weld for whom five generations of nephews were given his name.

FRANCIS MINOT WELD
and his descendants

FIRST GENERATION

1.FRANCIS MINOT WELD (H 1835) was born in Boston, MA on 27 April 1815 and died in Jamaica Plain, MA on 4 February 1886, son of William Gordon Weld and Hannah Minot. Married in New Bedford, MA on 1 October 1841 ELIZABETH RODMAN, who was born in New Bedford, MA on 24 February 1821 and died in Boston, MA on 28 February 1897, daughter of Benjamin Rodman and Susan W. Morgan.

Five children:

    i.   BENJAMIN RODMAN was born in New Bedford, MA on 2 July 1842 and died in Boston, MA on 27 November 1909. (Unmarried).

2.   ii.   GERTRUDE, born in Boston, MA on 29 January 1844. Married JOHN PARKINSON.

3.   iii.   CORA, born in Boston, MA on 4 January 1848. Married FRANCIS GREENWOOD PEABODY.

    iv.   FRANCIS MINOT, JR.(H'72) was born in Jamaica Plain, in June 1851 and died in Boston, MA on 18 March 1882. (Unmarried).

4.   v.   CHRISTOPHER MINOT, born in West Roxbury, MA on 2 December 1858. Married MARIAN LINZEE.

SECOND GENERATION

2. GERTRUDE WELD was born in Boston, MA on 29 January 1844 and died in Boston, MA on 18 June 1904. Married in Boston, MA on 1 June 1881 JOHN PARKINSON, who was born in Roxbury, MA on 1 September 1843 and died in Bourne, MA on 31 October 1918, son of John Parkinson and Anne Outram (Davis).

One child:

5.   i.   JOHN, born in Boston, MA on 20 October 1883. Married MARY ANN WALES EMMONS.

3. Cora Weld was born in Boston, MA on 4 January 1848 and died in North East Harbor, ME on 5 September 1914. Married in Jamaica Plain, MA on 11 June 1872 Francis Greenwood Peabody (H'69) who was born in Boston, MA on 4 December 1847 and died in Cambridge, MA on 28 December 1936 son of Ephraim Peabody and Mary Jane Darby.

Four children:

6.   i.   William Rodman, born in Boston, MA on 3 March 1874. Married Katharine Putnam Peabody.

      ii.   Gertrude Weld was born in Boston, MA on 4 November 1877 and died in Boston, MA on 3 December 1938. (Unmarried).

7.   iii. Francis Weld, born in Boston, MA on 24 November 1881. Married Virginia Grigsby Chandler.

      iv.   John Derby was born in Boston, MA on 19 November 1885 and died in Boston, MA on 27 May 1899.

4. Christopher Minot Weld (H'80) was born in West Roxbury, MA on 2 December 1858 and died in Boston, MA on 27 August 1918. Married in Boston, MA on 24 April 1889 Marian Linzee, who was born in Boston, MA on 11 May 1862 and died in Boston, MA on 5 February 1942, daughter of Thomas Coffin Amory Linzee and Sarah Parker Torrey.

Five children:

8.   i.   Marian Linzee, born in Boston, MA on 17 May 1890. Married George Richards Minot.

      ii.   Elizabeth Rodman was born in Boston, MA on 26 July 1892 and died in Bar Harbor, ME on 30 August 1961. (Unmarried).

9.   iii. Margaret Minot, born in Boston, MA on 12 October 1893. Married Francis Tennery Hunter.

10.   iv.   Francis Minot, born in Milton, MA on 5 July 1895. Married Elizabeth Burgess.

11.   v.   John Linzee, born in Milton, MA on 10 November 1896. Married (1) Barbara Foster. Married (2) Rose C. Loveland (Toulmin).

THIRD GENERATION

5. JOHN PARKINSON (H'06) was born in Boston, MA on 20 October 1883 and died in Boston, MA on 11 April 1953. Married in Falmouth, MA on 26 June 1905 MARY ANN WALES EMMONS, who was born in Boston, MA on 11 Novmeber 1886 and died in Boston, MA on 29 December 1957, daughter of Nathaniel Henry Emmons and Eleanor G. Bacon.

Four children:

12.   i.   JOHN, JR. born in Boston, MA on 4 June 1906. Married (1) ELIZABETH ADDISON BLISS. Married (2) WINIFRED LOEW (TRIMBLE).

    ii.   NATHANIEL EMMONS (H'31) was born in Boston, MA on 29 November 1907 and died in Norwood, MA on 4 March 1980. Married in Beverly Farms, MA on 26 July 1941 ELLEN LOVERING (CHILD), born in Boston, MA on 5 August 1904, and died circa 1985, daughter of Charles Taylor Lovering (H'02) and Ellen Brewer Lyman. (No children.)

13.   iii.   MARY EMMONS, born in Boston, MA on 15 April 1911. Married JOHN GREW.

14.   iv.   ROBERT, born in Dover, MA on 13 July 1915. Married (1) DOROTHEA DEAN. Married (2) FAY J. WILDERSTORM-WILSON. Married (3) FRANCESCA CAROL NAGLE (PORTER).

6. WILLIAM RODMAN PEABODY (H'95) was born in Boston, MA on 3 March 1874 and died in Milton, MA on 12 January 1941. Married in Boston, MA on 8 October 1908 KATHARINE PUTNAM PEABODY, who was born in Brookline, MA on 3 January 1877 and died poss. Milton, MA after 1945, daughter of Robert Swain Peabody and Anne Putnam.

Four children:

    i.   GERTRUDE was born in Boston, MA on 4 September 1910 and died in Boston, MA on 4 February 1987 (Unmarried).

15.   ii.   ANNE PUTNAM, born in Boston, MA on 25 August 1912. Married FREDERICK EMERSON DONALDSON, JR.

16.   iii.   KATHARINE, born in Milton, MA on 17 November 1913. Married HENRY HODGE BREWSTER.

17.   iv.   CORA WELD, born in Boston, MA on 13 February 1917. Married ROBERT LUKENS EMLEN.

7. FRANCIS WELD PEABODY (H'03) was born in Boston, MA on 24 November 1881 and died in Boston, MA on 13 October 1927. Married in Chicago, IL on 18 December 1919 VIRGINIA GRIGSBY CHANDLER, who was born in Chicago, IL on 22 April 1886 and died in Brookline, MA on 17 Decamber 1982, daughter of Reuben Grigsby Chandler and Emma Virginia Hamilton.

Two children:

18.   i.   FRANCIS WELD, JR. born in Boston, MA on 22 April 1924. Married (1) MADELEINE EVANS. Married (2) SARA T. WEEKS (WARD) (SWETZOFF).

19.   ii.   GRIGSBY CHANDLER, born in Boston, MA on 16 December 1925. Married PAMELA TOWNSEND DIX (LEE).

8. MARIAN LENZEE WELD was born in Boston, MA on 17 May 1890 and died in Brookline, MA on 29 July 1979. Married in Boston, MA on 29 June 1915 GEORGE RICHARDS MINOT (H'08) (Nobel'31) who was born in Boston, MA on 2 December 1885 and died in Brookline, MA on 25 February 1950, son of James Jackson Minot and Elizabeth Whitney.

Three children:

    i.   MARION LINZEE was born in Boston, MA on 6 October 1918. Married in Dedham, MA on 16 October 1987 DAVID CHEEVER, JR. (H'31) who was born in Boston, MA on 21 May 1908 son of David Cheever (H'93) and Jane Welles Sargent.

20.   ii.   ELIZABETH WHITNEY, born in Boston, MA on 4 December 1920. Married CHARLES PARLIN GRAVES.

21.   iii.   CHARLES SEDGWICK, born in Boston, MA on 18 March 1930. Married CHARLOTTE NICKERSON.

126

9. MARGARET MINOT WELD was born in Boston, MA on 12 October 1893 and died in Boston, MA on 8 November 1970. Married in Boston, MA on 17 December 1925 FRANCIS TENNERY HUNTER (H'19) who was born in North Amherst, OH on 22 October 1896 and died in Chestnut Hill, MA on 7 September 1954, son on William Hunter and Dorabelle Tennery.

Two children:

22.   i.   MARGARET, born in Boston, MA on 25 October 1929. Married DICK HOEFNAGEL.

23.   ii.   JOHN BARRINGTON, born in Boston, MA on 28 April 1931. Married (1) JEAN DOROTHY FAWCETT. Married (2) RITA HINES (SMITH).

10. FRANCIS MINOT WELD (H'17) was born in Milton, MA on 5 July 1895 and died in Beverly, MA on 20 February 1963. Married in Dedham, MA on 10 February 1951 (divorced 1957) ELIZABETH BURGESS, who was born in Berlin, NH on 22 May 1897, daughter of Theodore Phelps Burgess and Elizabeth Slade.

Two children:

24.   i.   PATRICIA, born in Boston, MA on 20 April 1929. Married (1) CHARLES GRENFILL WASHBURN, II. Married (2) CLARK DOUGLAS SAMPSON.

25.   ii.   CHRISTOPHER MINOT, born in Boston, MA on 20 July 1932. Married SUSANNA ROSS BOOCOCK.

11. JOHN LINZEE WELD (H'18) was born in Milton, MA on 10 November 1896 and died in Boston, MA on 19 February 1956. Married (1) in Boston, MA on 31 October 1925 BARBARA FOSTER who was born in Brookline, MA on 19 June 1899 and died in Newton, MA on 25 February 1952, daughter of Charles Henry Wheelwright Foster (H'1881) and Mary Chase Hill. Married (2) in Dover, MA on 11 December 1954 ROSE C. LOVELAND (TOULMIN) who was born in Wilkes Barre, PA on 28 July 1903, daughter of Charles L. Loveland and Mabel Bond.

Two children of Barbara Foster:

26. i. BARBARA, born in Boston, MA on 9 October 1927. Married GEORGE PUTNAM, JR.

27. ii. JANE LINZEE, born in Boston, MA on 23 January 1932. Married SHEPARD BROWN.

FOURTH GENERATION:

12. JOHN PARKINSON, JR.(H'29) was born in Boston, MA on 4 June 1906 and died in New York, NY on 22 February 1973. Married (1) in Westbury, NY on 18 December 1932 (divorced 1945) ELIZABETH ADDISON BLISS who was born in New York, NY on 25 April 1907, daughter of Cornelius Newton Bliss (H'27) and Zaidee C. Cobb. Married (2) in New York, NY on 9 October 1947 WINIFRED LOEW (TRIMBLE), born in New York, NY on 18 April 1909 and died in Oyster Bay, NY on 12 April 1982, daughter of William Goadby Loew and Florence Baker. (Elizabeth A. Bliss Parkinson subsequently married Henry Ivy Cobbs. Winifred Loew Parkinson was the widow of Richard Trimble who died 17 July 1941).

Two children by Elizabeth Addison Bliss:

28. i. JOHN, III, born in New York, NY on 8 August 1934. Married CHARLOTTE BOYER.

     ii. ZAIDE COBB PARKINSON was born in New York, NY on 2 July 1936.

One child by Winifred Loew (Trimble):

29. i. MARY ANN, born in New York, NY on 12 May 1953. Married (1) ALAIN OHNENWALD. Married (2) JEAN HACHE.

13. MARY EMMONS PARKINSON was born in Boston, MA on 15 April 1911. Married in Dover, MA on 20 January 1935 JOHN GREW (H'31) who was born in Dover, MA on 23 June 1907 and died in Aiken, SC on 29 May 1985, son of Edward Wigglesworth Grew (H 1889) and Ruth Dexter.

Two children:

30. i. JOHN, JR (H'59), born in Boston, MA on 6 February 1936. Married LYDIA KATHERINE GRIMES.

31.   ii.   NATHANIEL, born in Boston, MA on 20 September 1939. Married (1) MEREDITH EMERSON PAUL. Married (2) ROSAMOND MARGUERITE METCALFE.

14. ROBERT PARKINSON was born in Dover, MA on 13 July 1915. Married (1) in Boston, MA on 19 May 1939 (divorced) DOROTHEA DEAN who was born in Brookline, MA on 26 April 1913, daughter of James Dean (Manchester, NH) and Agnes Williams Lincoln. Married (2) in Wareham, MA on 14 August 1948 (divorced 1964) FAY J. WILDERSTROM-WILSON who was born in Red Bank, NJ in 1927, daughter of Ernest F. Wilderstrom-Wilson and Marguerite Whitte. Married (3) in Reno, NV on 26 January 1965 FRANCESCA CAROL NAGLE (PORTER) who was born (nee Fannie) in Brockton, MA on 21 May 1919, daughter of Isadore Nagle and Sophie Kamras (of Russia).

Three children by Fay J. Wilderstrom-Wilson:

32.   i.   MARTHA EMMONS, born in Wareham, MA on 28 July 1949. Married ROBERT PARADIES.

33.   ii.   ROBERT WELD, born in Wareham, MA on 5 January 1958. Married JEAN MARIE RICHARDSON.

       iii.   NATHANIEL EMMONS was born in Wareham, MA on 17 August 1959.

15. ANNE PUTNAM PEABODY was born in Boston, MA on 25 August 1912 and died in New Canaan, CT on 25 September 1985. Married in Milton, MA on 22 September 1945 FREDERICK EMERSON DONALDSON, JR. who was born in New York, NY on 12 October 1911 and died in Fairfield, CT on 1 December 1986, son of Frederick Emerson Donaldson and Marie H. Winkhaus (New York, NY).

Two children:

34.   i.   ALAN PEABODY, born in New York, NY on 29 October 1947. Married BARBARA RIDDELL THATCHER.

       ii.   SUSAN RODMAN (H'71) was born in New York, NY on 16 October 1949.

16. KATHARINE PEABODY was born in Milton, MA on 17 November 1913. Married in Milton, MA on 23 June 1936 (divorced 1963) HENRY HODGE BREWSTER (H'35) who was born in Boston, MA on 20 October 1912, son of George Washington Wales

Brewster (H'89) and Ellen Wilson Hodge.

Three children:

35.   i.   RODMAN PEABODY, (adopted) born in Cleveland, OH on 15 August 1942. Married PATRICIA DAMIEN.

36.   ii.   ELLEN HODGE, (adopted) born in Cambridge, MA on 16 August 1946. Married ALEXANDER JOHN MAKKAI, JR.

    iii.   HENRY HODGE, JR. was born in Boston, MA on 29 July 1952. Married in Mobile, AL on 20 May 1989 BARBARA A. WHITE.

17. CORA WELD PEABODY was born in Boston, MA on 23 February 1917. Married in Milton, MA on 21 July 1943 ROBERT LUKENS EMLEN who was born in Germantown, PA on 23 September 1915, son of Geroge Williams Emlen and Eleanor Clark.

Four children:

37.   i.   GEORGE WILLIAMS, born in Hagerstown, MD on 13 May 1944. Married JANETTE E. HOLLAND.

38.   ii.   ROBERT PEABODY, born in Chestnut Hill, PA on 11 September 1946. Married JULIA SEALEY.

39.   iii.   KATHERINE PEABODY, born in Bryn Mawr, PA on 3 April 1950. Married ROBERT MARTIN CHAMBERLIN.

    iv.   NICHOLAS RODMAN was born in Bryn Mawr on 23 May 1952.

18. FRANCIS WELD PEABODY, JR.(H'46) was born in Boston, MA on 22 April 1924. Married (1) in Williamsville, NY on 26 June 1949 (divorced) MADELEINE EVANS, who was born in Buffalo, NY in 1930, daughter of James C. Evans and Eleanor M. Carnochan (Scaife). Married (2) in Boston, MA on 16 June 1968 SARA T. WEEKS (WARD) (SWETZOFF) who was born in Boston, MA on 17 February 1926, daughter of Edward A. Weeks and Frederica Wartiss.

Two children by Madeleine Evans:

    i.   GEROGE SHATTUCK was born in Boston, MA on 22 June 1953.

ii.   CARY EVANS was born in Boston, MA on 22 May 1955.

Two stepchildren of Francis Weld Peabody, Jr. and children of Sara T. Weeks (Swetzoff):

i.   DAVID WULF SWETZOFF was born in Boston, MA on 9 March 1957.

ii.   MARTHA WARTISS SWETZOFF was born in Boston, MA on 4 September 1958.

19. GRISBY CHANDLER PEABODY (H'48) was born in Boston, MA on 16 December 1925. Married in Bradford, NY on 21 April 1956 PAMELA TOWNSEND DIX (LEE) who was born in New York, NY on 19 March 1925, daughter of John Adams Dix (H'02) and Sophie Witherspoon Townsend.

Two children:

i.   VIRGINIA SHATTUCK was born in Mt. Kisco, NY on 1 March 1957.

ii.   VERLINDA CHANDLER was born in Mt. Kisco, NY on 13 December 1958. Married in Manchester, MA on 13 May 1989 THOMAS B. MOORE, son of John L. Moore, Jr.

Two stepchildren of Grigsby C. Peabody and children of Pamela Townsend Dix (Lee):

40.   i.   HENRY LEE born in Mt. Kisco, NY on 28 April 1950. Married SUSAN GIBB DILLON.

ii.   LOWELL MASON LEE was born in Mt. Kisco, NY on 11 August 1951.

20. ELIZABETH WHITNEY MINOT was born in Boston, MA on 4 December 1920. Married in Boston, MA on 11 April 1953 CHARLES PARLIN GRAVES who was born in Apalachicola, FL on 23 January 1911 and died in New York, NY on 1 August 1982, son of John E. Graves and May Parlin.

Two children:

i.   ELIZABETH WELD was born in New York, NY on 13 February 1954.

41.   ii.   JOHN PARLIN, born in New York, NY on 10 July 1956. Married DONNA MARIE SCHNEIDER.

21. CHARLES SEDGWICK MINOT was born in Boston, MA on 18 March 1930 and died in Gloucester, MA on 20 February 1989. Married in Dedham, MA on 7 June 1958 (divorced 1972) CHARLOTTE NICKERSON who was born in Boston, MA on 14 March 1935, daughter of Henry Greenough Nickerson (H'33) and Leatietia Orlandini.

Two adopted children:

i.   MICHAEL WELD was born in Massachusetts on 4 December 1962.

ii.   ANITA LINZEE was born in Massachusetts, on 10 September 1964.

22. MARGARET HUNTER was born in Boston, MA on 25 October 1929. Married in Chestnut Hill, MA on 5 May 1956 DICK HOEFNAGEL, who was born in Madioen, Java, Indonesia on 25 September 1922, son of Jacobus Andries Hoefnagel and Roelina Kreulen.

Two children:

i.   ERICA ROELINA was born in Little Rock, AR on 8 May 1957. Married in Middletown, CT on 28 February 1981 JAVIER LUIS DE LA UZ who was born in Havana, Cuba on 14 August 1945, son of Javier E. de la Uz and Maria del Pilar Gomez.

ii.   HANS KREULEN was born in Boston, MA on 27 January 1959. Married in Columbus, GA on 10 September 1988 KAREN ELIZABETH LaRUE who was born in Pittsburgh, PA on 31 December 1963, daughter of Capt. John Robert LaRue and Etta Soltis.

23. JOHN BARRINGTON HUNTER was born in Boston, MA on 28 April 1931. Married (1) in Watertown, MA on 2 October 1954 (divorced) JEAN DOROTHY FAWCETT who was born in Newton, MA on 7 September 1930, daughter of Lionel F. Fawcett and Elizabeth E. McGerigle. Married (2) in June 1976 RITA HINES (SMITH) born in Richmond, VA, daughter of Henry Hines.

Four children by Jean Dorothy Fawcett:

i.   JEFFREY WELD was born in High Point, NC on 1 September 1956. Married in Pocasset, Bourne MA on 26 October 1985 LYDIA CLARK, born in Wilkes Barre, PA on 8 December 1953 daughter of H.B. Clark and Mary Wilcox Clemens.

42.   ii.   EDWARD BARRINGTON, born in Needham, MA on 27 January 1959. Married CHERI LYNN TEIXEIRA.

         iii.   JAMES LIONEL was born in Needham, MA on 8 September 1960 and died in Ft. Lauderdale, FL in August 1984.

         iv.   JOHN TENNERY was born in Needham, MA on 22 May 1968.

24. PATRICIA WELD was born in Boston, MA on 20 April 1929. Married (1) in Boston, MA on 10 February 1951 (divorced 1957) CHARLES GRENFILL WASHBURN, II (H'51) who was born in Worcester, MA on 3 April 1926 and died in Madrid, Spain on 14 May 1967 son of Slater Washburn and Beulah McClellan. Married (2) in FL, on 3 February 1961 (divorced 1964) CLARK DOUGLAS SAMPSON who was born in Concord, MA on 21 December 1934 and died in Boston, MA on 24 February 1967, son of James Harold Sampson and Ethel Massie.

Two children by Chalres Grenfill Washburn, II:

     i.   CHALRES GRENFILL, III was born in New York, NY on 7 September 1951.

     ii.   SANDRA L. (H'78) was born in New York, NY on 3 May 1953.

25. CHRISTOPHER MINOT WELD (H'54) was born in Boston, MA on 20 July 1932. Married in Fishers Island, NY on 13 September 1955 SUSANNA ROSS BOOCOCK (R'55) who was born in New York, NY on 2 August 1933, daughter of Kenyon Boocock and Glenn Helen Winnett.

Four children:

     i.   SUSANNA LINZEE was born in Charlottesville, VA on 12 June 1956.

     ii.   AMORY was born in Salem, MA on 25 July 1957.

     iii.   FRANCIS MINOT was born in Salem, MA on 21 January 1960.

     iv.   KATE WINNETT was born in Beverly, MA on 9 March 1970.

26. BARBARA WELD was born in Boston, MA on 9 October 1927. Married in Wellesley, MA on 23 June 1949 GEORGE PUTNAM, JR.(H'49) who was born in Manchester, MA on 30 August 1926, son of George Putnam and Katharine Harte.

Three children:

43.   i.   GEORGE, III born in Boston, MA on 10 August 1951. Married KAREN D. HUNZICKER.

44.   ii.   BARBARA ("BAMBI"), born in Boston, MA on 16 May 1954. Married LINCOLN PERKINS LYMAN.

      iii.   SUSAN WELD (H'79) was born in Boston, MA on 18 January 1957.

27. JANE LINZEE WELD was born in Boston, MA on 23 January 1932. Married in Wellesley, MA on 26 June 1954 SHEPARD BROWN (H'50), who was born in New York, NY on 25 November 1927, son of Charles Stelle Brown Jr. (H'08) and Mary Jane Schieffelin.

Four children:

      i.   LOUISE SHEPARD was born in Boston, MA on 15 March 1956.

      ii.   JOHN LINZEE was born in Boston, MA on 15 September 1958.

      iii.   SHEPARD JR. was born in Boston, MA on 1 June 1961.

      iv.   ELIZABETH WELD was born in Boston, MA on 17 February 1963.

FIFTH GENERATION:

28. JOHN PARKINSON, III (H'57) was born in New York, NY on 8 August 1934. Married in New York, NY on 10 May 1958 CHARLOTTE BOYER, who was born in New York, NY on 12 March 1936, daughter of Allston Boyer (H'35) and Charlotte Young.

Three children:

      i.   JOHN BLISS was born in Caracas, Venezuela on 2 June 1961.

      ii.   ALLSTON BOYER was born in Caracas, Venezuela on 23 May 1963.

      iii.   ELIZABETH CHARLOTTE was born in Bogota, Columbia on 8 June 1966.

29. MARY ANN PARKINSON was born in New York, NY on 12 May 1953. Married (1) in 1975 ALAIN OHNENWALD (divorced). Married (2) in 1979 JEAN HACHE, who was born in Paris, France.

Two children by Jean Hache:

i.   KOLYA was born in Paris, France in 1979.

ii.   DAVID ALEXANDER was born in Paris, France in 1982.

30. JOHN GREW, JR.(H'59) was born in Boston, MA on 6 February 1936. Married in Sherborn, MA on 15 July 1967 (divorced 1981) LYDIA KATHERINE GRIMES, who was born in Bloomington, IN on 21 March 1933, daughter of John G. Grimes and Violet Kern.

One child:

i.   JOSEPH GRIMES was born in West Newbury, MA on 16 February 1973.

31. NATHANIEL GREW was born in Boston, MA on 20 September 1939. Married (1) in Sherborn, MA on 20 June 1964 MEREDITH EMERSON PAUL who was born in Philadelphia, PA in 1942, daughter of William Henry Paul and Harriet Bates Moodie. Married (2) in Cheam, Surrey, England on 6 August 1977 ROSAMOND MARGUERITE METCALFE who was born in Cheam, Surrey, England on 22 August 1948.

Two children by Meredith Emerson Paul:

i.   ASHELY was born in San Jose, Costa Rica on 3 July 1967.

ii.   NATHANIEL, JR. was born in San Jose, Costa Rica, on 9 December 1970.

Four children of Rosmond Marguarite Metcalfe:

i.   ANNE CHRISTINA was born in San Jose, Costa Rica on 27 August 1979.

ii.   CAROLINE MARY was born in San Jose, Costa Rica, on 20 June 1981.

iii.   NICHOLAS JAMES was born in San Jose, Costa Rica, on 17 November 1982.

iv.　　　DANIEL was born in San Jose, Costa Rica, in January 1988.

32. MARTHA EMMONS PARKINSON was born in Wareham, MA on 28 July 1949. Married in Centerville, MA on 19 July 1969 ROBERT PARADIES, who was born in Cebu City, Philippines in 1945, son of William A. Paradies and Carmen Aboitiz.

Four children:

i.　　　NICHOLAS EMMONS was born in Manila, Philippines on 9 October 1970.

ii.　　　CHRISTINA WALES was born in Manila, Philippines on 15 December 1972.

iii.　　　WILLIAM WELD was born in Manila, Philippines, on 9 February 1977.

iv.　　　EMILY WALES was born in Manila, Philippines on 14 December 1981.

33. ROBERT WELD PARKINSON was born in Wareham, MA on 5 January 1958. Married in Independence, MO on 31 March 1984 JEAN MARIE RICHARDSON, who was born in Independence, MO.

One child:

i.　　　Child expected in February 1991 in Baltimore, MD.

34. ALAN PEABODY DONALDSON (H'40) was born in New York, NY on 29 October 1947. Married in Greenwich, CT on 30 May 1981 BARBARA RIDDELL THATCHER, who was born in New York, NY on 29 January 1954, daughter of John M. P. Thatcher, Jr. and Dorothy Riddell.

One adopted child:

i.　　　HOLLY THATCHER was born in New York, NY on 15 December 1988.

35. RODMAN PEABODY BREWSTER was born in Cleveland, OH on 15 August 1942. Married in Denver, CO on 24 November 1965 PATRICIA DAMIEN who was born in Chicago, IL on 28 July 1943, daughter of Michael Damien and Anne_____.

Two children:

i.　　　RODMAN PEABODY, JR. was born in Denver, CO on 8 April 1970.

ii.　　　MICHAEL G., was born in Denver, CO on 23 August 1973.

36. ELLEN HODGE BREWSTER WAS born in Cambridge, MA on 16 August 1946. Married in Denver, CO on 2 August 1969 ALEXANDER JOHN MAKKAI, Jr. who was born in NJ on 30 April 1943, son of Alexander John Makkai and May Butkocy.

Two children:

i.   ADAM JAMES was born in Denver, CO on 20 May 1973.

ii.   MARY KATHERINE who was born in Denver, CO on 22 March 1976.

37. GEORGE WILLIAM EMLEN was born in Hagerstown, MD on 13 May 1944. Married in Exeter, NH in February 1968 JANETTE E. HOLLAND who was born in Exeter, NH, daughter of Everett Holland.

Two children:

i.   HANNAH ("SASHOO").

ii.   SAMUEL.

38. ROBERT PEABODY EMLEN was born in Chestnut Hill, PA on 11 September 1946. Married in Orfordville, NH JULIA SEALEY.

One child:

i.   NICHOLAS QUINN was born in Providence, RI in October 1980.

39. KATHERINE PEABODY EMLEN was born in Bryn Mawr, PA on 3 April 1950. Married in Lyme, NH on 26 August 1989 ROBERT MARTIN CHAMBERLIN who was born in Millbrae, CA on 15 April 1957, son of Robert Simons Chamberlin and Mary Hill.

One child:

i.   ELIZABETH GREENWOOD was born in Hanover, NH on 12 December 1990.

40. HENRY LEE PEABODY was born in Mt. Kisco, NY on 28 April 1950. Married (before 1978) SUSAN GIBB DILLON. Divorced 1985.

Two children:

i.   HENRY LEE, JR.

ii.   JOHN G.

41. JOHN PARLIN GRAVES was born in New York, NY on 10 July 1956. Married in Bristol, NH on 12 June 1982 DONNA MARIE SCHNEIDER who was born in Franklin, NH on 14 September 1958 daughter of Fred Schneider and Elizabeth McCarthy.

Two children:

i.   CATHARINE ELIZABETH was born in Danvers, MA on 19 August 1986.

ii.   CHARLES MINOT was born in Beverly, MA on 6 September 1990.

42. EDWARD BARRINGTON HUNTER was born in Needham, MA on 27 January 1959. Married in Falmouth, MA on 1 September, 1984 CHERI LYNN TEIXEIRA, who was born in Falmouth, MA on 19 March 1964, daughter of Frank Manuel Teixeira and June Christine Chase.

One child:

i.   JAMIE was born in Ft. Lauderdale, FL on 25 August 1985.

43. GEORGE PUTNAM, III (H'73) was born in Boston, MA on 10 August 1951. Married in Wellesley, MA on 23 June 1977 (divorced) KAREN D. HUNZICKER who was born in Spokane, WA on 5 November 1949, daughter of Warren J. Hunzicker and Marjorie J. Owen.

One child:

i   WARREN LOWELL was born in London, England on 31 October 1982.

44. BARBARA PUTNAM was born in Boston, MA on 16 May 1954. Married LINCOLN PERKINS LYMAN (H'74) who was born in Boston, MA on 29 October 1951, son of Theodore Lyman (H'42) and Joan Morison Lincoln.

FRANCIS MINOT WELD ❧ SIXTH BROTHER

Three children:

ii.   DAPHNE WELD was born in New York, NY on 16 July 1983

ii.   OLIVIA LINCOLN was born in New York, NY on 26 April 1985.

iii.   VICTORIA CABOT was born in New York, NY on 25 April 1987.

The Seventh Weld Brother
JOHN GARDNER WELD
and his descendants

FIRST GENERATION

1. JOHN GARDNER WELD was born in Lancaster, MA on 19 August 1818 and died in Boston, MA on 29 September 1876, son of William Gordon Weld and Hannah Minot. Married in New York, NY on 4 May 1848 ANNA JANE SPALDING who was born in New York, NY on 12 January 1827 and died in Mt. Vernon, NY on 21 September 1914, daughter of Asa Spalding and Cornelia V. Thane.

Four children:

2. i. ASA SPALDING born in St. Louis, MO on 7 November 1849. Married ELINOR LOUISE MERRIAM.

3. ii. ELIZA FRANKLIN born in West Roxbury, MA on 19 June 1853. Married JAMES MAURAN BETTON.

4. iii. HENRY GARDNER born in West Roxbury, MA on 24 February 1856. Married MARY LODICE LARRABEE.

 iv. CORNELIA THANE was born in West Roxbury on 28 December 1859 and died in West Roxbury, MA on 27 September 1862.

SECOND GENERATION

2. ASA SPALDING WELD was born in St. Louis, MO on 7 November 1849 and died in Boston, MA on 21 October 1915. Married in West Roxbury, MA on 25 September 1872 ELINOR LOUISE MERRIMAN who was born in West Roxbury, MA on 20 January 1850 and died in Jamaica Plain, MA on 3 April 1944, daughter of Ephram Merriam and Martha Curtis.

Three children:

 i. CORNELIA SPALDING was born in Boston, MA on 14 August 1874 and died in Boston, MA on 2 November 1877.

 ii. ANNA SPALDING was born in Boston, MA on 20 December 1877 and died in Jamaica Plain, MA on 22 December 1965. (Unmarried.)

5   iii.   JOHN GARDNER born in Boston, MA on 19 December 1879. Married circa 1905 VIVIAN WARREN.

3. ELIZA FRANKLIN WELD was born in West Roxbury, MA on 19 June 1853 and died in Washington, DC on 13 October 1929. Married in Boston, MA on 9 October 1878 JAMES MAURAN BETTON (H'1873) who was born in New York, NY on the same day as his wife, 19 June 1853, son of Turbitt Lane Betton and Marie (or Mary) Mauran.

One child:

i.   ELINOR WELD was born poss. in Williamsburg, VA (where her father was living when married) on 16 January 1882 and died in New York, NY on 7 February 1954. (Unmarried.)

4. HENRY GARDNER WELD was born in West Roxbury, MA on 24 February 1855 and died in Norwalk, CT on 9 April 1919. Married prob. in Albany, NY MARY LODICE LARRABEE who was born in Albany, NY on 27 July 1855 and died in Norwalk, CT on 26 January 1928, daughter of Edward J. Larrabee and Maryetta Wilson.

Seven children:

i.   EDWARD LARRABEE who was born in poss. Ticonderoga or Albany, NY on 2 November 1880 and died probably in Norwalk, CT where he lived with his mother after 1928. He is not listed in the Norwalk City Directory of 1929. (Unmarried.)

6.   ii.   HENRY GARDNER, JR. born in Ticonderoga, NY on 19 June 1882. Married FLORA REMSTER SMALLWOOD.

iii.   MORTON BUTLER born in Ballston Spa, NY on 28 February 1883 and died in Ballston Spa, NY on 2 March 1886. (Interesting coincidence: There was a Morton Butler who was vestryman in the Episcopal Church in Ticonderoga in 1884. Was he a friend or relative of the family, thus, naming the child after him?)

iv.   MARYETTA LARRABEE (twin) was born in Ballston Spa, NY on 7 May 1886 and died in Ballston Spa, NY on 15 January 1887.

v.   MARGARET MINOT (twin) was born in Ballston Spa, NY on 7 May 1886 and died poss. in New Canaan/Westport/Norwalk, CT after 1941 (and before 1956). Worked in Norwalk, CT as a nurse. Lived with her sister Mary Lodice. (Unmarried.)

vi.   RACHEL LARRABEE was born in Ballston Spa, NY on 22 December 1889 and died in Norwalk, CT on 19 October 1930. (Unmarried.)

vii.   MARY LODICE was born in Ballston Spa, NY on 16 October 1894 and died in Norwalk, CT on 16 February 1975. Buried in family plot in Albany, NY Rural Cemetery. (Unmarried.)

THIRD GENERATION

5. JOHN GARDNER WELD was born in Boston, MA on 19 December 1879 and died in Boston, MA on 27 February 1969. (His death certificate states he was single but this probably means that he was widowed.) According to *Weld Collections* by Charles Frederick Robinson, JOHN GARDNER WELD married circa 1905 VIVIAN WARREN. There is no marriage certificate in Massachusetts. Therefore, at this time we do not know dates of birth or marriage or the parents of VIVIAN WARREN. *Weld Collections* also states that there were:

Two children:

i.   ANNA LOUISE who died young. (No birth or death record in MA.)

ii.   WARREN who was born (not in Massachusetts) on 8 October 1908. As of 1939 he was living in Havana, Cuba (according to *Weld Collections*).

6. HENRY GARDNER WELD, JR. was born in Ticonderoga, NY on 19 June 1882 and died possibly West Virginia after 1930. Married (according to *Weld Collections*) on 29 November 1905 to FLORA REMSTER SMALLWOOD. (Marriage not recorded in Massachusetts. Their son's Social Security birth place is West Virginia.)

One child:

7.   i.   WILLIAM H. born in West Virginia on 27 April 1915. Married MARY ANDRADE.

FOURTH GENERATION

7. WILLIAM H. WELD was born in West Virginia on 27 April 1915 and he died 1 May 1988 in Millville, NJ. He married MARY ANDRADE circa 1940 possibly in West Virginia or New Jersey.

FIFTH GENERATION

Probably two daughters based on the following information:

William H. Weld's widow, Mary Andrade Weld, still living in 1995, stated in a brief telephone conversation that her husband's father was Henry Gardner Weld. She was living in Millville, NJ at that time.

The obituary notice for Mary Lodice Weld (sister of Henry Gardner Weld) in the *Norwalk (CT) Hour* of 2/18/1975 states that she "is survived by a nephew, William H. Weld of Millville, NJ and two grand nieces. Since Henry, Jr was the only member of the Henry Gardner Weld family to marry, the obituary strongly suggests that William H. Weld is his son and that the two grand nieces are William's daughters.

SOURCES

Sources for the descendants of
William Fletcher Weld

Albright, Lars L.—MA VR: Birth: 1974/24/26.

Albright, Martina B.—MA VR: Birth: 1968/28/378.

Albright, Nile Ludlow—MA VR: Marriage: 1963/17/524.

Albright, Tara L. MA VR: Birth: 1969/31/203.

Anderson, Isabel Weld Perkins—MA VR: Death: 1948/24/243.

Under the Black Horse Flag by Isabel Anderson, 1926

Baker, Roy W. (See Brandegee, Edith S.).

Bingham, William John, Jr. MA VR: Birth: 1921/6/458.

Boit, Charles Sprague—MA VR: 1st Marriage: 1955/42/201. 3rd Marriage: 1980/Cert.#000947.

Boit, Charles-Frederick David—MA VR: Birth: 1967/20/219.

Boit, Christopher Sprague—MA VR: Marriage: 1987/Cert.#035119.

Boit, Marion Sprague—MA VR Death: 1968/15/449. Forest Hills Cemetery, MA.

Boit, Marka Spalding—MA VR: Marriage: 1955/42/201

Boit, Nancy Kunkle (Stout)—MA VR: Marriage: 1980/Cert.#000947.

Boit, Robert Sprague—MA VR: 1st Marriage: 1955/29/164; 2nd Marriage: 1968/9/450

Brandegee, Edith S. (Brooke) MA VR: Marriage: 1946/62/372. (In Antrim, NH in 1960-61).

Brandegee, John Langdon—MA VR: Marriage (*); Death: 1964/30/24.Crem. Mt. Auburn

Brooke, Edith S. (See Brandegee, Edith S.).

Brown, Amy Grace—MA VR: Birth: 1959/47/510. Marriage: 1987/Cert.#035119.

Buffington, Druscilla Moore—MA VR: Marriage: 1955/29/164.

Burgin, Clarence Rogers—Harvard Class of 1921 Reports.

Burgin, Jane Scudder—(See Lawrence, Jane Scudder Burgin).

Duryea, Humanus B. (See Winchester, Ellen Homer). Soc. Reg. Summer 1895.

Ford, Janet—MA VR: Birth: 1928/82/467.

Goddard, Caroline Langdon—MA VR: Marriage: 1854/79/176. Death: 1918/1/331. Goddard
   Geneal. Manuscript (NEHGS).

Grew, Joseph G.—MA VR: (*).

Harding, Agnes Bunty—MA VR: Marriage: 1968/9/450.

Hoagland, Jimmy Lee—Birth: Who's Who 1978-79. Pulitizer Prize winner.

Kunkle (Stout), Nancy—(See Boit, Nanct Kunkle (Stout).

Lane, Thomas Francis, Jr.—MA VR: Birth: 1925/2/30.

Lane, Thomas Francis, III—MA VR: Birth: 1956/28/100.

Lawrence, Abbott Wells Lawrence—MA VR: Birth: 1970/31/009

Lawrence, Eloise Paul—MA VR: Birth: 1973/17/98.

Lawrence, James, III—MA VR: Birth: 1936/23/464.

Lawrence, James, Jr.—Harvard Class of 1929 Reports.

Lawrence, Jane Scudder Burgin—Harvard Class of 1962 Reports.

Lawrence, Martina Lee—MA VR: Marriage: 1963/17/524.

May, Penelope Theobald—Marriage: NH Cert.#4M373

May, Thomas Allen—Marriage: NH Cert.#4M373.

Payson, William Francis—Brown Un. Class of 1935.
Perkins, George Hamilton—MA VR: Death: 1899/495/468.
Perkins, Isabel Weld—(See Anderson, Isabel Weld Perkins).
Pingree, Alexander Weld—MA VR: Birth: 1958/171/365.
Pingree, Charles Ford—MA VR: Birth: 1952/13/35.
Pingree, Charles Weld—MA VR: Birth: 1930/75/501.
Pingree, Christopher Weld—MA VR: Birth: 1959/168/333
Pingree Family—Our Branch of the Family Weld by Mary Weld Pingree, 1970.
Pingree, Jay Copeland—MA VR: Birth: 1961/180/165.
Pingree, John Randolph—MA VR: Birth: 1933/18/196.
Pingree, Mary Orr—MA VR: Birth: 1960/168/150.
Pingree, Mary Weld—MA VR: Death: 1978/Cert.#025488.
Pingree, Sumner Arthur—MA VR: Marriage: 1927/1/95. Death: 1965/6/159.
Pingree, Sumner III—MA VR: Birth: 1953/33/117.
Pingree, Sumner—MA VR: Birth: 1928/44/368.
Pingree, William Lewis—MA VR: Birth: 1958/172/276.
Pratt, Mary Bryant (See Sprague, Mary Bryant Pratt).
Sefton, Katharine—1st Marriage: NT Times 4/5/45.
Spalding, Marka (See Boit, Marka Spalding).
Spalding, Oakes Ames—Harvard Class 1927 Reports.
Sprague, Eleanor—MA VR: 2nd Marriage: 1936/27/497. Death: Soc. Reg. Sum. 1959.
Sprague, Marion (See Boit, Marion Sprague).
Sprague, Mary Bryant Pratt—MA VR: Birth: 1871/234/192
Stewart, Eleanor Sprague—(See Sprague, Eleanor).
Stewart, John Henderson—MA VR: Marriage: 1936/27/497.
Talmadge, Edward Taylor Hunt, Jr.—Death: NY Times 6/29/64. Soc. Reg. 1965.
Theobald, Katharine Sefton (See Sefton, Katharine).
Theobald, Penelope—(See May, Penelope, Theobald).
Theobald, Richard Jackson—Marriage: NY Times 4/5/45. Harvard Law School 1938.
Train, Hannah Putnam—MA VR: Death: 1943/31/436.
Walker, Isabella Melissa (See Weld, Isabella Melissa Walker).
Weld, Caroline Goddard (See Goddard, Caroline Langdon).
Weld, Charles Goddard—Harvard Class 1879 Reports.
Weld, Ellen Homer Winchester—MA VR: Birth: 1861/143/100; Marriage 1886/372/88. NYC Death Index 1927.
Weld, George Walker—MA VR: Death: 1905/7/338.
Weld, Isabella Melissa Walker—Boston Transcript Obituary Index 1900-1930
Weld, Mary—(See Pingree, Mary Weld).
Weld, William Fletcher—MA VR. Marriage: 1886/372/88. Death: 1893/437/487.
Weld, William Gordon—MA VR: Marriage: 1854/79/176. Death: 1896/465/154.
Whittemore, Margaret Dobbins—MA VR: Birth: 1921/91/9A. Death: 1976/042/153.
Winchester, Ellen Homer—(See Weld, Ellen Homer Winchester).

(*) = No records found in Massachusetts Vital Records.

SOURCES

Sources for descendants of
George Richards Minot Weld

Alcorn, Ellen Siff—NY VA: Birth: Cert. # 46138; Marriage: Tivoli, NY Clerk confirmed.

Alcorn, Harbert Richard—Florida VR: Marriage: State File #: 80-041774.

Alcorn, John Weld—Marriage: County of St. Charles, MO, Book 1983, page 25.

Alcorn, Matthew—Marriage: Tivoli, NY Clerk confirmed date & place.

Alcorn, Rosetta Elizabeth Falkenrath (Kreisel)—FL VR: Marriage: File # 80-041774.

Alcorn, Tracia R. Wafe—Marriage: County of St. Charles, MO. Book 83, page 25.

Bird, William David—IL VR: Marriage: 1952/Cart.36441.

Bird, Patricia Minot Woodbury—IL VR: Marriage: Cert.36441.

Brown, Charles Farwell, Jr.—MA VR: Marriage: 1944/60/3.

Brown, Charles Farwell—MA VR: Marriage: 21/7/172 (Brookline); Death:. 62/79/149.

Brown, Diana de Grout—MA VR: Birth: 38/7/401 (Boston).

Brown, Edward Jackson—MA VR: Marriage: 1863/164/121.

Brown, Edward Lyman, Jr.—MA VR: Marriage: 37/5/208 (Beverly).

Brown, Edward Lyman—MA VR: Birth: 1867/198/23 (Boston); Death: 42/10/243.

Brown, Edward Reid—MA VR: Birth: 39/5/67 (Beverly).

Brown, Eliot Weld—MA VR: Marriages: (1) 1933/19/257; (2) 46/144/308; Death: 1987/Cert.015399. Buried in Duxbury, MA.

Brown, Elizabeth de Grout—MA VR: Death: 1938/7/479 (Boston).

Brown, Isabel Walter Weld—MA VR: Death: 23/9/261 (Brookline). Age 56 yrs.

Brown, James Southwick—MA VR: Birth: 48/24/396 (Boston).

Brown, Mary E.—MA VR: Marriage: 1863/164/121.

Brown, Richard Stone (*)—b. 14 June 1974, Washington, D.C.

Brown, Stephen St.Clair (*)—b. 18 December 1978, Washington, D.C.

Caldwell, Charles—CA VR: Mariage: File #: 69-006620, Registrar's #: 183-560-213.

Caldwell, Nancy Maddock—CA VR: Marriage: File # 69-006620, Registrar's # 183-560-213.

Christensen, Helen Eddy—Soc. Sec. : Death: September 1973 (Groton).

Christensen, Minot Holmes—MA VR: Death: 1933/44/221 (Groton).

Claghorn, David Townsend MA VR: Birth: 53/27/509 (Boston).

Claghorn, Edward Taws—Marriage: NY Times 7/20/75.

Claghorn Family—*The Family of Claghorn* (page 106) by William Crumby Claghorn, 1912.

Claghorn, John Winthrop, III—Marriage: NY Times 5/27/79.

Claghorn, Katrina Elizabeth Van Buren—Marriage: NY Times 7/20/75.

Claghorn, Margaret Ellen Jump—Birth: NY Cert # 47704; Marriage: NY Times 5/27/79.

Claghorn, Susan Strawbridge—(See Ferguson, Susan Strawbridge Claghorn).

Clews, Mancha Madison—MA VR: Marriage: 40/46/474 (Woods Hole).

Clews, Margaret Strawbridge—MA VR: Marriage:40/46/474 (Woods Hole). NY Times: 9/6/40.

Clothier, Emily—(See Strawbridge).

Comstock, Marguerite (See Peck, Marguerite Peck).

Corey, Lucy Ann—(See Eddy, Lucy Ann Corey).

De Grout, Elizabeth—MA VR: Marriage: 1933/19/257. (B. 1901 in Passaic, NJ).

Dunlap, Terry—Ohio VR: Marriage: Volume 784, Page 110.

Dunlap, Elizabeth G. Peck—Ohio VR: Marriage: Volume 784, Page 110.

Eddy, Benjamin (*).

Eddy, Caleb—Buried at Mt. Auburn, Lot 362.

Eddy, Charles Benjamin—MA VR: Birth: 1854/82/134.

Eddy, Ellen Minot Weld (*).

Eddy Family—*The Eddy Family in America* by Ruth Story Devereaux Eddy, 1930.
   Genealogical Memoir of Rev. William Eddy by Robert Henry Eddy, 1881.

Eddy, Helen—(See Helen Eddy Christensen).

Eddy, Lucy Ann Corey—Groton Cemetery. Gravestone gives birth year 1858.

Eddy, Mary Caroline—U.S. Census 1860.

Eddy, Nellie—MA VR: Birth: 1860/134/130. (Chelsea).

Eddy. Charles B.—MA VR: Death: 1936/45/215 (Groton). Buried in Groton, MA Cemetery.

Etter, Bertha Walter—MA VR: Birth: 1912/609/252; Marriage: 1957/69/9.

Etter, Howard Ernest—MA VR: Birth: b. 1913/615/545 (Everett); Marriage: 1957/69/9.

Falkenrath, Rosetta Elizabeth—(See Alcorn, Rosetta Elizabeth).

Fenninger, Peter Laurence—MA VR: Birth: 42/

Ferguson, Stuart William—Marriage: NY Times 9/11/83.

Ferguson, Susan Strawbridge Claghorn—Marriage: NY Times 9/11/83.

Fisher, Elizabeth A. (Maddock)—(See Strawbridge, Elizabeth Fisher [Maddock]).

Fruit, Helen—(See Strawbridge).

Hampton, Edith Powell—(See Tripp, Edith Powell Hampton).

Helm, Alma—(See Peck, Alma Helm).

Hobart, Miriam Clara—(See Stearns, Miriam Clara Hobart).

Jack, Elizabeth May—MA VR: Birth: 1907/566/611 (Manchester, MA); Marriage: 37/5/208.

Jump. Margaret Ellen—(See Claghorn, Margaret Ellen Jump).

LaRue, Margaret—(See Strawbridge).

Louder, Harriet—(See Weld, Harriet Louder).

Maddock, Nancy Ellen—(See Caldwell, Nancy Ellen Maddock).

May, Thomas Lester, Jr.—Kentucky VR: Birth: District 9, Registration # 3922.

Minor, Patience Harper—MA VR: Birth: 1954/143/424 (Newton).

Mochak, Teresa Marie—(See Tripp, Teresa Marie Mochak).

Moeser, Barbara Ann—(See Peck, Barbara Ann Moeser).

Newlin Family—*The Newlin Family* by Alexander DuBin, 1942.

Newlin, Hannah Ann—(See Newlin Family).

North, Wallace—Kentucky VR: Registration #: 93294.

Wafe, Tracia R.—(See Alcorn, Tracia R. Wafe).

Peck, Alma Helm—OH VR: Death: State File #: 063782, Registrar's #: 4889.

Peck, Arthur Minot—OH VR: Death: State File #: 074441.

Peck, Barbara Ann Moeser—OH VR: Birth: File # 64784, Reg. # 4723.

Peck, Elizabeth Graves (See Dunlap, Elizabeth Peck).

Peck Family—*A Genealogical History of the Descendants of Joseph Peck* by Ira B. Peck, 1868.

Peck, Harriet Emily Weld—MA VR: Marriage: 1868/210/156.

Peck, Hiram David—MA VR: Marriage: 1868/210/156. *Who Was Who*, Vol. I.

Peck, Janet Ann Schoenberg (Robinson)—Birth: OH File # 112937, Reg.# 3631.

Peck, John Weld—*Who Was Who*, Vol. I.

Peck, Marguerite Comstock—OH VR: Death: Hamilton Cty. File # 24677, Register # 2276.

Pelfry, Arturo Ray—Tennessee VR's has 1969 death certificate (File # 69-030736) for a Samuel James Pelfry. Question: Arturo's father? Or relative?

Pilling, Richard E.—Death : Philadelphia Soc. Reg. January 1952.

Powell, Edith—MA VR: Birth: 1924/138/154 (Everett).

Price, Elizabeth Ann—(See Tripp, Elizabeth Ann).

Price, Walter Coachman, Jr.—MA VR: Marriage: 1968/34/135.

Richards, Alice Winchester—(See Walter, Alice Winchester Richards).

Rogers, Grace Hovey—MA VR: Birth: 1881/323/260 (Brookline).

Schoenberg, Janet Ann—(See Peck, Janet Ann Schoenberg).

Siff, Ellen (See Alcorn, Ellen Siff).

St. Clair, Janice—MA VR: Marriage : 1944/60/3 (Newton).

Stearns, Edna Waters—OH VR: Death: State File #: 060497, Registrar's # 4895.

Stearns Family—*Geneal. & Memoirs Of Isaac Stearns* by Avis Stearns Wagenen, 1901; *Memoranda of the Stearns Family* (pg.83) by W.E. Stearns,'01.

Stearns, George Weld (*).

Stearns, Mabel E. (See Stonehill, Mabel E. Stearns).

Stearns, Miriam Clara Hobart—MA VR: Birth: 1885/359/205 (Newton); Marriage: 1904/555/642 (Newton); Death: 1973/74/18 (Newton).

Stearns, Miriam Vere—MA VR: Birth: 1907/567/623 (Newton); Marriage: 1935/15/194.

Stonehill, Mabel E. Stearns—MA VR: Marriage: 1918/2/183 (Boston); CA VR:Death: File #: 4472-107974. Buried: Mt. Auburn, Cambridge, MA.

Stonehill, Winaloe—MA VR: Marriage: 1918/2/183 (Boston).

Strawbridge, A. Clayton—RI VR: Informant of wife's death. (See Strawbridge, Helen Fruit).

Strawbridge, Alexandra Cummins—(See Wright).

Strawbridge, Elizabeth Fisher (Maddock)—CA VR: Marriage: File: 63-049753; Reg.'s # 380.

Strawbridge, Emily Clothier—Marriage: Philadelphia Soc. Reg.(Radnor).

Strawbridge Family—*Early Friends Families of Upper Bucks County, PA* (page 600) by Clarence V. Roberts, 1925.

Strawbridge, Frederic Heap—MA VR: Marriage: 1894/443/414. Death: Soc. Reg. Jan.'59.

Strawbridge, Frederic Heap, Jr.—Marriage: Philadelphia Soc. Reg. 1921.

Strawbridge, Gordon Weld—Divorce: S.F. Chronicle 8/3/60; 3rd Marriage: Marin County, CA File # 49753, Registrar's # 380.

Strawbridge, Helen Fruit—RI VR: Death: 1974/Cert.138-74-003258.

Strawbridge, J. Clayton—Marriage: Philadelphia Soc. Reg. 1918 (Germantown).

Strawbridge, Margaret—(See Clews).

Strawbridge, Margaret La Rue—Marriage: Philadelphia Soc. Reg. 1918 (Germantown).

Swanson, Martha J.—MA VR: Marriage: 1938/35/331 (Falmouth) to Minot Weld Tripp.

Tripp, Cornelia Franklin Walter—MA VR: Death: 1966/49/273.

Tripp, Edith Powell Hampton—MA VR: Birth (*); Marriage: 1965/29/501.

Tripp, Edwin P., Jr.—MA VR: Birth: 1912/609/325; 1st Marriage: 1965/29/501; Divorce: 1965, Docket # 04940; 2nd Marriage: 1965/29/501.

Tripp, Edwin Prescott, III—MA VR: Birth: 1945/141/106.

Tripp, Edwin Prescott—MA VR: Birth: 1876/277/133 (New Bedford); Death: 1953/45/329.

Tripp, Elizabeth Ann—MA VR: Birth: 1943/145/215; Marriage: 1968/34/135.

Tripp, Minot Weld, Jr.—NEHGS *NEXUS*, Vol. XIII, No.6, Page 192.

Tripp, Minot Weld—MA VR: Marriage: 1938/35/331.

Tripp, Teresa Marie Mochak—MA VR: Birth: 1914/623/277 (Westfield).

Turnbull, Guy Hobart Heatherington.—MA VR: Birth: 1938/7/122; Marriage: 1974/15/282.

Turnbull, Gwendolyn Stearns—MA VR: Birth: 1940/33/297.

Turnbull, Kathleen E. Neate:—MA VR: Death: 1950/36/173.

Turnbull, W. Hetherington—MA VR: Death: 1952/35/529.

Turnbull, Walter Jack Hetherington—MA VR: Birth: 1907/569/34; Death: 1980/Cert. #016175.

Turnbull. Miriam Vere Stearns—MA VR: Death: 1973/19/230.

Van Buren, Katrina Elizabeth—(See Katrina E. Van Buren Claghorn).

Walter, Alice Winchester Richards—MA VR: Birth: 1867/196/22. Marriage: 1890/407/340. Death: 1894/446/639.

Walter, Anne V. F.—MA VR: Death: 1958/38/205.

Walter, Bertha Gordon—MA VR: Marriage: 1894/443/414. Death: NY Times: 11/13/46.

Walter, Bertha Gordon (b.1912)—MA VR: Birth: 1912/609/252; Marriage: 1957/69/9.

Walter, Cornelia Franklin (See Tripp, Cornelia Franklin Walter).

Walter, Franklin, Jr.—MA VR: Marriage: 1902/526/20; Death: 1932/28/329.

Walter, Franklin—MA VR: Marriage: 1863/162/128; Death: 1903/541/12.

Walter, Harry—(Born 1880) MA VR: 1st marriage: 1910/596/29; 2nd marriage: 1918/5/41.

Walter, Henrietta Mallison—MA VR: Death: 1914/14/251.

Walter, Isabelle Weld—MA VR: Marriage: 1893/434/44.

Walter, Minot Weld—MA VR: Marriage: 1890/407/340; Death: 1905/24/321.

Walter, Susan Minot Weld—MA VR: Marriage: 1863/162/128.

Waters, Edna (Gimble)—(See Stearns, Edna Waters).

Weld, Ellen Minot—MAQ VR: Marriage: 1854/80/30.

Weld Family—*Weld Collections* by Charles Frederick Robinson, 1938.

Weld, Gordon Elliot—MA VR: Death: 1889/402/28.

Weld, Harriet Louder—MA VR: 2nd Marriage: 1870/228/114. Death: (*).

Weld, Harriet Emily—(b.1845) (See Peck, Harriet Emily Weld).

Weld, Susan Minot—(See Walter, Susan Minot Weld).

Willard, Ammi—MA VR: Marriage: 2nd Marriage: 1870/228/114.(His first name difficult to read on marriage record).

Woodbury, Patricia Minot—(See Bird).

Wright, Cyrus Mansfield—*Who Was Who*, Vol. I.

Wright, Thomas Joseph—Marriage: Philadelphia Soc. Reg. 1954.

Wright, Alexandra Cummins Strawbridge—Marriage: Philadelphia Soc. Reg. 1954.

(*) No records found in Massachusetts Vital Records.

SOURCES

Sources for the descendants of
Stephen Minot Weld

Astuto, Maria Blance—(See Astuto Family).

Astuto Famuily—*Libro d'oro della Nobiltà* 1969-1972 edition, page 88, 1995-1999 edition, pages 94 & 95.

Bacon, Katherine Weld—Marriage: NY Times: 3/3/40.

Bacon, Martha—(See Martin.)

Bacon, Nathaniel—MA VR: Death: 87/Cert.001856.

Bacon, Penelope Shaw Crittenden—MA VR: Birth: 46/11/418; Marriage: 66/27/56.

Bacon, Priscilla—(See Woods.)

Bacon, Susan Moreland Makrianes—MA VR: Birth: 56/179/287. Marriage: NY Times: 9/12/1982.

Bacon, William Benjamin—(b. 1911)—MA VR: Birth: (*). Marriage: NY Times: 3/3/40. Death: Boston Globe: 4/4/91.

Bacon, William Benjamin, Jr. (b. 1940)—MA VR: Birth: 40/32/412; Marriage: 66/27/56. Death: Boston Globe: 2/10/89.

Bacon. Daniel Carpenter—MA VR: Birth: 44/30/221. Marriage: NY Times: 9/12/1982.

Bader, Nancy Ellen—(See Gardiner.)

Bailey, Margherita—(see Baldwin.)

Baldwin, Benjamin—NY VR: Birth: 1967/Cert.16631.

Baldwin, Helena-Margherita—MA VR: Birth: 1975/109/434.

Baldwin, Howard Lapsley—NY VR: Birth: 1942/Cert.14203.

Baldwin, Howard Lapsley, Jr. (b. 1971)—MA VR: 71/151/260.

Baldwin, Ian (b. 1912)—MA VR: Marriage: 37/83/33.

Baldwin, Ian, Jr. (b. 1938)—NY VR: Birth: 1938/Cert.32491. MA VR: Marriage: 62/19/184.

Baldwin, Karen Elise Mulvihill—MA VR: Birth: 64/31/115.

Baldwin, Margherita Bailey—MA VR: Birth: 47/44/399. Marriage: NY Times: 3/4/73.

Baldwin, Michael—NY VR: Birth: 1940/Cert.32039. Marriage: NY Times: 3/4/73.

Baldwin, Nathaniel Kinsman—MA VR: Birth: 80/104/473.

Baldwin, Philip Weld—Marriage: Soc. Reg. 1970.

Baldwin, Rose Weld—MA VR: Marriage: 37/83/33.

Baldwin, Sybil Kane Jay Kinnicutt—NY VR: Birth: 1938/Cert.11302; Marriage: 62/19/184.

Baldwin, Taylor Converse—MA VR: Birth: 77/107/228.

Baldwin, Victoria Monroe Cunningham—NY VR: 1948/Cert.11153. Marriage: Soc. Reg. 1970.

Bank, Linda Ruth—(See Weld.)

Bell, Anne Weld—MA VR: 48/50/245; Marriaage: 79/Cert.028843.

Bell, Morris Mac Stewart—MA VR: Birth: 52/10/92; Marriage: 79/Cert.028843.

Bell, Philip Franklin Morris—MA VR: Birth: 81/98/53.

Bell, Sylvie Anne Katherine Crockett—MA VR: 87/Cert.018536.

Bell, Winnie Fay Lumpkin—MA VR: Birth: 82/64/179.

Benton, Emily Weld—NY VR: Birth: 1962/Cert.105994.

Benton Family—*A Benton Heritage* by Nicholas Benton, 1964; *Samuel H. Benton* by J. H.

Benton, Jr. 1901

Benton, Frances Hill (b. 1955)—NY VR: 1955/Cert.136125.

Benton, Kate (b. 1958)—(See Doughan.)

Benton, Kate Bigelow (b. 1935)—MA VR: Birth: 1935/38/484; Marriage: 1954/27/388.

Benton, Louisa Barclay—NY VR: 1964/Cert.113181.

Benton, Nicholas—MA VR: 1926/2/120; Marriage: 1954/27/388. *Who's Who In America,* 1997

Bigelow, Albert Smith—MA VR: Birth: 1906/560/18; Marriage: 1931/65/511. Death: NY Times:
    10/8/93.

Bigelow, Kate—(See Benton, Kate Bigelow.)

Bigelow, Lisa Barclay—(Married to Edge, Leslie, Roberts, Rodriquez) MA VR: Birth: 32/45/129;
    Marriage: 51/73/441.

Bigelow, Mary DeFord—MA VR: Birth: 1946/39/239; Death: 1947/48/231.

Bigelow, Sylvia Weld—NY VR: Birth: 1909/Cert.45417; MA VR: Marriage: 31/65/511.

Brewster, Charles Erskine Scott—NY VR: 1971/Cert.20759.

Brewster, Michelle Grosjean—NY VR: Birth: 1943/Cert.14792.

Brewster, Richard—NY VR: Birth: 1941/Cert.32716.

Brewster, Sylvia Weld—(See O'Connor.)

Burnes, Daniel Carney—MA VR: Birth: 46/27/397.

Burnes, Holly Gardiner—MA VR: Birth: 48/16/102.

Casey, Cecily Jay Paschal—Marriage: NY Times: 7/19/87.

Choate, Arthur Osgood, Jt.—NY VR: Birth: 11911/Cert.59834. MA VR: Marriage: 1951/27/499.

Choate, Eloise Rodman Weld—NY VR: Birth: 1911/Cert.21494. MA VR: Marriage: 1951/27/499.

Clark, Jonathan Bruce—NY VR: Birth: 1963/Cert.31370. Marriage: Social Register 1991

Clark, Michael Weld—NY VR: Birth: 1959/Cert.45829. Marriage: NY Times: 8/25/85.

Clark, Pamela Ryder Van Hoven—Marriage: NY Times: 8/25/83.

Clark, Sarah Jean Hlvaka—Marriage: NY Times: 8/25/83.

Clark, Timothy Adams—NY VR: Birth: 1966/Cert.2311.

Clark William Goodman—Marriage: NY Times: 4/14/57.

Clark, William Goodman, Jr.—(b. 1957)—Marriage: NY Times: 8/21/83.

Colt, Samuel Sloan—Death: NY Times: 5/3/75. *Who Was Who,* Vol.VI.

Cooper, Howard Morton—NY VR: Marriage 1964/28635.

Cooper, Neal Stuyvesant—NY VR: Birth: 1966/Cert,568.

Crawford, William, III (b. 1932)—NY VR: 1932/Cert.22957.

Crawford, William Jr. (b. 1908)—MA VR: Death: 1971/104/126.

Crittenden, Penelope Shaw—(See Bacon.)

Cross, Virginia Gay (Guild)—(See Weld.)

Cunningham, Victoria Monroe—(See Baldwin)

Doughan, James Francis—MA VR: Marriage: 1988/039743.

Doughan, Kate Benton—NY VR: Birth: 1958/Cert.140691. MA VR: Marriage:1988/Cert.039743.

Durini Family—*Libro d'oro della Nobiltà* 1969-1972 edition (page 548).

Eaton, Elizabeth Stevens—(See Weld.)

Edge, Albert Smith Bigelow—MA VR: Birth: 1953/24/281.

Edge, Dena Sue Gewanter—NY VR: 1953/Cert.5827.

Edge, Joshua Paris—MA VR: Birth: 1982/12/129.

Edge, Kimberly Anne—NY VR: Birth: 11953/Cert.21698.

Edge, Lisa Howard—(See Schraeter.)

Edge, Loyall Howard—MA VR: Marriage: 51/73/441.

Edge, Nancy Jean Kimberly—MA VR: Marriage: 1988/Cert.039720.

Edge, Walter Evans, II—MA VR: Birth: 52/14/47; Marriage: 1988/Cert.039720.

Elkins, Carol—(See Stout.)

Elkins, Eloise Rodman Weld—NY VR: Birth: 1911/Cert.21494.. MA VR: Marriage: 1931/21/85.

Elkins, William Lukens, Jr. (b.1932)—MA VR: Birth: 1932/25/525.

Elkins, William Lukens—MA VR: Marriage: 1931/21/85.

Emerick, Katharine Woods—NY VR: Birth:1970/Cert.04944.

Eyre Family—Personal family chart of William Richard Eyre, London, England; See Astuto Family,

Field, Augustus Bradhurst, III—NY VR: Birth: 1934/Cert.1000; Marriage: NY Times: 11/27/77.

Field, Barbara Bruce Weld—(See Weld)

Fingleton, Anthony James—MA VR: Marriage: 67/51/355.

Fingleton, Pamela Wolcott—MA VR: Birth: 41/30/283; Marriage: 67/51/355.

Fingleton, Priscilla—NY VR: Birth: 1971/Cert.2777427.

Fingleton, Samantha—NY VR: Birth: 1969/Cert.01075.

Fleming, William Thomas, Jr.—Death: Philadelphia Enquirer: 2/3/1977

Flynn, Barbara—(See Wolcott.)

Fitz Herbert Family—Personal Family Tree of William Richard Eyre, 20 Parsons Green Lane, London, England.

Gardiner, Alison—(See Pierson.)

Gardiner, Frances Weld (also McDermott)—MA VR: Birth: 22/1/86. Marriage: NY Times: 6/8/41. Death: Boston Globe: 12/17/93.

Gardiner, Holly—(See Burnes.)

Gardiner, Nancy Ellen—NY VR: Birth: 1956/Cert.42061. Marriage: NY Times: 4/29/84.

Gardiner, Nathaniel Saltonstall—MA VR: Birth: 53/31/471. Marriage: NY Times: 4/29/84.

Gardiner, Phyllis—(See Johnston.)

Gardiner, Robert Hallowell, Jr. (b. 1944)—Harvard Class of 1966 Reports.

Gardiner, Robert Hallowell (b. 1914)—MA VR: Birth: 14/624/65. Marriage: NY Times 6/8/41. Death: NY Times: 11/20/84.

Gewanter, Dena Sue—(See Edge.)

Gleason Family—(See Astuto Family).

Grandchamps, Marc de Villers—Marriage: NY Times: 7/27/63.

Grandchamps, Claire Weld Grosjean de Villers—NY VR: Birth: 1940/Cert.29436. Marriage: NY Times: 7/27/63.

Grassi, Louise Purcell—(See Whitney.)

Gray, Caroline Balch Weld—MA VR: Death: 1912/13/628 (Boston). Mt. Auburn.

Gray, Georgina Hemingway (Merriam)—MA VR: Birth: 1881/322/402; Death:Soc. Reg.: April 1971 (Boston)

Gray, Hope—MA VR: Death: 1979/Cert.000952 (Boston). Buried at Mt. Auburn.

Gray, Marjorie Whiting—(See Weld)

Gray, Ralph Weld—MA VR: Marriage: 1921/62/543 (Weston).

Gray, Samuel Shober—MA VR: Death: 1926/2/332 (Boston). Buried: Mt. Auburn.

Gray. Marjorie Whiting—(See Weld, Marjorie Whiting Gray.)

Grosjean, Charles Adolphe—MA VR: Marriage: 39/14/168.

Grosjean, Claire Weld—(See Grandchamps.)

Grosjean, Daphne—(See Hamaide.)

Grosjean, Michelle—(See Brewster.)

Grosjean, Priscilla Alden Weld—MA VR: Birth: 17/1/71; Marriage: 39/14/168.

Hallet, Georgiana—MA VR: Marriage: 1856/100/281 (West Roxbury).

Hamaide, Daphne Grosjean de La—NY VR: Birth: 1946/Cert.

Harding, Goodwin Warner, Jr.—MA VR: Birth: 47/18/469; Marriage: 72/29/6.

Harding, Katherine Weld—MA VR: Birth: 47/35/404; Marriage: 72/29/6.

Harz, John Claude—NY VR: Marriage: 1965/Cert.27104.

Harz, Tuesday Weld—(See Susan Ker Weld.)

Hemmingway, Georgina (Merriam)—(See Gray, Georgina Hemmingway.)

Hlavka, Sarah Jean—(See Clark.)

Hodges, Arthur Carlisle—MA VR: Marriage: 61/33/198.

Hodges, Eloise Weld—MA VR: Marriage: 61/33/198.

Hodges, Sunhee Juhon—Marriage: NY Times: 8/20/89.

Hodges, Susanna—(See Salk.)

Hodges. Alexander Weld—MA VR: Birth: 68/8/387.

Horsburgh, Emily Robbins—NY VR: Marriage:1980/Cert.12553.

Horsburgh, Jennifer Weld Robbins—NY VR: Birth: 1953/Cert. 14544

Johnston, Phyllis Gardiner—MA VR: Birth: 55/39/509.

Juhon, Sunhee—(See Hodges.)

Keeney, Nancy Jean—(See Edge.)

Ker, Yosene Balfour (See Weld.)

King, Sarah Lothrop—(See Weld.)

Kinnicutt, Sybil Kane Jay—(See Baldwin.)

Knott, Adelaide Weld (Whitney)—MA VR: 1st Marriage: 39/92/234. 2nd Marriage: NY Times: 10/25/54.

Knott, James, Jr. (b. 1955)—NY VR: Birth: 1955/Cert.22295. Death: NY Times: 6/7/95 obit classified.

Knott, James—NY VR: Birth: 1916/Cert.58913. Marriage: NY Times: 10/25/54. Death: NY Times: 4/23/89.

Ladd, Adelaide Watson—(See Weld.)

Lamb, Sandra Crain—(See Wolcott.)

Lapsley, Adelaide Weld—(See Mulry.)

Lapsley, Hope Whiney—NY VR: Birth: 1940/Cert.33301. Marriage: NY Times: 9/25/60.

Lapsley, John Willard—NY VR: Birth: 19935/Cert.15683. Marriage: NY Times: 9/25/60.

Lentz, Patricia (Martin)—(See Weld.)

Leslie, Alfred (b. Alfred Morton Lippitz)—Bronx VR: Birth: 1927/Cert.14761. CT VR: Marriage: 1960/Cert.4629.

SOURCES

Leslie, Joseph—NY VR: Birth: 1961/Cert.49564.

Makrianes, Susan Moreland—(See Bacon.)

Martin, David Briton Hadden, Jr.—MA VR: Birth: 46/9/364; Marriage: 69/7/124.

Martin, Martha Bacon—MA VR: Birth: 47/27/210; Marriage: 69/7/124.

Maynard, Hope—(See Weld.)

McDermott, William Vincent, Jr.—MA VR: Birth: 17/640/740. *Who's Who in America*, 1986-87.

Merriman, Elizabeth Barbara—(See Weld.)

Moore, Dudley Stuart John—*Who's Who in Entertainment*, Vol. 2, 1992-93.

Moore, Tuesday Weld—(See Susan Ker Weld.)

Morris, Andrew Raphael, Jr—NY: Marriage: Christ Church, United Methodist, 1957.

Morris, Sarah Ann—(See Rousso.)

Mulry, Adelaide Weld Lapsley—Marriage: NY Times: 9/25/88.

Mulry, Sean Francis—NY VR: Birth: 1963/Cert.37099. Marriage: NY Times: 9/25/88.

Mulvihill, Karen Elise—(See Baldwin.)

New, Elizabeth Stayer—(See Weld.)

O'Connor, Sylvia Weld Brewster—NY VR: Birth: 1969/Cert.35415.

Parsons, Sylvia Caroline—(See Weld.)

Pascal, Guy—Marriage: NY Times: 6/22/58.

Paschal, Cecily Jay (See Casey.)

Paschal, Dorothy Islelin—NY VR: Birth 1963/35400. (Twin)

Paschal, Eleanor Merriman—(See Reich.)

Paschal, Elizabeth Weld—NY VR: Birth: 1963/35439. (Twin)

Paschal, Helen Merriman Weld—NY VR: Birth: 1938/Cert.8558. Marriage: NY Times: 6/22/58.

Peters, Priscilla Quincy (Loburg)—(See Weld.)

Pierson, Alison Gardiner—NY VR: Birth: 1942/Cert.29154.

Pierson, Arthur Campbell—NY VR: Birth: 41/Cert.24376.

Reich, Christopher Verrill—NY VR: Birth: 1958/Cert.34587. Marriage: NY Times: 5/19/91.

Reich, Eleanor Merriman Paschal—MA VR: Birth: 1959/36/55. Marriage: NY Times: 5/19/91.

Robbins, Jennifer Weld—(See Horsburgh.)

Robbins, John Garside—NY VR: Marriage: 1952/10177; Death: 1970/Cert. 17003.

Roberts, Martin Hugh—NY VR: Birth: 1949/Cert.46203.

Rodman, Eloise (b. 1850)—(See Weld, Eloise Rodman.)

Rous Family—Debrett's Peerage and Baronetage 2000 (pages 78ff).

Rousso, Louis Eli—NY VR: Birth: 1951/Cert.58338.

Rousso, Sarah Ann Morris—NY VR: Birth: 1957/Cert.42887.

Salk, Eric David—NY VR: Birth: 1961/Cert.31972. Marriage: NY Times: 11/3/91.

Salk, Susanna Hodges—MA VR: Birth: 64/34/122. Marriage: NY Times: 11/3/91.

Saltonstall, Katharine Leverett—(See Weld.)

Schraeter, Jack Martin—MA VR: Birth: 1949/155/366; Marriage: 1978/Cert.019464.

Schraeter, Lisa Howard Edge—MA VR: Marriage: 1978/Cert.019464.

Silva, Bradford Richard—MA VR: Birth: 66/128/436.

Smith, Alice Van B.—Marriage: (See Jonathan Bruce Clark).

Smith, Donna Bell—(See Weld)

Smith, Kimberly Anne—(See Edge.)

Stewart, Craig Marwin—MA VR: Marriage: 75/31/382.

Stout, Andrew Varick, Jr.—NY VR: Birth: 1930/Cert.24602. Marriage: NY Times: 9/22/57.

Stout, Carol Elkins—Marriage: NY Times: 9/22/57.

Strachan, Helen Warren (Stewart)—MA VR: Birth: 54/25/456. Marriage: 75/31/382.

Van Hoven, Pamela Ryder—(See Clark.)

Warren, Anne—(See Weld.)

Waterbury, Susan Edith—(See Weld, Susan Edith Waterbury.)

Weld, Adelaide—(See Knott.)

Weld, Adelaide Watson Ladd—MA VR: Marriage: 1900/502/61; Death: 1942/61/511.

Weld, Alfred Rodman (b.1870)—MA VR: Birth: 1870/224/307; Marriage: 1900/502/61; Death: 02/530/39.

Weld, Alice Balch—MA VR: Birth: 1843 or 44/5/139; Death: 1902/531/408.

Weld, Alice Gordon—Personal family chart of William Richard Gordon, London, England; See Astuto Family.

Weld, Anne (b. 1948)—(See Bell.)

Weld, Anne King—(Married to Crawford, McLane and Colt); NY VR: Birth: 1910/Cert.20683. 1st Marriage: Soc. Reg. Summer 1931.

Weld, Anne Warren—MA VR: Birth: 12/609/82; Marriage: 37/7/161. Death: Boston Globe: 10/20/92.

Weld, Arthur Carlisle, Jr. (b. 1963)—MA VR: Birth: 63/16/122. Marriage: NY Times: 8/20/89.

Weld, Arthur Cyril Gordon—MA VR: (*); Death: NY Times: 10/12/1914.NY Surrogate Court: Will filed:11/30/1914.

Weld, Barbara Bruce—NY VR: Birth: 1936/Cert.6544; 1st Marriage: NY Times: 4/14/57; 2nd Marriage: NY Times: 11/27/77. Death: NY Times Obit Classified 1/18/98.

Weld, Caroline Balch—MA VR: Marriage: 1879/309/5 (Boston).

Weld, Cyril Gordon—Death: NY Times: 1/14/1936.

Weld, David Balfour—MA VR: Birth: 37/8/331. Las Vegas, NV VR: Marriage: 1962/Book 139/Cert.224161.

Weld, Donna Bell Smith—AR VR: Marriage: (Miller County) 33/QQ/446.

Weld, Dorothy Livermore Wells—MA VR: Birth: 1900/499/4; Death: 1963/43/385.

Weld, Edith—MA VR: Birth: 1848 or 49/36/69 (Roxbury); Death: 1938/27/270.

Weld, Edward Motley, Jr (b. 1906)—NY VR: Death: 1969/Cert. 12145.

Weld, Edward Motley (b. 1872)—MA VR: Birth: 1872/242/338; Marriage: 1897/470/467; NY VR: Death: NYC Cert.30676.

Weld, Elizabeth Barbara Merriman—Death: NY Times: 10/12/84.

Weld, Elizabeth Stayer New—MA VR: Marriage: 63/28/384.

Weld, Elizabeth Stevens Eaton—MA VR: Marriage: 45/66/309; Death: 64/75/185.

Weld, Eloise—(See Hodges.)

Weld, Eloise Minot—MA VR: Birth: 1879/305/246; Death: NY Times: 1/7/1908.

Weld, Eloise Rodman (b.1850)—MA VR: Birth: 1850/43/191; Marriage: 1869/218/302; Death:1898/482/338/339.

Weld, Eloise Rodman—(b. 1911) (See Elkins, Fleming, Choate.)

SOURCES

Weld Family—*Weld Collections* by Charles Frederick Robinson, 1938

Weld, Frances—(See Gardiner.)

Weld, Georgiana Hallet Weld—MA VR: Death: 1867/203/277 (West Roxbury).

Weld, Hannah Minot—MA VR: Death: 1923/1/210. Age 84 yrs, 9 mos. 20 dys.

Weld, Helen Merriman—(See Paschal.)

Weld, Helen Warren—(See Strachan.)

Weld, Henry Hallet—MA VR: Birth: 1861/142/330; Death: 1868/212/283.

Weld, Hope Maynard—MA VR: Birth: 1933/10/468; Marriage: 1953/36/400.

Weld, Katharine Leverett Saltonstall—MA VR: Birth: 111891/413/479; Marriage: 12/612/73; Death: 1987/Cert..035734.

Weld, Katherine—(See Bacon.)

Weld, Katherine—(See Harding)

Weld, Linda Ruth Bank—MA VR: Marriage: 87/Cert.031271.

Weld, Lothrop Motley, Jr.—MA VR: Birth 1922/1/164; 1st Marriage: 1953/36/400; 2nd Marriage: 1959/13/321; 3rd Marriage: 1986/Cert.028254..

Weld, Lothrop Motley (b. 1898)—MA VR: 1st Marriage: 1921/1/258; 3rd Marriage: AR 33/QQ/446; 4th Marriage NY VR: 1934/Lic. 2041; Death: 1947/Cert.12975.

Weld, Marjorie Whiting Gray—MA VR: Death: 1987 Cert.033869 (Wayland).

Weld, Mary Elizabeth (See Wolcott.)

Weld, Patricia Lentz (Martin)—Las Vagas NV VR: Marriage: 1962/Book 139/Cert.224161.

Weld, Philip Balch—MA VR: Birth: 1887/377/335; Marriage: 12/612/73; Death: 64/6/190.

Weld, Philip Saltonstall—NY VR: 1914/Cert.63819. MA VR: Marriage: 37/7/161; Death: 1984/Cert.050358.

Weld, Philip Saltonstall, Jr. (b. 1938)—MA VR: Marriage: 63/28/384.

Weld, Priscilla Alden—(See Grosjean.)

Weld, Priscilla Quincy (Loburg)—MA VR: Birth: 1923/126/452; Marriage: 1986/Cert. 028254.

Weld, Rose—(See Baldwin.)

Weld, Rudolph—MA VR: Birth: 1883/341/282; Death: 1941/27/499.

Weld, Sarah King (b. 1935)—MA VR: Birth: 35/17/481; NY VR: 1st Marriage: 1952/10177; 3rd Marriage : 1964/28635.

Weld, Sarah Lothrop King (b.1874)—Birth: MA VR: 1874/261/179; Marriage: 1897/470/467.

Weld, Stephen Minot—(b. 1806)—MA VR: 2nd Marriage: 1856/100/281 to G. Hallet.

Weld, Stephen Minot—(b. 1901)—MA VR: Birth: 01/66/288; Marriage: 45/66/309; Death: 82/Cert.049045.

Weld, Stephen Minot, Jr.—(b. 1842)—MA VR: 1st Marriage: 1869/218/302; 2nd Marriage: 04/549/110; Death: NY Times: 3/17/20. *Who Was Who*, Vol I.

Weld, Stephen Minot, Jr., Descendants—*The Call of the Weld* by Nicholas Benton, 1999.

Weld, Stephen Minot II—(b. 1870) MA VR: Birth: 1870/224/307; Death: 1887/338/282.

Weld, Stephen Minot, Jr.—(b. 1947)—MA VR: Birth: 47/57/363; Marriage: 87/Cert.031271.

Weld, Susan Edith Waterbury—MA VR: Marriage: 04/549/110; Death: 60/25/8.

Weld, Susan Ker (a/k/a Tuesday Weld) (See also Harz, Moore, Zuckerman)—NY VR: Birth: 1943/Cert.28544.; Marriage: 1965/Cert.27104. *Who's Who in Entertainment*, 1992-93.

Weld, Sylvia—(See Bigelow.)

Weld, Sylvia Caroline Parsons—(See *My New England Ancestors* by Anna Reed Parsons, 1958.)

Weld, Virginia Gay Cross (Guild)—MA VR: Birth: 1934/24/244; Marriage: 1959/13/321; Death: 1978/Cert.000797.

Weld, Yosene Balfour Ker—NY VR: Marriage: 1934/Lic. 2041.

Wells, Dorothy Livermore—(See Weld)

Whitney, Hope—(See Lapsley.)

Whitney, Jason—NY VR: Birth: 1972/Cert.23732.

Whitney, Louise Purcell Grassi—Marriage: NY Times: 11/17/68.

Whitney, Robert Bacon, Jr.—(b. 1943)—NY VR: Birth: 1943/Cert.1813; Marriage: NY Times: 11/17/68.

Whitney, Robert Bacon (b. 1916)—NY VR: Birth: 1916/Cert.58913; MA VR: Marriage: 39/92/234.

Whitney, Stephen Weld (b. 1970)—NY VR: Birth: 1970/Cert.35877.

Whitney, Stephen Weld (b. 1944)—NY VR: Birth: 1944/Cert.27093.

Williams, Hugo Andrew Younger—Marriage: NY Times: 7/11/93.

Williams, Natalie Wolcott—Marriage: NY Times 7/11/93.

Wolcott, Barbara Flynn—MA VR: Birth: 39/51/213. Marriage: (*).

Wolcott, Jessica Lamb—MA VR: Birth: 71/010/288.

Wolcott, Mary Elizabeth Weld—MA VR: Marriage: 34/76/92.

Wolcott, Natalie—(See Williams.)

Wolcott, Pamela—(See Fingleton.)

Wolcott, Philip Weld—MA VR: Birth: 36/27/213.

Wolcott, Samuel Huntington, Jr.—MA VR: Birth: 10/592/66; Marriage: 34/76/92.

Wolcott, Samuel Huntington, III—MA VR: Birth: 35/18/166. *Who's Who in America*, '95.

Wolcott, Sandra Crain Lamb—Marriage: NY Times: 6/4/67.

Wolcott, William Prescott—MA VR: Birth: 44/39/103. Marriage: NY Times 6/4/67. Death: NY Times: Obit Classified.

Wolcott, William Prescott, Jr. (b. 1968)—MA VR: Birth: 68/26/227.

Woodbury, Kate de Rosset—Personal family chart of her great-grandson, William Richard Eyre

Woods, Alexandra—NY VR: Birth: 1972/Cert.14071.

Woods, Katharine—(See Emerick.)

Woods, Priscilla Bacon—MA VR: Birth: 42/34/559; Marriage: 67/6/395.

Woods, Ward Wilson, Jr.—MA VR: Marriage: 67/6/395. *Who's Who in America*, 1997.

Zuckerman, Pincas—*Who's Who in Entertainment*, Vol. 2, 1992-93.

Zuckerman, Tuesday Weld—(See Susan Ker Weld.)

(*) = No record found in Massachusetts Vital Records.

SOURCES

Sources for the descendants of
THOMAS SWAN WELD

Alexandre, Anne Lenox—(See Brett).

Alverson, Brenda Louise—(See Austin).

Austin, Brenda Louise Alverson—MA VR: Marriage: 1986/Cert.050317.

Austin, Francis Reed, Jr.—MA VR: Birth: 53/20/525.

Austin, Marjory Weld (See Johnson).

Austin, Richard W.—MA VR: Birth: 1959/51/114 (Boston).

Austin, William Fisher—MA VR: Birth: 55/30/176 (Boston); Marriage: 1986/Cert.05317.

Austin, William Mason—MA VR: Birth: 1902/523/214 (Boston).

Bandanza, Deborah Claire Marriage: NY Times 6/2/91.

Blake, Charles Chandler—MA VR: Marriage: 1905/556/25.

Blake, Sarah Swan Weld (b. 1873)—MA VR: Marriage: 1905/556/25.

Blyth, Howard Alden—Marriage: NY Times: 6/24/34; Death: NY Times: 6/22/87.

Blyth, Serena Weld—Marriage: NY Times: 6/24/34 (Bedford, NY).

Brett, Anne Lenox Alexandre—Marriage: 1970 Soc. Reg. (New York).

Brett, Philip Milledoler III—Marriage: 1970 Soc. Reg. (New York).

Carret, Anna Weld—(See Dunlap).

Carret, Elizabeth Calkins—(See Smith).

Carret, Elizabeth Hammil Calkins—Not in the Social Security Death Index.

Carret, Jose Francisco—MA VR: Marriage: 1864/172/235; Death: 1897/473/165 (Cambridge). 63 yrs, 8 mos, 5 days. Buried at Forest Hills Cemetery, Jamaica Plain, MA.

Carret, Sarah Swan Weld—MA VR: Marriage: 1864/172/235 (West Roxbury).

Crawford, Alexander Iselin—Marriage: NY Times 6/2/91.

Dunlap Family—*The Descendants of Ensign Robert Dunlap,*(updated insertions into *The House of Dunlap* by The Rev. James Arthur MacClellan Hanna, A.B., B.D.) by Charles Dawes Dunlap, 1991.

Dunlap, Elizabeth Nason—MA VR: Birth: 39/21/282 (Boston).

Dunlop, Anna Weld Carret—MA VR: Marriage: 1902/525/341 (Cambridge).

Dworetz, Stephen—NY VR: Birth: 1947/Cert.16212.(Spells surname: Dwaretz.) MA VR: Marriage: 1969/10/440 (Newton).

Dworetz. Serena Weld Granberry—MA VR: Marriage: 1969/10/440 (Newton).

Garrison, Margaret—(See Poutrides).

Granberry, Serena Weld—(See Dworetz).

Hambly, Harry Bishop III—MA VR: Marriage: 62/42/234 (Nantucket).

Hambly, Margot Weld Smith—MA VR: Marriage: 62/42/234 (Nantucket).

Haskell, Joseph Farrell—Death: NY Times: 10/11/83. *Who's Who in America*, 1970-1971.

Jeffries, Jean Carolyn MacDowell—MA VR: Marriage: 1989/Cert.031024.

Jeffries, William Q.—MA VR: Marriage: 1989/Cert.031024 (New Marlborough).

Johnson, Marjory Weld Austin (b. 1927)—MA VR: Death: 1988/Cert.008640 (Boston). Buried at Mt. Auburn, Cambridge. MA.

Johnson, Marjory Weld (b. 1956)—MA VR: Birth: 56/38/40.

Johnson, Richard Irwin—MA VR: Birth: 1925/32/501 (Everett). Harvard Magazine, January 1994.

Johnson, Richard Minot Weld—Harvard Magazine, January 1994.

Johnson, Sally Weld—MA VR: Birth: 55/14/50. Harvard Magazine, January 1994.

Lurie, David—Harvard Magazine, January 1994

MacDowell, Anne Katherine—MA VR: Birth: 56/49/377 (Boston).

MacDowell, Jean Carolyn—(See Jeffries).

McCrary, Jane M. (Rohrbaugh)—(See Smith).

O'Leary, Karen—Harvard Magazine, January 1994.

Phoutrides, Margaret Garrison—MA VR: Marriage: 21/8/343 (Cambridge), Also 21/3/358 (Wiano, Barnstable).

Phoutrides, Aristides Evangelus—MA VR: Marriage: 21/8/343 (Cambridge). Also 21/3/358 (Wiano, Barnstable).

Russ, Tobey J.—NH VR: Marriage: 58/Cert.60415.(New Ipswich).

Smith, Elizabeth Calkins Carret—MA VR: Birth: 1908/576/20 (Brookline); Marriage: 32/18/426.

Smith, Jane M. McCrary (Rohrbaugh)—NH VR: Marriage 1980/Cert.32425 (New Ipswich).

Smith, Jennifer Haynes (See Stiefel).

Smith, Kilby Page III (b.1933)—NH VR: Marriage: 1980/Cert.32427. (New Ipswich).

Smith, Kilby Page, Jr. (b. 1904)—MA VR: Birth: 1904/543/672; Marriage: 32/18/426. Death: 1980/Cert.003716.

Smith,Margot Weld—(See Hambly).

Stiefel, Jennifer Haynes Smith—MA VR: Birth: 44/26/126 (Boston); Marriage: 69/23/097.

Stiefel, Robert E.—MA VR: Marriage 69/23/097.

Van Winkle, Grace L.—(See Weld).

Webster, Jerome Pierce, Jr.—NY VR: Birth: 1938/Cert.28599.

Webster, Sally Ann Weld—Death: NY Times: 3/4/67 page 22.

Weld, Christopher Minot (b.1876)—NY VR: Marriage: 1924/Cert.14335.

Weld, David Minot—MA VR: Birth: 76/19/264 (Boston).

Weld, Ethel Derby—MA VR: Birth: 77/23/187 (Boston).

Weld, Frances Wylie—MA VR: Birth: 83/25/314 (Boston).

Weld, Grace L. Van Winkle—NY VR: Marriage: 1924/Cert.14335.

Weld, Mary Blake—MA VR: Birth: 1979/6/477 (Boston).

Weld, Quentin Roosevelt—MA VR: Birth: 1981/18/339 (Boston).

Weld, Sally Ann—(See Webster).

Weld, Sarah Swan (b.1839)—(See Carret).

Weld, Sarah Swan (b. 1873)—(See Blake).

Weld, Serena—(See Blyth).

(*) = No record found in Massachusetts Vital Records.

SOURCES

Sources for the wife of
Christopher Minot Weld

Weld, Mary Jane Jarvis—MA VR: Death: 1898/483/511 (Boston). Age 83 yrs, 4 mos.
Jarvis, Mary Jane—(See Weld).

The Seven Weld Brothers

Sources for the descendants of
Francis Minot Weld

Brown, Elizabeth Weld—MA VR: Birth: 1963/16/300 (Boston).

Brown, John Linzee—MA VR: Birth: 1958/45/202 (Boston).

Brown, Louisa Shepard: MA VR: Birth: 1956/21/178 (Boston).

Brown, Shepard, Jr.—MA VR: Birth: 61/33/157 (Boston).

Burgess, Elizabeth—(See Weld).

Carter, John Boyd, Jr.—*Who's Who in America*, 1984-85.

Cheever, David, Jr.—MA VR: Marriage: 1987/Cert.041119.

Cheever, Marion Linzee Minot—MA VR: Marriage: 1987/Cert.041119.(Dedham).

Clark, Lydia—(See Hunter).

Dean, Dorothea—(See Parkinson).

Donaldson, Anne Putnam Peabody—MA VR: Marriage: 1945/66/310 (Milton).

Donaldson, Frederick Emerson, Jr.—MA VR: 1945/66/310 (Milton).

Emlen, Cora Weld Peabody—MA VR: Marriage: 43/62/252.

Emlen, Robert Lukens—MA VR: Marriage:1943/62/252 (Milton).

Emmons, Mary Ann Wales—(See Parkinson).

Fawcett, Jean Dorothy—(See Hunter).

Foster, Barbara (b. 1925)—MA VR: Birth: 1925/14/117 (Boston).

Foster, Barbara (b. 1899)—(See Weld).

Graves, Charles Parlin—MA VR: Marriage: 1953/11/178.

Graves, Elizabeth Whitney Minot—MA VR: Marriage: 1953/11/178 (Boston).

Graves, Elizabeth Whitney Minot—MA VR: Marriage: 53/11/178.

Grew, John Grimes: MA VR: Birth: (*).

Grew, John, Jr. (b. 1936)—MA VR: Marriage: 1967/28/119.

Grew, Joseph Grimes: MA VR: Birth: (*).

Grew, Lydia Katharine Grimes—MA VR: Marriage: 1967/28/119 (Sherborn).

Grew, Meredith Emerson Paul—MA VR: Marriage: 1964/54/480.

Grew, Nathaniel—MA VR: Marriage:1964/54/480.

Grimes, Lydia Katherine—(See Grew).

Hoefnagel, Dick—MA VR: Marriage: 1956/69/338 (Newton).

Hoefnagel, Margaret Hunter—MA VR: Marriage: 56/69/338.

Hunter, Cheri Lynn Teixeira—MA VR: Birth: 64/78/336; Marriage: 1984/Cert.3985.

Hunter, Edward Burrington—MA VR: Birth: 1959/136/440; Marriage: 1984/Cert.3985.

Hunter, James Lionel—MA VR: Birth: 1960/140/8 (Needham).

Hunter, Jean Dorothy Fawcett—MA VR: Birth: 1930/112/344; Marriage: 54/69/407.

Hunter, Jeffrey Weld—MA VR Marriage: 1985/Cert.049196 (Bourne).

Hunter, John Barrington—MA VR: Birth: 4/28/31 Boston; Marriage: 1954/69/407 (Watertown).

Hunter, John Tennery—MA VR: Birth: 1968/112/153 (Needham).

Hunter, Lydia Clark—MA VR: Marriage: 1985/Cert.049196 (Bourne).

Hunter, Margaret—(See Hoefnagel).

Hunter, Margaret Minot—MA VR: Death: 70/28/89 (Boston). 77 years of age.

SOURCES

Hunzicker, Karen D.—(See Putnam).

Linzee, Marian—(See Weld).

Loveland, Rose—(See Toulman).

Lovering, Ellen (Child)—(See Parkinson).

Lyman, Barbara Putnam—MA VR: Birth: 54/28/197 (Boston); Marriage: 1979/Cert.016952.

Minot, Charles Sedgwick—MA VR: Marriage: 1958/25/321.

Minot, Charlotte Nickerson—MA VR: Marriage: 1958/25/321.

Minot, Elizabeth Whitney—(See Graves).

Minot, George Richards—MA VR: Death: 50/32/400 (Brookline).

Minot, Marion Linzee Weld (b. 1890)—MA VR: Death: 1979/Cert. 037011 (Brookline) 89 years.

Minot, Marion Linzee (b. 1918)—(See Cheever).

Nagle, Francesca C.—(See Parkinson).

Nickerson, Charlotte—(See Minot).

Paradies, Martha Emmons Parkinson—MA VR: Marriage: 1969/5/326.

Paradies y Aboitiz, Robert John—MA VR: Marriage: 1969/5/326.

Parkinson, Dorothea Dean—MA VR: Birth: 1913/616/16 (Brookline); Marriage:1939/24/25.

Parkinson, Ellen Lovering (Child)—MA VR: Marriage: 41/9/61.

Parkinson, Fay J. Wilderstrom-Wilson—MA VR: Marriage: 1948/31/40 (Wareham).

Parkinson, Francesca C. Nagle—MA VR: Birth: (nee Fannie Nagle) 1919/47/76 (Brockton); Marriage: 1941/34/216 (as Frances Carol Nagle).

Parkinson, John—(b. 1843)—MA VR: Death: 1918/7/52 (Bourne).

Parkinson, John, Jr.—MA VR: Birth: 1883/342/93 (Boston); Marriage: 1905/554/5 (Falmouth).

Parkinson, Martha Emmons—(See Paradies).

Parkinson, Mary Ann Wales Emmons—MA VR: Marriage: 1905/554/5 (Falmouth); Death: 1957/31/246 (Boston).

Parkinson, Nathaniel Emmons—MA VR: Marriage: 1941/9/61 (Beverly).

Parkinson, Robert—MA VR: Marriage: 39/24/25 (Brookline).

Parkinson, Robert—MA VR: Birth: 1915/630/41 (Dover); Marriage: (1st) 1939/24/25 (Brookline); (2nd) 1948/31/40 (Wareham).

Paul, Meredith Emerson—(See Grew).

Peabody, Anne Putnam—(See Donaldson).

Peabody, Cora Weld—(See Emlen).

Peabody, Francis Weld, Jr.—MA VR: Marriage: 1968/12/214 (Boston).

Peabody, George Shattuck—MA VR: Birth: 1953/32/333.

Peabody, Gertrude—MA VR: Death: 1967/10/37 (Boston).

Peabody, Gertrude Weld (b. 1877)—MA VR: Death: 1938/23/251. (Boston).

Peabody, Sara Weeks Swetzoff—MA VR: Birth: 1926/102/274; Marriage: 1968/12/214 (Boston)

Putnam, Barbara—(See Lyman).

Putnam, Barbara Weld—MA VR: Marriage: 449/65/281.

Putnam, George III—MA VR: Birth: 1951/37/408 (Boston).

Putnam, George, Jr.—MA VR: Birth: 1926/49/726 (Manchester); Marriage: 49/65/281.

Putnam, Karen D.Hunzicker—MA VR: Marriage: 1977/Cert.040576.

Putnam, Susan Weld—MA VR: Birth: 57/15/54 (Boston).

Runnells, Clive, Jr.—*Who's Who in America*, 1964-65.

Sampson, Clark Douglas—MA VR: Birth: 1934/44/586; Death: 1967/11/344.

Shattuck, George Cheever—MA VR: Marriage: 1932/19/21; Death: 1972/34/284 (Brookline).

Shattuck, Virginia Chandler Peabody (widow of Francis Weld Peabody, Jr.)—MA VR: Marriage to Shattuck: 32/19/21; Death: 1982/Cert.055040.

Swetzoff, Sara Weeks—(See Peabody).

Teixeira, Cheri Lynn—(See Hunter).

Toulman, Rose Loveland—(See Weld).

Trimble, Winifred—NY VR: Birth: 19932/Cer.10904

Washburn, Charles G. II—MA VR: Birth: 1926/102/274; Marriage: 1951/11/13.

Washburn, Patricia Weld—MA VR: Birth: 29/1/142; Marriage: 1951/11/13.

Weeks, Sara—(See Peabody).

Weld, Amory—MA VR: Birth: 57/169/451 (Salem).

Weld, Barbara (b. 1927)—(See Putnam).

Weld, Barbara Foster—MA VR: Birth: 1899/486/15; Death: 52/72/268 (Newton).

Weld, Christopher Minot—(b. 1932—MA VR: (*).

Weld, Elizabeth Burgess—MA VR: Marriage: 28/14/123. (Dedham).

Weld, Elizabeth Rodman—(b. 1892)—MA VR: Death: 1961/36/36. Buried at Forest Hills, Jamaica Plains, MA.

Weld, Elizabeth Rodman—(b. 1821)—MA VR: 1897/474/87 (Boston).

Weld, Francis Minot—(b. 1960)—MA VR: Birth: 1960/167/240 (Salem).

Weld, Francis Minot—(b. 1895)—MA VR: Marriage: 28/14/123 (Dedham); Death: 63/6/83 (Beverly). Age 68 yrs, 7 mos, 15 days.

Weld, John Linzee—MA VR: Marriage: 1954/66/23 (Dover).

Weld, Kate Winnett—MA VR: Birth: 70/7/193 (Beverly).

Weld, Marion Linzee—(See Minot).

Weld, Marion Linzee—MA VR: Death: 42/8/69 (Boston).

Weld, Patricia—(See Washburn).

Weld, Rose Loveland Toulman—MA VR: Marriage: 54/66/23 (Dover).

Wilson, Fay J. Wilderstrom—(See Parkinson).

(*) = No records found in Massachusetts Vital Records.

SOURCES

Sources for the descendants of
HENRY GARDNER WELD

Betton, Elinor Weld—Death: Soc. Reg. Summer 1954. Forest Hills Cemetery (MA) Records.

Betton, Eliza Franklin Weld—MA VR: Birth: 1853/73/258. Death : Forest Hills Cemetery Records.

Betton, James Mauran—Harvard Class Reports/1871 and 1873. Death: Forest Hills Records.

Larrabee, Mary Lodice—(See Weld).

Mauran Family—*Memorials of the Mauran Family* by James Eddy Mauran, 1893.

Merriam, Elinor Louise—(See Weld).

Mirrian Family—*Mirriam Family Genealogy* by Charles Henry Pope, 1906.

Spalding, Anna Jane—(See Weld).

Spalding, Cornelia V. (Mother of Anna Jane Splading Weld.)—Death: 11/22/1881, 87 yrs. 6 months, 11 days. Forest Hills Cemetery (Jamaica Plains, MA) Records.

Weld, Anna Jane Spalding (b. 1823)—Death: New York Times: 9/22/14, page 9. Forest Hills Cemetery (Jamaica Plains, MA) Records.

Weld, Anna Spalding (b.1877)—MA VR: Birth: 1877/288/48; Death: 1965/32/260. (Lived in Jamaica Plain with brother, John G. II.) Forest Hills Cemetery Records.

Weld, Asa Spalding—MA VR: Death: 1915/2/508. (See *Merriam Genealogy*.)

Weld, Cornelia Spalding (b.1874)—MA VR: Birth: 1874/261/227; Death: 1877/294/232. Forest Hills Cemetery (Jamaica Plains, MA) Records.

Weld, Cornelia Thane (b. 1859)—MA VR: Death: 1862/157/315. Buried at Forest Hills Cemetery, Jamaica Plains, MA.

Weld, Elinor Louise Merriam—MA VR: Death: 1944/12/90. Forest Hills Cemetery Records.

Weld, Eliza Franklin—(See Betton).

Weld Family—*Weld Collections* by Charles Frederick Robinson, 1938. (Several dates in this volume differ with those of the Albany (NY) Rural Cemetery Records which are given here.)

Weld, Henry Gardner family—(Norwalk, CT City Directories 1928, 1929 & 1976. Death Records:Albany (NY) Rural Cemetery: 1994 Cemetery Custodian:
John Bustza, (Tel: (518) 463-4017).

Weld, Henry Gardner, Jr. MA VR: Birth: 1882/333/196.

Weld, Henry Gardner (b.1855)—Death: Albany, NY Rural Cemetery Records.

Weld, John Gardner—(b. 1818)—Death: Forest Hills Cemetery (Jamaica Plains, MA) Records.

Weld, John Gardner II—(b. 1879) MA VR: Birth: 1879/306/74; Marr: (*); Death: 1969/11/164.

Weld, Margaret—Death: Albany, NY Rural Death Records.

Weld, Mary Lodice—Death: *Norwalk Hour* (CT): 2/18/75, Obit page 6. Buried in Albany, NY.

Weld, Mary Lodice Larrabee—Death: Albany, NY Rural Cemetery Records.

Weld, Maryetta—Death: Albany, NY Rural Death Records.

Weld, Morton—Death: Albany, NY Rural Cemetery Records.

Weld, Rachel Larrabee—Death: *Norwalk Hour* (CT): 10/20/1930. Buried Albany, NY.

Weld, William H.—NJ VR: Death: 5/1/88 Cert: 00255753.

(*) Records not found in Massachusetts Vital Records.)

INDEX

INDEX

Rohrer, Sonia 30
Roosevelt, Frances Blanche Webb 108
Roosevelt, Quentin 108
Roosevelt, Susan 98, 109
Rous, Elizabeth Alice Mary Fraser 80
Rous, Peter James Mowbray 80
Rous, Phillipa Mary Katherine 64, 79
Rousso, Eli 80
Rousso, Eli Louis 80
Rousso, Julia Saporta 80
Rousso, Louis Eli 66, 80
Rousso, Sarah Ann Morris 66, 80
Russ, child expected of Tobey 118
Russ, Elizabeth Haynes Short 105, 118
Russ, Gloria Boisvert 118
Russ, Jon R. 118
Russ, Margot Weld 118
Russ, Tobey J. 105, 118
Russell, Elizabeth 1
Rust, Kathleen 88
Ruter, Chester 43
Ruter, Christopher Clothier 43
Ruter, Elizabeth Ann Smith 31, 43
Ruter, Jessica Mae 43
Ruter, Kenneth 31, 43
Ruter, Leona McGraw 43

S

Salk, Eric David 72, 87
Salk, Kerstin Andersson 87
Salk, Lee 87
Salk, Susanna Hodges 73, 876
Salk, Oliver Lee Warren 86
Saltonstall, Frances A.F. Sherwood 55
Saltonstall, Katharine Leverett 52, 55
Saltonstall, Philip Leverett 55
Sampson, Clark Douglas 127, 133
Sampson, Ethel Massie 133
Sampson, James Harold 133
Sampson, Patricia Weld 117, 123
Sanborn, Cynthia J. MacDowell 102, 114
Sanborn, Harold Wayne 102, 114
Sanborn, Jared Weld 115

Sanborn, Meghan Elizabeth 114
Saporta, Julia 80
Sargent, Barbara 70, 85
Sargent, Barbara Brown 85
Sargent, Jane Wells 116
Sargent, Talbot Hill 85
Saunders, Julia Born 16
Sawicki, Arlene Virginia Teir 117
Sawicki, Janet Elizabeth 105, 117
Sawicki, Joseph Adam 117
Saxton, Anne Kemble 113
Saxton, George Albert 113
Saxton, Melinda Harly 100, 113
Sayre, Dorothy 84
Schauffler, Bennet Fellows 30
Schauffler, Marjorie Page 30
Schauffler, Mary Strawbridge 23, 30
Schauffler, Peter Page 23, 30
Schieffelin, Mary Jane 134
Schlauffler, David Estes 30
Schlauffler, Florence 30
Schlauffler, Richard Page 30
Schneider, Donna Marie 131, 138
Schneider, Elizabeth McCarthy 138
Schneider, Fred 138
Schneiders, Jennifer L. 8, 13
Schoenberg, Corinda Lee 28
Schoenberg, George Walter 28
Schoenberg, Janet Ann 21, 28
Schraeter, Arnold Hirsh 83
Schraeter, Hannah Lake 83
Schraeter, Jack Martin 68, 83
Schraeter, Lisa Howard Edge 68, 83
Schraeter, Louise Belle Shankman 83
Schraeter, Sophie Loyall 83
Scirotto, Angeline 41
Scott, Mary Helen Stewart 46
Scott, Mary Holt 33, 46
Scott, Watson Guerrant 46
Scruggs, Mary Olive 37
Sealey, Julia 130, 137
Sefton, Eleanor Sprague 3, 5
Sefton, Katharine 5, 8

T

Y

0-595-31390-6